PERFECT CONDUCT

PERFECT CONDUCT

Ascertaining the Three Vows

NGARI PANCHEN, PEMA WANGYI GYALPO

Commentary by

HIS HOLINESS DUDJOM RINPOCHE,
JIGDRAL YESHE DORJE

Translated by

KHENPO GYURME SAMDRUB AND SANGYE KHANDRO

Wisdom Publications • Boston

WISDOM PUBLICATIONS
361 Newbury Street
Boston, Massachusetts 02115
USA

Library of Congress Cataloging-in-Publication Data

Mṅa'-ris Paṇ-chen Padma-dbaṅ-rgyal , 1487 or 8–1542 or 3.
[Sdom gsum rnam ṅes. English]
Perfect conduct : ascertaining the three vows / Ngari Panchen Pema Wangyi Gyalpo ; with commentary by Dudjom Rinpoche Jigdral Yeshe Dorje ; translated by Khenpo Gyurme Samdrub and Sangye Khandro.
p. cm.
ISBN 0-86171-083-5 (alk. paper)
1. Trisaṃvara (Buddhism)—Early works to 1800. 2. Vows (Buddhism)—Early works to 1800. 3. Buddhism—Discipline—Early works to 1800. I. Bdud- 'joms 'Jigs-bral-ye-śes-rdo-rje, 1904– . II. Gyurme Samdrub, Khenpo. III. Khandro, Sangye. IV. Title.
BQ6135.M5713 1996
294.3'444—dc20 96–20917

0 86171 083 5

01 00 99 98 97
6 5 4 3 2

Designed by: L·J·SAWLIT

Cover: thangka painting of Ngari Panchen Pema Wangyi Gyalpo by Kunzang Dorje; photograph courtesy of Pacific Region Yeshe Nyingpo.

Wisdom Publications' books are printed on acid-free paper and meet the guidelines for permanence and durability of the Committee on Production Guidelines for Book Longevity of the Council on Library Resources.

Printed in the United States of America.

Contents

Preface *vii*
Introduction *xv*
Translator's Note *xix*

The Commentary, Including the Root Text *1*
First: The Initial Virtue *3*
Second: The Intermediate Virtue *7*
Chapter One: A Brief Explanation of the Stages of the Main Teaching *7*
Chapter Two: An Explanation of the Prātimokṣa-vinaya *14*
Chapter Three: The Bodhisattva Vows *63*
Chapter Four: Secret Mantra *100*
Chapter Five: An Explanation of How to Practice the Three Vows Together without Conflict *141*
Third: The Concluding Virtue *149*
Commentator's Note *153*

Translation of the Root Text, *Ascertaining the Three Vows* *155*

Outline of the Commentary *175*

Notes *191*

Publisher's Acknowledgment

The publisher gratefully acknowledges the generous help of the Hershey Family Foundation in sponsoring the production of this book.

Preface

Commitment, as the essence of the Buddhist vows, demonstrates the dedication of one's life to refraining from harmful deeds and to fostering peace and joy in oneself and others. These aims are accomplished by disciplining the mind, which is the key to all spiritual actions, experiences, and attainments. Lord Buddha said:

> Not committing any evil deeds,
> fostering all that is virtuous, and
> taming one's own mind
> are the teachings of the Buddha.

Buddhist discipline begins with taming the mind, because the mind is the source of all mental events and physical actions. If a person's mind is open, peaceful, and kind, all his or her thoughts and efforts will benefit self and others. If a person's mind is selfish and violent, all his or her thoughts and physical actions will manifest as harmful. Lord Buddha said:

> Mind is the main factor and forerunner of all (actions).
> If with a cruel mind one speaks or acts,
> misery follows, just as the cart follows (the horse)...
> If with a pure mind one speaks or acts,
> happiness follows, as the shadow never departs.

Although the mind is the main factor, for those whose spiritual strength is limited, the physical discipline of living in solitary peace and refraining from indulgence in violent actions is crucial. Mental attitudes and concepts are formed by habits that are totally conditioned by physical and external circumstances and are enslaved by those circumstances. We cannot think, act, or function independently of them. Physical disciplines protect us from becoming prey to the so-called sources of emotions, such as enmity, beauty, ugliness, wealth, power, and fame, which give the mind a craving and aggressive nature, resulting in harmful physical reactions. Thus, physical discipline is an essential means of avoidance and a mechanism of defense.

In order to refrain from committing any negative deed, one must persistently follow the guideline of physical and mental disciplines. There are different sets of disciplines in Buddhism, especially in *tantra*, but their classification into three vows is universal in the Tibetan Buddhist tradition. For the Nyingma school of

Tibetan Buddhism, *Ascertaining the Three Vows* (*sDom-gSum rNam-Nges*) by Panchen Pema Wangyal (1487–1542) of Ngari province has for centuries been the root text for learning the codes of the three vows. In this text, the author elucidates each vow together with its history, nature, and divisions: how to receive the vow, how to observe the vow, how to repair a broken vow, and the result of observing the vow. The three vows are the vows of *prātimokṣa, bodhisattva*, and tantra.

The prātimokṣa vow: The vow of prātimokṣa (individual liberation) mainly emphasizes disciplining one's physical behavior and not harming others. Prātimokṣa discipline is called the foundation of Buddhism, because for ordinary people physical discipline is the beginning of spiritual training and the basis of spiritual progress. The aspiration of the pure prātimokṣa discipline is the achievement of liberation for oneself, as it belongs to the *śrāvaka* training. However, since Tibetan Buddhists are automatically followers of the Mahāyāna, they emphasize taking the prātimokṣa vows with the attitude of *bodhicitta.* Thus, the vows are taken and observed so that all beings may know happiness and achieve enlightenment.

In prātimokṣa there are eight precept categories. The *upavāsika* observes eight vows for twenty-four hours. The *upāsaka* (male lay householder) and *upāsikā* (female lay householder) observe five precepts. These three are the precept categories for lay householders. The *śrāmaṇera* (male novice) and *śrāmaṇerikā* (female novice) observe ten, thirteen, or thirty-six vows. The *śikṣamānā* (female novice in training) observes twelve vows in addition to the precepts of a śrāmaṇerikā. The *bhikṣu* (fully ordained monk) observes 253 vows, and the *bhikṣuṇī* (fully ordained nun) observes 364 vows. These five are the precept categories for those who are celibate and have renounced the lifestyle of lay householders. In Tibetan monastic practice, the last seven prātimokṣa categories are taken for the duration of one's life. Some do not count the upavāsika vow as a prātimokṣa category since it is a temporary precept.

In essence, the training in observing the prātimokṣa vow is to avoid any cause for negative action, which is the source of mental affliction and of pain for oneself and others. In this way, the chain of negative causes and habits is broken, establishing a spiritual basis, which is the source of peace, joy, and benefit for oneself and all parent sentient beings. It is important to remember that unless we can improve our own life, step by step, we will not be properly equipped to be a perfect tool for bringing true joy to others.

As long as one's mind is weak and attracted to the sources of emotions, it will be easily influenced or overwhelmed by anger, lust, and confusion. Thus, it is most important to hold back from the sources of emotions by observing the prātimokṣa vows. For example, if we are weak, it is wiser not to confront powerful enemies but to avoid them. The prātimokṣa vows are a way to defend ourselves from encountering the mental afflictions or their sources. These vows are easy to observe, because they are apparent as physical disciplines such as refraining from killing and stealing. Then, when one's mind is strong enough to stand on its own with less influence from physical activities or external influences, one can put more emphasis on the disciplines of the bodhisattva.

The bodhisattva vow: The vow of the bodhisattva (adherent of enlightenment) mainly emphasizes observing bodhicitta, or the mind of enlightenment. Bodhicitta is the mental attitude of taking responsibility for bringing happiness and enlightenment to all beings, with love and compassion free from any trace of selfish interest, as well as putting this into practice.[1] So here we are not just refraining from harming others, but dedicating ourselves to serving them.

The bodhisattva precept has three major divisions. The first is "refraining from harmful deeds," which has two traditions. According to the tradition of Nāgārjuna, there are eighteen major precepts to observe. According to the tradition of Asaṅga, for the vows of aspirational bodhicitta, there are four general precepts for not losing the vows and eight precepts for not forgetting them. For the vow of practical bodhicitta, there are four root downfalls and forty-six auxiliary faults from which to refrain.

The second division is "the amassing of virtuous deeds." This is the training in the six perfections: generosity, moral discipline, patience, diligence, contemplation, and wisdom.

The third division is "the service of others." This is the practice of the four means of gathering or bringing others to Dharma. These four are the practice of generosity, pleasing speech, leading others to the meaningful path of Dharma, and remaining oneself on the same path.

According to Longchen Rabjam,[2] the vow for the bodhicitta of aspiration is to contemplate the four immeasurable attitudes: love, compassion, joy, and equanimity. The vow for the bodhicitta of practice is to train in the six perfections.

The bodhisattva vow should be maintained until one reaches enlightenment. Unless we abandon bodhicitta, it will remain in us through death and birth, pain and joy. Its force of merit increases in us, even in sleep or distraction, as trees grow even in the darkness of night. Here, people might have a problem with the concept of maintaining the vows after death. According to Buddhism, physical attributes such as body, wealth, and friends will not accompany us into our next lives; but mental habits, convictions, strengths, and aspirations—together with their effects, their *karma*—will stay with us until they are ripened or destroyed. So if we make powerful aspirations and efforts, the vows will remain with us and will form the course of our future lives.

The bodhisattva vow is much harder to observe than the vow of prātimokṣa, as its main discipline is maintaining the right mental attitude and understanding, which is subtle and difficult to control. However, it is also more powerful and beneficial, since if we have bodhicitta in our mind, we cannot do anything harmful to anyone and can only be of benefit. This is not a matter of avoiding mental afflictions or their sources, but of destroying or neutralizing them. For example, a compassionate attitude pacifies anger, seeing the impermanent nature of phenomenal existence alleviates desire, and realizing the causation and/or absence of a "self" ends ignorance. When an aspirant with true bodhicitta awareness is exceptionally intelligent and diligent, full of energy and enthusiasm, and totally open and appreciative, then he or she qualifies to enter and put more emphasis on the disciplines of tantra.

The tantric vow: The vow of tantra (esoteric continuum) mainly emphasizes realizing and perfecting the union of wisdom and skillful means and accomplishing simultaneously the goal of oneself and others.

Tantric training begins with receiving empowerment (*abhiṣeka*) from a highly qualified tantric master. In the transmission of the empowerment, the master's enlightened power causes the disciple's innate primordial wisdom nature to awaken, which is the meaning of empowerment. Such wisdom, although inherent in every being, remains hidden like a treasure buried in the walls. With the power of awakened wisdom one trains in the two stages of tantra, the development stage and perfection stage, and accomplishes the goal: the attainment of buddhahood for the benefit of oneself and others. In order to preserve, develop, and perfect such awakened wisdom, one must observe the *samayas* (esoteric precepts), as these are the heart of tantric training. Breaking tantric samaya is more harmful than breaking other vows. It is like falling from an airplane compared to falling from a horse. Tantric realization and transmission are full of power, depth, and greatness. There is no way of giving up tantric vows except to break them and fall.

For tantric samaya there are numerous precepts to observe, but Ngari Panchen presents the main ones. These include the precepts of twenty-five esoteric activities, the five buddha families, the fourteen root downfalls, and the eight auxiliary downfalls of tantra in general. In addition, he presents the twenty-seven root downfalls and twenty-five auxiliary precepts unique to the vehicle of the Great Perfection.

Without taking and maintaining samaya, there is no way of accomplishing any tantric attainments. Lord Buddha said:[3]

> For those who have impaired the samaya,
> the Buddha never said that they could accomplish tantra.

Je Tsongkhapa writes:[4]

> Those who claim to be practicing tantra without observing the samaya have strayed from it, since in *anuttara* tantra it is said, "The tantra will never be accomplished by those who do not observe samaya, who have not received proper empowerments, and who do not know the suchness (the meaning of empowerment, the wisdom), even though they practice it."

The three vows are steps that lead to the same goal, enlightenment. The stream of lower vows merges into the higher vows, and the higher vows embody all the vows and the merits of the lower ones. Furthermore, when we are empowered in tantra, we are also ordained in the prātimokṣa and bodhisattva disciplines. Ngari Panchen writes:[5]

> By receiving empowerment, all three vows are born simultaneously.

Tibetan Buddhists, as followers of tantra, must observe all three vows. Most lay practitioners observe the upāsaka or upāsikā vows of prātimokṣa, the bodhisattva vows, and tantric vows. Most monks physically observe each moral code of the *vinaya* in order to tame the mind. Mentally they uphold the aspiration of bodhisattvas, the aspiration to be of benefit to others with love and compassion. With wisdom awareness, they are also tantrics accepting all appearances as the path of pure perception. Longchen Rabjam writes:[6]

> With the unconflicted three vows of
> śrāvaka, bodhisattva, and *vidyādhara*,
> tame your mind stream, benefit others,
> and transform every appearance into the path of pure nature.

Highly accomplished tantrics, through their power of realization, can maintain the vow of celibacy even if they have consorts, but such claims of attainment are authentic only if they are also able to bring the dead back to life. So for a highly perfected trainee of higher tantra, all other vows are perfected. The *Māyājālatantra* states:[7]

> In the vow of unexcelled tantra,
> all the disciplines of vinaya and
> the disciplines of the bodhisattva
> are entirely embodied and are pure.

Many of us, who are so-called Dharma followers, are mediocre with respect to true discipline and realization but have the tendency to boast about our wisdom. We become lax about the guidelines of the precepts and indulge in craving for sensual phenomena under the guise of transmuting everything into the means of training. Some of us adopt this attitude intentionally in order to polish our ego or for the sake of worldly pleasures. Others have deviated into these wrong notions because they are confused by the darkness of ignorance. Rather than being like eyes searching out others' faults, we should strive to be like a mirror that sees our own inadequacies.

The lineage of the three vows: The prātimokṣa lineage came to Tibet in three different traditions from the Sarvāstivāda school of ancient India, in the same way that it went to Thailand, Burma, and Sri Lanka from the Theravādin school.

The first tradition is the Lower Lineage of Vinaya (sMad-'Dul). This lineage was passed from the Buddha down to my teacher through the following succession: Buddha, Śāriputra, Prince Rāhulagupta, Brāhman Rāhulagupta, Nāgārjuna, Bhāvaviveka, Śrīgupta, Jñānagarbha, and Śāntarakṣita (who brought the lineage to Tibet in the 9th century C.E.), Ba Ratna, Tsang Rabsal, Lachen Gongpa Rabsal, Lume Tsultrim Sherab, Dorje Gyaltsen, Newo Trakpa Gyaltsen, Dre Sherab Bar, Cha Duldzin Tsöndru Bar, Zhönu Senge, Tromo Chewa Dudtsi Trak, Chimchen Namkha Trak, Trakpa Sherab, Chimtön Lobzang Trakpa, Kunga Gyaltsen, Trupa Sherab (the last six masters were throneholders of Narthang monastery), Gendun Trub (the first Dalai Lama), Kunga Gelek of Nenying, Gendun Gyatso (the second Dalai Lama), Gelek Palzang of Dewachen, Paljor Gyatso, Könchok Chöpel (the last three masters were throneholders of Ganden monastery), Könchok Tendzin, Lochen Dharmaśrī (1654–1717),[8] Chökyi Trakpa, Gyurme Chöden, Orgyen Tendzin (the last four were abbots of Mindröling monastery),[9] Rigdzin Zangpo, Sengtruk Pema Tashi (both were abbots of Dzogchen monastery),[10] Domtsa Khenpo of Shechen monastery, Sershul Khenpo Ngawang Kunga of Dodrupchen monastery, and Khenpo Chöyak (living) of Shukchung monastery. Additionally, after Sengtruk Pema Tashi, a lineage of vinaya ordination descended through Gyalse Zhenphen Thaye (1800–?) of Dzogchen monastery, Lingtul Gyaltsen Palzang, Khenpo Dorje Palzang of Kathok monastery, Khenpo Kalzang Wangchuk of Nyakrong, Situ Chökyi Gyatso (1880–1925) of Kathok monastery, and Choktrul Chökyi Dawa (1894–1959) of Tarthang monastery to Kyabje Jigme Thubten Shedrub (1932–), the Third Pema Norbu, who is the current head of the Nyingma school. Nyingmapas and most of the Gelukpas are ordained in the Lower Lineage.[11]

The second tradition is the Middle Lineage of Vinaya (Bar-'Dul), also known as the Khache or Panchen Lineage. This lineage came from the Buddha through Śāriputra, Prince Rāhulagupta, Brāhman Rahulagupta, Nāgārjuna, Guṇajñāna (Guṇamati), Ratnamitra, Dharmabhadra (Dharmapāla), Guṇapati (Guṇasagara), Dharmamālā, Śāntākaragupta (Ākaragupta), and Panchen Śakyaśrībhadra of Khache (Kaśmīr),[12] who brought it to Tibet and ordained Sakya Paṇḍita (1181–1251), Dorje Palzang, and others. Most of the Sakyapas and Kagyupas are ordained in this lineage.[13]

The third tradition is the Upper Lineage of Vinaya (sTod-'Dul), brought to Tibet by an Indian scholar named Dharmapāla. However, this lineage no longer exists[14] in Tibet so that the Middle Lineage has become popularly known as the Upper Lineage.

As mentioned earlier, the bodhisattva vow has two major lineages. The Lineage of Nāgārjuna came from the Buddha to Mañjuśrī and then to Nāgārjuna, and the Lineage of Asaṅga came from the Buddha to Maitreya and then to Asaṅga.[15] These lineages later came to Tibet from the Mahāyāna masters of ancient India.

Tantras of various types appeared in the world and also came to Tibet through numerous lineages. But the major tantras of *mahāyoga* and *anuyoga* of Nyingma came from Samantabhadra of the *dharmakāya* through the buddhas of the five families of the *sambhogakāya,* the three bodhisattvas, the five classes of beings, and King Dza of Oḍḍiyāna, the first human recipient. Later, Vimalamitra, Guru Padmasambhava, and Nub Sangye Yeshe brought them to Tibet. Nyingthik Tantras, the innermost teachings of *atiyoga,* came from Samantabhadra of the dharmakāya through the peaceful and wrathful deities, Vajradhara, Vajrasattva, Vajrapāṇi, and Garab Dorje, the first human recipient. Later, Vimalamitra and Padmasambhava brought them to Tibet.

Maintaining the vows: It is essential to learn each code of law of the three vows, as explained in *Ascertaining the Three Vows,* and to observe them accordingly. However, because of limitations of knowledge, time, atmosphere, dedication, and energy, it might be hard for many of us to observe them. I like to quote the advice of H. H. Dodrupchen Rinpoche given at the end of the empowerment of the *Nyingthik Yabshi,* bestowed in 1989 in the temple of the Mahāsiddha Nyingmapa Center in Massachusetts. He said: "It is difficult to learn the names of the vows, let alone observe them. So at least you should strive to be loving to people, especially those who are close to you such as friends, relatives, Dharma brothers and sisters, and neighbors. Try to avoid harming them. Be respectful to them, as all are enlightened in their true nature. Then, in a simple way, you are moving toward fulfilling the prātimokṣa vow of not harming others, the bodhisattvas' vow of being loving to others, and the tantric vow of pure perception."

Restoring the vows: After taking the vows, we must learn how to repair any decay and ruptures of the vows, for we will undoubtedly be causing these to happen. Otherwise, it will be like an explosive in the hand of a deranged person. Each of the three vows has its own methods of purification. However, since the followers of Tibetan Buddhism are tantric practitioners, it is proper to use a tantric means of purification, as this is more powerful and purifies the faults committed in any of the vow categories. For many of us, the purification through Vajrasattva recitation is familiar. It is also one of the most powerful means of purification. This purification must be practiced with "the four forces." "The force of the source of the power of purification" is total reliance on Vajrasattva with convinced faith, devotional warmth, and one-pointed concentration. One should see Vajrasattva as the embodiment of the power of purification of all the buddhas, who possess perfect wisdom, infinite power, and ceaseless compassion. "The force of sincere regret" is the strong feeling of remorse for whatever faults one has committed, knowingly or unknowingly, as if poison had been consumed. "The force of promising not to repeat the fault again" is the determination from the depths of one's heart that now, even at the cost of one's life, one won't commit such a fault again. If we have strong, sincere regret and determination not to commit faults again, like using brakes and steering when driving, this will gradually force us to change the direction of our life. "The force of purification" is the actual recitation and meditation of Vajrasattva. One should visualize Vajrasattva and consort above the crown of one's head and repeat prayers and *mantras* with faith and devotion. With sincere regret for past misdeeds and a total commitment not to repeat them, one should pray for their blessing, which is the power of purification. One should feel devotion and openness and the compassion and power of Vajrasattva and his consort. Then, as the result, the purification power descends from the body of Vajrasattva in the form of streaming nectar, washing down all impurities of our body, speech, and mind without leaving any trace. Feel certain that you are then free from all defilements. Finally, fill your body with the nectar and the feeling of peace, bliss, and openness, the blessing power of Vajrasattva. Confession and purification is not just the act of telling the person involved, even if it's a lama, that (for example) "I hate you" or "I did hate you," but is the meditation and experience of the four forces experienced from the depths of one's heart.

The benefits of observing the vows: The achievement of happiness and enlightenment is the result of maintaining vows. Remember that maintaining a vow is making a strong commitment to live only with proper and virtuous deeds and to refrain from wrong and evil deeds. In this way, we will create good karma or, in the case of tantra, pure samaya, and this will result in happiness, wisdom, and buddhahood, the source of joy for all. Ngari Panchen Pema Wangyal writes:

> Then one will spontaneously achieve the goals of oneself and of others.

This timely book is composed of a translation of the root text, *Ascertaining the Three Vows,* and the wonderful commentary on it by H. H. Dudjom Rinpoche. It fulfills a crucial need for serious Western students of Tibetan Buddhism. Sangye Khandro, with her gift for language and knowledge of Buddhist wisdom, has made every word of these most important texts available to English readers. At last we have a handbook in English that explains the full code of discipline of the prātimokṣa, bodhisattva, and tantric trainings, along with an elucidation of their philosophical principles and historical background.

Tulku Thondup
Buddhayana, Massachusetts

INTRODUCTION

With the coming of the fourth Buddha into this world of human beings, in order to reveal the mode through which one may accomplish buddhahood and in accordance with the needs and responsibilities of the limitless beings to be tamed, Lord Buddha turned the Dharma wheel on three great occasions. Although inconceivable numbers of methods to reach freedom were revealed, these teachings are grouped into eighty-four thousand categories, which comprise the four baskets.[16] These four baskets are further condensed into the prātimokṣa, bodhisattva, and mantra vehicles, each of which has been the basis for innumerable commentaries written by many learned scholars and accomplished masters since the time of the Buddha. Of these many commentaries, there are few that reveal the manner through which an individual can engage in the vows and practice of prātimokṣa, bodhisattva, and mantra by incorporating the essence of all three. Also, few commentaries have been able to present an accurate overview of all three vehicles (within which the nine vehicles exist) unmistakenly and without confusion in as stainlessly clear a way as the root text, *Ascertaining the Three Vows.*

In fact, *Ascertaining the Three Vows* came about exactly in accordance with the intention of the great Mañjuśrī. It was written by an emanation of the royal line of King Trisong Detsen: the powerful scholar, realized master, and holder of the rare title Mahā Paṇḍita known as Ngari Panchen Pema Wangyi Gyalpo (1487–1542). This great Mahā Paṇḍita wrote this text to clarify how an individual can indeed embrace all three vows by simultaneously incorporating them into practice without conflict. In addition, the text presents an unmistaken and detailed description of each vow category, arranged like a wish-fulfilling jewel. All followers of the Dharma will regard this text as a lamp that illuminates the true path and will utilize it in the same way that they would put on a beautiful ornament. Indeed, this presentation, which unites the three vows, is the mother source of the practice of all three vows, as well as the supreme crown ornament of all vehicles of practice.

Concerning the life of the illustrious author, Ngari Panchen was himself the ninth emanation of the Dharma King Trisong Detsen. He emanated into this world for the general welfare and purpose of mankind, and specifically, to further the propagation of the doctrine in the land of Tibet. He was born in the region known as Ngari Lowo, and his father, Jamyang Rinchen Gyaltsen, a great scholar and practitioner, was the last in the line of the ancestral religious heritage of Marpa Lotsawa. His mother's name was Drompa Gyen. At the time of his conception both parents received marvelous signs in their dreams, as well as the appearance of a rainbow over the roof of their house. In addition, the sound of roaring dragons was heard arising from the natural elements. The child was born in the Female Fire Sheep year (1487) and was given the name Pema Wangyal. In his eighth year he received the precepts of lay ordination from his own father. After taking bodhisattva vows, uncontrived bodhicitta spontaneously awakened in him. Then, again from his own father, he received all the transmissions for the three inner yogas of mahā, anu, and ati, which included the entire transmission of the *Chido Gongdu* (*sPyi-mDo dGongs-'Dus*) [*The Sūtra that Gathers All Intentions*]; *Gyutrul Drawa* (*sGyu-'Phrul Dra-wa*) [*Net of Illusory Manifestations*]; and *Semde* (*Sems-sDe*) [*Mind Class*]. Following this, through his diligent enthusiastic effort and training, he fully mastered everything contained in the Nyingma lineages of *kama* and *terma.* He realized all essential instructions in exact accordance with the scriptures. He received teachings from countless scholars and meditation masters, and he contemplated and proceeded through the stages of training without any laziness or hesitation. By his twentieth year he had fully realized the prātimokṣa vinaya, *madhyamaka*, and hundreds of scriptures, and had mastered all the major and minor sciences. Then, after impartially accomplishing each of the later translation schools, he was given the title Mahā Paṇḍita, and his fame spread in the ten directions.

At the age of twenty-one he began an extensive retreat of Red Yamāntaka, completing both the generation and completion cycles. The wrathful Mañjuśrī Yamāntaka appeared directly before him. At age twenty-five he received full ordination from Lowo Khenchen Khenpo Sönam Lhundrub and embraced all two-hundred and fifty precepts, which he immaculately guarded from deterioration. It was at that time in Tibet that Ngari Panchen became known far and wide as the purest upholder of the prātimokṣa discipline. From then onward, having completely forsaken the eight worldly attitudes, he never remained in any one location for very long. As a true renunciate he roamed from one uncertain place to another, traveling to all the sacred power places where he remained in retreat performing various accomplishment ceremonies.

After this practice pilgrimage he journeyed to Nepal, where he studied under and received transmissions from the greatest lamas in the region. After this, there was nothing in the early and later translation schools that he had not received, so he entered into an extended retreat. While in retreat, Ngari Panchen received unceasing visions of each deity that he accomplished. In particular, Guru Padmasambhava came to him in both visions and dreams time and time again to bestow empowerments and blessings. It was then that he was fully able to recall his past life as King Trisong Detsen, along with many others.

During the construction of Samye monastery, at the time when Guru Padmasambhava was bestowing empowerment upon the twenty-five great disciples, King Trisong Detsen's flower fell in the *maṇḍala's* center. This destined him to accomplish all eight wrathful meditational deities in the practice known as *Deshek Dupa* (*bDe-gShegs 'Dus-Pa*) [*Gathering of All the Sugatas*]. This is why during his life as Ngari Panchen he received the *Deshek Dupa* empowerment some twenty-five times. The twenty-fifth time, he received it from the unequaled great *mahāsiddha* of Lodrak Gönkar, Namkhai Naljorpa, who himself was a lineage holder of the ancestral heritage of the king. With that transmission, Ngari Panchen felt satisfied that the lineage he was holding was perfectly pure. Having received all that this great yogin's mind contained, Ngari Panchen then entered into seclusion to practice until he had visions of each of the eight *herukas*. He went on to accomplish both common and supreme attainments.

At age thirty-eight he himself began to give many transmissions from the early and later traditions. With a pure, impartial attitude he performed enlightened activities like a downpour of Dharma rain that brought countless aspirants to fruition. In this way he began the period of his life known as "accomplishing the purpose of others extensively in all directions."

At this time in central Tibet, both the early and later traditions had deteriorated, so Ngari Panchen traveled there to restore the doctrines of both, bringing immeasurable benefit.

At age forty-six he began to reveal his own profound treasures, beginning with the entire cycle of *Rigdzin Yongdu* (*Rig-'Dzin Yongs-'Dus*) [*Condensed Essence of the Pure-Awareness Holders*], revealed from within the upper palace of Samye where it had been buried in a secret casket between the four images of Vairocana.

At age fifty-six he demonstrated the signs of passing into *nirvāṇa*, after which many relics issued from his body and all regions of space were filled with marvelous rainbows and various signs of the highest level of attainment. An orb of light then arose from his body and traveled into the southwestern direction of space, where it disappeared. This was witnessed by the many people who had gathered, who then recalled that prior to his passing he had proclaimed: "Now it is time to depart for the copper-colored mountain" (Guru Rinpoche's southwestern pure realm). The gathered disciples then realized the significance of the mysterious orb of light.

Ngari Panchen, Pema Wangyi Gyalpo, having fully accomplished the deeds of a great scholar and realized being, is praised by those of nonsectarian views as the greatest scholar and master of his time.

The path of the three vows brings all eighty-four thousand categories of the precious Dharma together as one path. This is certainly the supreme path if practiced accordingly. This text, *Ascertaining the Three Vows*, is the very source of all commentaries written on the subject of the three vows. By understanding how to utilize all three vows simultaneously, one is able to maintain the moral ground of the Vajrayāna, which transforms the essence and increases all noble qualitites. This is just like finding a wish-fulfilling jewel. For those who truly wish to obtain freedom in this life, this text is a cause for joyful celebration.

Initially by emerging from the mark of the three realms of existence, and eventually by possessing the wealth of the awakened mind of aspiration and practice, and finally by arriving in the pleasure-garden continent of the mantra precepts and training, the purpose of oneself and others is spontaneously fulfilled and one arrives at the stronghold of all the conquerors.

For all who wish to travel to this continent of all-knowing omniscience, this text is the guide to that unmistaken path. It is my wish that all fortunate aspirants whose minds are renounced will study this text with great diligence.

Yangthang Tulku Rinpoche
Tashi Chöling, Oregon

Translator's Note

Although I possess few qualities, due to some small knowledge of the Tibetan written and oral language and the sincere wish to bring benefit to those of Western countries who desire to learn the precious Dharma, I have attempted to translate this invaluable text into English. This book contains a translation of the root text, *Ascertaining the Three Vows*, as well as a commentary to the root text based primarily on H. H. Dudjom Rinpoche's commentary and the explanations given by Khenpo Gyurme Samdrub. The commentary explains each word found in the root text, which is outlined in five chapters. The first chapter gives an overview of the stages of the main teaching, which is, of course, the subject of the three vows. It also clearly points to the view that this teaching is based on, which is the ultimate goal of Vajrayāna practice, the achievement of the status known as vajra-holder of the three categories, or vidyādhara (intrinsic-awareness holder). The status of a vidyādhara is no minor accomplishment; it is the ultimate goal of those who practice the Nyingma tradition of the Great Perfection. It is therefore extremely important for sincere aspirants on this path to possess the basic knowledge that this book presents as the very ground of their spiritual pursuit. The three vows and the many commentaries written on them by such celebrated masters as Lochen Dharmaśrī, Kunzang Sherab, and Je Mipham is the first course of study pursued in Nyingma scholastic institutions. The second, third, and fourth chapters offer in-depth explanations of the prātimokṣa precepts, the bodhisattva vows, and the words of honor of secret mantra. These explanations elaborate how the vows are obtained and who is qualified to receive them, what the vows are, how they are damaged or lost, how they are restored, how they are maintained, and what their benefits are. The fourth chapter, on secret mantra, provides an in-depth explanation of the specific words of honor of the Great Perfection Vehicle. Finally, the fifth chapter explains the manner in which all three categories are practiced simultaneously and without conflict so that the status of a vidyādhara may be attained.

We are now experiencing the rapid spread of the profound traditions of Vajrayāna Buddhism in countries where they were previously nonexistent. As a result, many questions arise concerning the different vows and modes of practice. Many are interested in ordination, yet do not understand how this fits into the broader perspective of Vajrayāna practice. Others intend to maintain their lives as householders, yet wonder if this disqualifies them to practice and accomplish the advanced methods employed in Vajrayāna. Many simply wonder why some teachers have vows as monks and nuns and why others are householders. This text is written to lay out the ground for the path of Vajrayāna practice and to elucidate the methods through which one is able to develop the skillful means necessary to simultaneously uphold all three vows. As this is the path that leads to perfect liberation in one body and in one lifetime, knowledge of the basis for this accomplishment is essential.

The commentary on the three vows written by His Holiness Dudjom Rinpoche was chosen for this book because of Dudjom Rinpoche's unrivalled scholarship and the profundity of the blessings derived through any connection established with his enlightened awareness and aspirations. In addition, Dudjom Rinpoche dedicated a great part of the latter years of his life to the establishment of Vajrayāna Buddhism in the West. In fact, this was one of the last commentaries that he wrote and was one of the major works included in his revision of the Nyingma Kama.

I would like to thank Khenpo Gyurme Samdrub for all the help he has rendered in giving clear explanations of the root text and commentary. His excellent command of English Dharma vocabulary has been extremely useful throughout all stages of this translation. I would also like to thank Rick Finney for his editorial assistance, Kay Henry for her help in preparing this manuscript for publication, Vesna Wallace for checking all the Sanskrit terms and for entering the correct diacritical marks, and, finally, Ani Yeshe Lhamo for her many hours of work preparing the original rough draft of the manuscript. Although there are always many tireless helpers to acknowledge, I think it is more important that we all share prayers that the virtue from this translation and its propagation may increase and expand the Buddha's doctrine and bring long, firm lives to all the great practitioners who uphold it. We pray for there to be happiness in this world, as well as for the pacification of all disease, famine, war, and unrest.

In dependence upon this excellent text and all the desirable qualities that arise from it, may all beings see with clear faith the true path of knowing what to accept and what to reject and be swiftly led to the paradise of omniscient freedom.

From this life onward may we and all others always obtain the precious human rebirth; and by unmistakenly ascending the stages on the path, together may we pick the fruit of permanent peace.

Sangye Khandro
Tashi Chöling, Oregon

THE COMMENTARY

First: The Initial Virtue

The initial virtue, the intermediate virtue, and the concluding virtue are the three divisions in this and in all commentaries that are written based on the Buddha's spoken teachings. These three divisions are similar to the three pure recollections: those of motivation, nonconceptual awareness during the actual practice, and the concluding dedication of merit. In the initial virtue there are the three divisions that explain the title of the text, the homage, and the commitment to compose.

I. The Title of the Text:

> *A Branch on the Path of the Natural Great Perfection Called Ascertaining the Three Vows*

Within the profound expanse of the innate, unaltered, natural mind, all meanings, including the foundation, path, and result, are originally perfected. This spontaneous presence, which is unsurpassed by any other, is called "great." The unmistaken actualization of this nature is the ultimate fruit of all paths, the atiyoga. From anuyoga on down, all the paths of *sūtra* and tantra are practiced in order to realize this nature. In this way they are established as "branches" of the path. The three vows, the essence of the practice of all these paths, are the main subject at hand. To establish an accurate understanding of the view of the three vows through the three investigations—actual, inferential, and scriptural—is the meaning of "ascertaining."

Śāstra literally means that which has the potential to sever all negative emotions and grant refuge from rebirth in the three lower realms. Specifically, a śāstra is a commentary on the Buddha's teachings written by a perfect follower. There are three levels to be considered here. Ideally, the author of a śāstra must have realization of the nature of the *dharmatā*. To qualify as average the author should have had a vision of the deity. At least, the author should be perfectly learned in the five major sciences.[17] In addition, the commentary must be eloquently written with the qualities and ability to alleviate the causes of delusion, as well as to produce the results that grant protection from inferior rebirths in cyclic existence.

The purpose of the title will vary according to the sensibility of the reader. Those of superior sensibility, just by reading the title, will be able to realize the entire meaning of the text. Those of average sensibility will derive a general idea of its contents, and those of common sensibility will become interested and inspired to begin to study the text.

II. Homage:

A. General homage to the supremely kind guru:

> *Namo Guruve!*
> Homage to the Guru-Lama!

"Namo" means to pay homage. "Guru" describes an individual whose noble qualities are limitless, whose wisdom-knowledge is unsurpassed, and whose great loving-kindness is unequalled. To such a guru-lama, with great admiration and respect from the three doors of body, speech, and mind, homage is rendered.

B. Specific homage to the great master, Padmasambhava:

> By churning the treasure ocean of the glorious two accumulations, the white light of knowledge and loving-kindness brings forth the all-pervasive rain of the definitive secret vehicle. To the supreme crown jewel of all scholars and accomplished masters of Tibet's Land of Snow, to the guide of all sentient beings, the Lake-born Vajra (Guru Padmasambhava), I pay homage!

It is believed by the Vedic school of Hinduism that by churning the ocean the moon arose. The author draws from this example to poetically illustrate the qualities of Guru Padmasambhava. By churning the vast ocean of the accumulation of ordinary and wisdom merit, supreme wisdom and loving-kindness arise indivisibly, forming the maṇḍala of the moon with its cooling, moist, illuminating rays. The all-pervasiveness of a rain shower is likened to the spontaneity of the concerned action that arises from such a "moon" to reveal the secret mantra teachings in order to tame the minds of beings.

This analogy exemplifies the object of specific homage, the great master Padmasambhava, who is the very embodiment of the great ocean of the two accumulations of merit, the source from which all enlightened qualities of wisdom-knowledge and compassion arise. As the supreme crown jewel of all scholars and accomplished masters in the three realms, including the snow land of Tibet, he is well known as the Lake-born Vajra.[18]

The Lake-born Vajra, Padmasambhava, was born from the center of a lotus without depending on parents. The word "vajra" refers to this transcendence of the concept of birth and death. Because he possesses the wisdom to guide all beings on whatever level is necessary according to their specific needs, he is known as the supreme guide of beings.

III. The Commitment to Compose:

> This sage, skilled in knowing how to cleanse the mental stains of beings and upholding the lapis lazuli vase of supreme intelligence,

> bestows the ambrosia-like explanations of the three vows. May all those with sincere interest gather here to partake of this!

The author, Ngari Panchen, refers to himself as a sage, defined as one who is wise in the worldly knowledge of what to accept and reject. As is the case with all scriptural commentaries, the author's "commitment" must reveal with superiority the four necessities of this Dharma. The first necessity is the subject, in this case the three vows. The second necessity is a superior explanation of the subject so that the meaning and purpose can be fully understood, leading readers to embark upon the path to liberation. This bestows temporary benefit. Third, once the path is entered and perfected, perfect awakening is revealed as the ultimate benefit. Fourth, the interdependent relationship between each of these four is demonstrated, in that one arises in dependence upon the other and is accomplished accordingly.

Second: The Intermediate Virtue

The actual text is divided into three sections:

I. A brief explanation of the stages of the main teaching
II. An extensive explanation of the nature and precepts of each of the three vows
III. A concise explanation of the manner in which an individual practices the three vows together without conflict

Chapter One:
A Brief Explanation of the Stages of the Main Teaching

I. Chapter One: A Brief Explanation of the Stages of the Main Teaching, in three subdivisions:

A. Recognizing the basis for purification and the ultimate result:

> The general expression of primordial wisdom is the Great Perfection atiyoga. The perfectly pure embodiment, *kāya*, of the great Vajradhara is ultimate fruition, the oneness of *buddha*.

Generally, the Great Perfection is considered in three divisions: foundation, path, and result. The foundational Great Perfection is the fundamental nature of all living beings as the essential nature of the realized ones. The path of Great Perfection is the ultimate result sought by all the vehicles, namely the cleansing of the two obscurations and all habitual propensities, which overshadow the buddha nature. The resultant state of the Great Perfection is separation from all obscurity, and dwelling in the inner lucency of the ever-youthful vase presence, the unsurpassed nature of pure presence and primordial wisdom. This nature of truth, known here as the "general expression of primordial wisdom," is otherwise inexpressible, yet prevalent throughout existence and beyond.

The basis for the purification is the buddha nature itself. The object of the purification is the temporary veil through which all that appears as cyclic existence is perceived. The purification is the essence of the path of the three vows, the profound path of mantra, practiced by those who uphold pure awareness, the vidyādharas. Although the path itself is not inherently "true," it exists in order to fully purify the sudden stain of the two obscurations as well as all residual habitual propensities. The result of this purification is the spontaneous accomplishment of the two purposes, which manifests as the five states of pure presence, kāyas, and the five primordial wisdoms,[19] the nature of which is the Buddha. This buddha nature is also referred to as Samantabhadra or Mahāvajradhara. This is the result of all vehicles, the "ultimate fruition, the oneness of buddha."

B. A general explanation of the different aspects of the path to accomplish, in three subdivisions:

1. A brief revelation of the one and only path:

> Although the ways of entry into the profound and extensive Dharma are beyond number, without relying upon the great secret path of maturation and liberation (Vajrayāna), there is no attainment, the perfected Buddha said.

The reference to the profound Dharma indicates its ability to reveal the ultimate nature of emptiness, as it is. The reference to extensive Dharma indicates all conventional paths that comprise the multitudes of entranceways. However, without reliance upon the great secret vehicle of ripening empowerments, as well as the supreme paths of liberation, generation, and completion stage practice, enlightenment will never be obtained, because what binds us to cyclic existence is the extremely subtle red and white bodhicitta and the vital air, through which the three appearances[20] are generated at the time of transition from this life to the next. The methods that clear the obscurations created by these three appearances are found only in the Vajrayāna. This was clearly taught by the perfected Buddha, who actualized the primordial wisdom of being unimpeded by, and unattached to, all knowable things.

2. A specific explanation of how vehicle distinctions are merely steps on the path, in two subdivisions:

a. An explanation of the general characteristics of the foundational vehicles:

> Just as mental engagements are unceasing, one cannot possibly engage in all the inconceivable numbers of vehicles. As places to rest leading to the only true path, each one possesses its own corresponding pinnacle and result. Although these are obtainable as the individual renunciations of each vehicle, what result will be obtained without entering the one path of all vehicles?

Here it is clearly stated that it is characteristic of the foundational vehicles to serve as rest stops that eventually lead the aspirant to embark upon the only true path. Although each vehicle does bring its result, unless one enters and practices the Vajrayāna, the ultimate result of buddhahood remains unobtained.

b. A specific explanation of how all paths leading to liberation are included in the nine vehicles:

> Here, according to the tradition of the Great Perfection, the *śrāvakabuddhayāna, pratyekabuddhayāna,* and *bodhisattvayāna* are the three causal vehicles of characteristics; *kriyātantra, ubhayatantra,* and *yogatantra* are the three outer tantras; and the unsurpassed father tantra of mahāyoga, that known as the mother tantra (anuyoga), and the nondual tantric class of atiyoga are the three inner tantras (completing the nine vehicles).

The śrāvakayāna is generally characterized as the path of reliance upon the teacher's words, which, when understood, are then taught to others. The pratyekayāna is the path carried out independent of a spiritual mentor. Here, the aspirant seeks alone to achieve the result of victory over cyclic existence. Bodhisattvas aspire to accomplish perfect awakening by actively fulfilling the purpose of others without ever becoming fainthearted or apprehensive. This type of courageous intent and effort qualifies such aspirants as "brave awakened ones," the meaning of "bodhisattva."

The results obtained from practicing these three vehicles are similar to the ultimate result of buddhahood, but are not the ultimate result. Therefore, they are known as paths that possess "characteristics" (similar to those that produce awakening). They are also known as the three causal vehicles, because although each respective vehicle produces its own corresponding result, it is not the result of buddhahood.

The kriyātantra focuses primarily upon action and the *upatantra* (also known as the ubhayatantra) upon view and conduct. The yogatantra places emphasis upon internal meditation. These three are similar to the three vehicles below them because they seek for spiritual attainment to be received from an external source. Thus they are called the three outer tantras.

Although there are many ways in which the inner tantras are more exalted than the outer, the concise difference lies in the view, meditation, and conduct of the inner tantras. These possess uncommon power, qualifying them as unsurpassed tantras. The first inner tantra is the father tantra, mahāyoga, which focuses primarily upon the method of the generation stage. The mother tantra, anuyoga, focuses upon the wisdom nature of the completion stage. The nondual tantra, atiyoga (also known as *binduyoga*), focuses upon the stages of nondual clear light. Each of these three vehicles actualizes the view that realizes the equal nature of *saṃsāra* and nirvāṇa; hence, spiritual attainments are not searched for externally. This is the reason they are well known as the three inner tantras.

All paths that lead to liberation are found within these nine vehicles.

3. Revealing the manner in which the prātimokṣa and bodhisattva categories are branch precepts of mantra vows, in three subdivisions:

a. Showing how upholders of each of the three categories qualify to enter the path of mantra:

> It is taught that the individual upholders of the śrāvakabuddhayāna, pratyekabuddhayāna, and bodhisattvayāna can enter the path of the vajra-holders. This is clearly documented in the *Tantra of Five Hundred Thousand Verses* (*Pañcaśatasahasra*).

Although beings whose minds are still untamed possess myriad sensibilities, it is generally agreed that those of lower sensibility qualify as śrāvakas, those of middling sensibility as pratyekas, and those of superior sensibility as bodhisattvas. Each of these individuals may enter the Vajrayāna to become a vidyādhara.

For example, if you liken these differences in sensibility to types of metal, the inferior would be like iron, the middling would be like copper, and the superior would be like silver. If you add a chemical preparation that converts all metals into gold, each will become gold regardless of what its original status was. Likewise, after individuals enter the vajra-maṇḍala, there is no distinction among them, for they all attain the status of a vidyādhara.

b. Although the path of mantra has many entranceways, this is not the present subject of discussion:

> Since the mode of entering mantra depends on distinctions of sensibility, there exist many entranceways. However, this is not the principal subject of discussion.

Bearing in mind the immense varieties and differences in intelligence, receptivity, and faculties of all living beings, there must be a variety of modes through which they are able to enter the Vajrayāna. Nevertheless, those of superior sensibility may enter Vajrayāna directly without ever having engaged upon the paths that precede it.

Others may enter each path individually, ascending in progressive order as the ultimate result of each path is actualized.

Due to the different needs of each and every sentient being still on the path, there are countless ways to engage and eventually meet with the Vajrayāna. To elaborate upon this here would be to stray from the main subject of the three categories of vows.

c. Recognizing and establishing the purpose of this subject, in two subdivisions:

1. A general explanation of the manner in which the superior, average, and common receive the vows
2. A specific explanation of how the average aspirants receive the vows

1. A general explanation of the manner in which the superior, average, and common receive the vows, in two subdivisions:

1.a. Briefly revealed:

> Here, those of superior, average, and common sensibility,...

1.b. An extensive explanation in three parts:

1.b.1. The manner in which the superior receive all three vows simultaneously:

> ...those fortunate ones of superior intelligence who have previously perfected all training, by receiving empowerment, instantaneously develop all three vows. As was the case with Indrabhūti, realization and liberation are simultaneous.

Superior aspirants of supreme intelligence are those who possess the fortunate karma of having perfected the two accumulations of merit in previous lifetimes. Therefore, the necessary purification has already been completed. Such individuals with fortunate karma no longer need to rely upon the common paths for purification. Just by receiving empowerment, all three vows develop instantaneously. Such individuals then realize the purpose of the empowerment and are simultaneously liberated. This was the case with the king of Oḍḍiyāna, Indrabhūti. Prior to his realization, King Indrabhūti asked Lord Buddha if there was a method to achieve buddhahood without having to abandon desirable objects. Omnisciently perceiving that the king possessed fortunate karmic propensities, the Buddha manifested the empowerment-maṇḍala at that very moment. While receiving the empowerment, the king realized the nonduality of the two kāyas. In the context of the Vajrayāna vows, the total abandonment of harming others constitutes the prātimokṣa. The total accomplishment of the purpose of others constitutes the activity of a bodhisattva. And the essence of the mantra vow is the maintenance of the method of the great pure equality.

1.b.2. The manner in which the average receive the three vows individually:

> The average rely upon the individual ritual for each of the three vows, obtaining them progressively like Nāgārjuna.

An individual of average sensibility qualifies as a suitable vessel for the seven categories of precepts according to the prātimokṣa-vinaya. After embracing one or more of these seven categories, the individual then qualifies to receive bodhisattva vows from one or both of the two traditions (those of Nāgārjuna and Asaṅga). With these two vows (prātimokṣa and bodhisattva) as the basis, the individual may then receive mantra words of honor through empowerment in accordance with his or her capacity. In this way the three vows are received progressively, in dependence upon their respective rituals. This is exemplified by the life story of the great spiritual master Nāgārjuna.

1.b.3. The manner in which the common aspirants are led to gradually engage in the three vows:

> The less fortunate common aspirants, whose minds are more difficult to tame, must gradually familiarize themselves with the purification training of the ten precepts, the four philosophical doctrines, kriyātantra, ubhayatantra, and yogatantra, after which they engage in the unsurpassed. This is taught in the *Tantra of the Two Investigations* (*brTag-pa gNyis-pa*).

"Less fortunate common aspirants" refers to individuals who from the past and in the present life have a weak accumulation of the two merits. As a result of this lack of merit, their minds are more difficult to subdue, thus producing the need to be introduced to each path before being led to the next.

Initially the mind is prepared for practice by listening to teachings on the faults of cyclic existence and the benefits of liberation. After familiarizing oneself with the discipline of the eight twenty-four-hour precepts, the vows of lay ordination are taken. This is followed by embracing the ten precepts of a novice and, later, the precepts of full ordination. The stages of study include an investigation of the four Buddhist philosophical schools through which, according to the Vaibhāṣika and Sautrāntika, the lack of a truly existing self is proven and realized. Afterwards, with the taking of the bodhisattva vows, the views of the Cittamātra and Madhyamaka are established. After practicing the outer tantras of kriyā, upa, and yoga, one may enter the unsurpassed tantras.

C. A specific explanation of how the average receive vows, in five divisions:

1. An explanation of the higher and lower supports as well as the exception:

> Now, the specific method for the average will be discussed. Upholders of full, novice, and lay ordination qualify as superior, average, and common vajra-holders respectively. This is taught in the *Vajrakīlaya* and *Kālacakra-tantras*. However, those who possess primordial wisdom are held as foremost.

In this treatise, *Ascertaining the Three Vows*, the methods for those of average sensibility are the main subject of discussion. This is because the vast majority of practitioners fall within this category and embark upon the path accordingly.

The basis for entering the mantra path is prātimokṣa. This means that prātimokṣa precepts of either lay, novice, or full ordination must be embraced. Then, according to these three levels of precepts, an individual will qualify as a common, average, or superior vajra-holder upon entering mantra. The lay vajra-holder is inferior, the novice is mediocre, and the fully ordained is superior. This point is agreed upon in both the *Vajrakīlaya* and *Kālacakra-tantras*. However, there is one exception. Even if an individual is a lay vajra-holder but has realized the primordial wisdom of the level of the path of seeing,[21] he qualifies as "absolute fully ordained" and is respected as "foremost."

2. Revealing the individual philosophies of each of the three vows:

> According to the root text of the earlier translation tantric class, the *Sarvasamudita-sūtra*: "One's own purpose, the purpose of others, and great benefit" are explained as the nature of prātimokṣa, bodhicitta, and abhiṣeka respectively. The individual upholders are well known among the learned as śrāvakas, bodhisattvas, and vidyādharas.

According to prātimokṣa, the motivating force is one's own personal attainment of permanent peace. According to the bodhisattva training, it is both the wish that all others may obtain perfect awakening and the motivation to practice for their sake. Then, after receiving empowerment into mantra, one must constantly maintain skillful means and wisdom, bringing great waves of benefit to oneself and others alike. The individuals who uphold these moral principles as their spiritual pursuit are known first as śrāvakas, then as bodhisattvas, and finally as vidyādharas.

3. The manner in which the lower two are branches of the higher:

> Therefore, the two lower, common vows are understood here to be branches of the unsurpassed anuttara empowerment. This is taught according to the ocean-like explanations of the tantric classes.

If a prātimokṣa precept-holder obtains mantra precepts, the prātimokṣa vow of mantra becomes the vow to abstain from harming others. Likewise, the bodhisattva vow of mantra is the samaya of Buddha Vairocana. In fact, the essence of all precepts for the prātimokṣa and bodhisattva trainings are perfectly complete within mantra. In addition, even if the two lower vows of prātimokṣa and bodhisattva have not been previously taken, in order to become a vajra-holder one needs only to receive empowerment in which the prātimokṣa and bodhisattva vows are automatically received.

4. In order to easily understand each of the three vow categories, the following three chapters set forth each vow as follows:

> Penetrating the inner meaning and source of each of the three vows; initially, the way to receive vows that have not been previously obtained; afterwards, how to protect them from deterioration; and finally, if they become impaired, the way to restore them: These are the four steps that apply to each vow.

An extensive overview of each of the three vows is given in the next three chapters. "The four steps that apply to each vow" refers to the way in which each will be explained in its respective chapter. Initially, the source of the vow and its nature and distinctions will be discussed. Then, the manner through which one may obtain the vow for the first time, including the ritual for bestowing the precepts, will be discussed. Next, the different enumerations of vows and the methods through which to guard them from deterioration will be presented. Finally, in the case of a downfall or damaged vow, the methods of restoration will be revealed.

5. A recapitulation of the first chapter:

> This general explanation of the stages of the main teaching completes
> the recapitulation of the first chapter.

This recapitulation is simply a way of reiterating the theme of the first chapter, which serves the purpose of preparing the reader for the main subject to be covered in the remaining four chapters.

II. An extensive explanation of the nature and training of each of the three vows in three divisions, which comprise the second, third, and fourth chapters:

A. Chapter Two: Prātimokṣa
B. Chapter Three: Bodhisattva
C. Chapter Four: Secret Mantra

CHAPTER TWO:
AN EXPLANATION OF THE PRĀTIMOKṢA-VINAYA

A. Chapter Two: An Explanation of the Prātimokṣa-vinaya, in three subdivisions:

1. The manner in which Lord Buddha taught the precious doctrine of the vinaya:

> In Varanasi, the Buddha primarily taught the Four Noble Truths and
> the practice of higher morality to the Five Excellent Ones.[22]

The basket of morality, the Vinaya Piṭaka, was the subject of the first turning of the Dharma wheel, which occurred within the context of the five fully endowed circumstances. These five are the fully endowed teacher, the unequaled Lord Buddha Śākyamuni; the fully endowed place, the central land of the *arhats*, Varanasi, India (Varanasi is a sacred land, where many realized saints have vanished without leaving ordinary human remains); the fully endowed time, seven weeks after the Buddha achieved perfect awakening, on the fourth day of the sixth month of the lunar calendar; the fully endowed Dharma, the training in extraordinary discipline and the first Dharma discourse on the Four Noble Truths; and the fully endowed assembly, the gathering of eighty thousand celestial beings and the Five Excellent Ones of the human race.

2. After the teachings were compiled, the way in which the teachings and accomplishments were upheld:

> The teachings were compiled by Kāśyapa and others. The arhats composed the *Treasury of Particular Explanations* and other texts, which were propagated by Yönten Öd (Guṇaprabha) and Shakya Öd (Śākyaprabha). The precept lineage of the earlier translations was propagated by Śāntarakṣita and, later, by Śākya Śrī.

On three great occasions the spoken teachings of Lord Buddha Śākyamuni were compiled. The first council came about when the Buddha's foremost disciples, Śāriputra and Maudgalyāyana, along with countless arhats, passed into *parinirvāṇa* along with Lord Buddha. Many celestial beings proclaimed that since all the fully ordained disciples of Lord Buddha had passed into parinirvāṇa along with their teacher, the Dharma was like an extinguished fire, with only smoke remaining. In order to correct this view, shortly after the parinirvāṇa, in the Nyagrodha cave at Rājagṛha (in central India) and under the sponsorship of King Ajātaśatru, the great Kāśyapa along with five hundred arhats convened during the summer rainy retreat known as *yarney* (*vārṣika*).[23] It was during this gathering that Ānanda recalled from memory the entire teaching Lord Buddha had given on the Sūtra Piṭaka. Upāli recalled from memory the Vinaya Piṭaka, while the great Kāśyapa immaculately recited the Abhidharma Piṭaka. Afterwards, these three "baskets" were compiled with the assistance of the gathering of arhats.

The second council occurred some one hundred and ten years after Lord Buddha's parinirvāṇa. In Vaiśālī seven hundred arhats, under the sponsorship of the Dharma king Aśoka, gathered in the Kusmapurī monastery to clarify what had become known as the "ten prohibitions."[24] The entire Tripiṭaka was recited to clarify that these ten were indeed not permitted, and afterwards the *sojong* (*uposatha*)[25] (purification) rite was performed to create conducive, auspicious circumstances.

After the reign of King Aśoka's grandson, King Vīrasena, several bhikṣus—such as Mahādeva, Bhadra, Sthavira, Nāgasena, and others—became possessed by demonic forces. Due to this there came to be five major points of discrepancy[26] concerning the prātimokṣa training. The discrepancy originated with the bhikṣus whose minds were possessed by demonic forces so that their actions were not in accordance with the true teachings of Lord Buddha Śākyamuni. As a result of this, these wrong views became accepted as doctrine even though they were prohibited according to the Buddha's teachings. For four generations of anarchical leadership, the *saṅgha* was thrown into turmoil and conflict. Since the Buddha had never allowed the vinaya to be put into writing, the debate persisted for a very long time. Eventually there emerged four major systems that became known as the four root schools of the śrāvakas. From these four roots eighteen minor schools emerged. The four root schools are the Sarvāstivāda, the Mahāsāṅghika, the Sthavira, and the Saṃmitīya. Seven of the eighteen minor schools follow the Sarvastivāda school's principles, five follow the Mahāsāṅghika, and three each follow the final two root schools.

The Sarvāstivāda is the basis of all four schools. The philosophy of this tradition asserts that there are five knowable things: that appearances are the basis of form; that the basis is the mind, accompanied by secondary mental events; the existence of nonassociated compositional factors; the existence of uncompounded factors (those that exist without cause or condition); and that all of these constitute substantial reality or existent things. This lineage originates with Rāhula, the Buddha's son, and the Sanskrit language is used during recitation of the vinaya. The patched saffron robe, indicating full ordination, must be made of more than nine sections and fewer than twenty-five, with the symbols of a Dharma wheel and lotus sewn on the top corner. The Sarvāstivāda school's followers assert the view that the phenomena of the three times are substantial reality, yet that all compounded phenomena are self-destructing in each moment. They also believe in the nonexistence of the "self." After three countless eons of time, according to this system, buddhahood is attained.

The second school, the Mahāsāṅghika, derives its name from the fact that originally the majority of the ordained saṅgha belonged to this school. The lineage originated with Mahā Kāśyapa. The robe of full ordination must have at least seven sections and no more than twenty-three. The symbols sewn on it are the endless knot and white conch shell. The language used to recite the vinaya is the Prākrit dialect.

The founder-abbots of the Sthavira school were Kātyāyana and the arhats. While reciting the vinaya in this school the Piśācika dialect is used. The saffron robe must have at least five and no more than twenty-one partitions. The symbol sewn upon it is the white conch shell. The philosophy maintained is that during the experience of the "absorption of cessation" there is mind but no incorrect (deluded) awareness. Through this school, buddhahood is achieved in no fewer than ten and no more than thirty eons of time.

The Saṃmitīya school derives its name from the fact that its followers displayed tremendous devotion over an extended period of time. The vinaya is recited in the Apabhraṃśa dialect, and the founding abbot was Upāli. The style and manner of preparing and wearing the saffron robe is in accordance with the Sthavira tradition. The philosophy asserted is that the "self" exists but is inexpressible. All knowable things are included in that which can and cannot be expressed.

The vinaya tradition that was propagated in Tibet is that of the Sarvāstivāda school.

After four generations of kings had come and gone, the conflict began to decrease. During the reign of King Kaniṣka, the sponsor for the third great council, there were still many differences of opinion. Then, in the Kaśmīr Temple, Kuvana Vihāra, five hundred arhats, four hundred bhikṣus, and five hundred bodhisattvas gathered. According to the prophetic dream of King Kṛkin, quoted in the sūtras, it was agreed that all eighteen schools upheld the Buddha's utterance. All volumes that comprise the Vinaya Piṭaka were written down, and all remaining volumes of the Sūtra and Abhidharma Piṭakas were put into writing.

The authorized commentaries based on the Buddha's spoken teachings originated and were maintained as follows:

In northern India, the arhat Upagupta, together with five hundred arhats, composed the extraordinary commentaries of the śrāvakas, such as the *Mahāvibhāṣa* (*Treasury of Particular Explanations*) and others. In addition, many great śrāvakas with qualities similar to those of the Buddha, such as Guru Kṛti and his assembly of arhats, composed additional commentaries. In particular the spiritual master Guṇaprabha, attainer of the third *bhūmi*, composed the *Vinayamūla-sūtra* (*Root Text on the Vinaya*) and further commentaries upon it, such as the *Twelve Thousand Verses.*

The spiritual master Śākyaprabha wrote the advice to the novice called *Śrāmaṇeratriśata-kārikā* (*Three Hundred Verses of the Novice*) and the commentary *Prabhāvatī,* further propagating the doctrine. Due to the kindness of these two spiritual masters, countless upholders of the victory banner of full ordination filled the land from the southern reaches of India to as far north as Śambhala.

Then, in accordance with the wishes of the great Dharma King Trisong Detsen, the vinaya tradition known as Sarvāstivāda was first brought into Tibet by Abbot Śāntarakṣita. This was passed down to Ba Ratna and others, becoming the only vinaya tradition to enter Tibet. Later, after the evil King Langdarma nearly destroyed the presence of the Buddhadharma in Tibet, three men called Mar, Yo, and Tsang carried the entire vinaya by mule pack to the place called Riwo Dentik. It was there that the great lama Gongpa Rabsal bestowed the vows of full ordination upon ten men from central and upper Tibet. Lume Tsultrim Sherab and others propagated this lineage, which became known as the "vinaya lineage of the lower region of Tibet." It remains undeteriorated to the present day.

When Dharmapāla, the great *paṇḍita* from eastern India, came to Ngari in Tibet, he brought with him the pure vinaya lineage, which he propagated extensively. This in turn became known as the "vinaya lineage of the upper region of Tibet." Again, at a later time, the lineage that became known as the "vinaya lineage of the central region of Tibet" was brought by Khache Panchen Śākya Śrī at the invitation of Trophu Lotsawa Champa Pal. This lineage was passed on to Sakya Paṇḍita Kunga Gyaltsen Pal Zangpo, then to Changchub Pal and Dorje Pal, and down the line to the present day.

3. The main topic of discussion, in two subdivisions:
a. A general explanation of the nature and distinctions of vows
b. A specific explanation of the format for the vow-receiving ritual

a. A general explanation in two additional subdivisions:

1. The nature of the vows:

> The nature is to take up the thought of renunciation; the foundation is to abstain from harming others. If born from the body and speech, it is objective by belief. In addition, it is believed to be the seed of the continuum of the "abandoning mind." In our school, this is according to individual views of higher and lower traditions.

The nature of the prātimokṣa vows is total renunciation and abstinence from harming others. This is called the morality of abandoning harm, a discipline that is practiced by a human being of the desire realm. All philosophical doctrines agree that this constitutes the abandonment of nonvirtue that is accumulated through body and speech (comprising seven of the ten nonvirtues). Regarding what actually qualifies as the vow itself, there is a point of conflict as to whether this is a perceivable or mental form. The śrāvaka philosophical doctrine of the Vaibhāṣika asserts that the nature of the vow arises as both a perceivable and mental form at the moment it is received. In the second moment after the vow is received, it remains as a mental form. The śrāvaka philosophical doctrine of the Sautrāntika asserts that the nature of the vow is complete mental transformation.[27] The Mahāyāna school of Cittamātra asserts that the nature of the vow is the mental continuum that has rejected impure or immoral conduct, as well as the seed or source from which it arises. The Madhyamaka school asserts that the nature of the vow is the "abandoning mind," which means that the primary and secondary consciousnesses (subtle mind) have attained full renunciation. On the Buddhist path there exist higher and lower philosophical schools with differing views that ultimately meet the needs of the intellectual differences of the aspirants.

2. The distinctions of the vows:

> The twenty-four-hour and lay ordination for male and female are the categories for laymen. Novice (male and female), female novice in training, and full ordination (male and female) are the five categories for the completely renounced. These are the eight divisions of prātimokṣa. According to the *Abhidharmakośa* tradition, if condensed according to type, there are four categories.

The cause for accomplishing each of these vow categories must be perfectly complete. The morality of total renunciation is the very ground upon which all prātimokṣa precepts are built. To abandon all negativity, and specifically to promise to maintain eight precepts for the duration of twenty-four hours, is the time-based discipline of the twenty-four-hour precept (*upavāsa*).

If the aspirant has already received lay ordination, then this twenty-four-hour vow becomes known as the taking of sojong upavāsa (to restore and purify the unwholesome). To take from one to five precepts for the duration of one's lifetime is known as upāsaka and upāsikā (lay ordination for both male and female aspirants). In the vinaya texts, mention is made only of the perfectly complete lay ordination, which is to accept all five precepts. In the abhidharma[28] scriptures, the various distinctions of lay ordination are mentioned, such as refuge and so forth.

To promise to maintain ten precepts for the duration of one's lifetime is to become a śrāmaṇera or śrāmaṇerikā (novice male or female). Upon that basis, to promise twelve additional precepts for a duration of two years is to become a śikṣamānā (female novice in training). To abandon the seven categories of defeats and so forth for the duration of one's life is to become fully ordained as a bhikṣu (male or female). These are the categories for ordination. To condense these eight categories of prātimokṣa into types, the fully ordained male and female category is the first, the male and female novice as well as the female novice in training are the second, male and female lay ordination are the third, and the twenty-four-hour vow constitutes the fourth. Thus, although technically there are eight prātimokṣa categories, they are condensed into these four. Since these categories exist due to distinctions of gender, there is no contradiction in condensing them according to type.

b. The specific explanation of the format for the vow-receiving ritual in five additional subdivisions:

1. The manner in which to receive vows previously unobtained
2. The methods that guard the vows from deterioration
3. The physical support necessary to receive the vows
4. The methods for restoring damaged vows
5. The benefits of guarding the vows

1. The manner in which to receive vows previously unobtained, in two subdivisions:

1.a. Briefly revealed:

> First, the manner for receiving vows not previously obtained is explained according to two traditions.

The two traditions for obtaining vows refer to the rituals of the past and the present day. The ritual of the past was a specialized way of receiving vows based on previous realization and the extraordinary powers of the preceptors. Those who depend upon symbolic indication, which is the nature of the present-day ritual, must first know the manner in which to receive vows not previously obtained. In the ritual of the past, full ordination occurred effortlessly. In the ritual of the present time, hardships are a necessary factor in receiving ordination.

1.b An extensive explanation, in two subdivisions:

1.b.1 The ritual of the past
1.b.2 The present-day ritual

1.b.1 The ritual of the past:

> In the ritual of the past, through self-origination, primordial wisdom realization, a message, promising the Buddha, coming forward, the four requests, in response to the questions, taking the promise of the

> heavy dharmas, and so forth, the aspirants had pure minds and the preceptor was an arhat.

The time frame of the existence of what is termed the "ritual of the past" was prior to the birth of Lord Buddha Śākyamuni, during his life, after his enlightenment, and until his parinirvāṇa. According to the śrāvaka school of the Vaibhāṣika, there were ten ways in which ordination was received. The first, "through self-ordination," refers to both the "fully awakened" and the "personal victor" higher levels of realization, at which time ordination self-originated simultaneously.

The second, "through primordial wisdom realization," refers to the level of accomplishment of the Five Excellent Ones, who were on the path of seeing. On that level of accomplishment their primordial wisdom nature was realized. The Buddha himself, the pratyekas (personal victors), and the Five Excellent Ones—these three—all received their status of ordination due solely to their level of realization. Because of this, the ordination they received is called "absolute" ordination.

The third, "a message," refers to a circumstance during Buddha's life when the bhikṣuṇī Utpalā was refused permission by her parents to take ordination. The Buddha sent a messenger with a message through which she became ordained. "Promising the Buddha" refers to the promise Kāśyapa made as he declared to the Buddha, "You are my teacher. I am your disciple." With this statement his ordination was received. "Coming forward" refers to the incident with Śāriputra and several others of pure karmic propensities whom the Buddha commanded to come forward and to uphold pure conduct. At that very moment, each of them became fully ordained. "The four requests" refers to asking four times for full ordination in the presence of ten other fully ordained, if it is a Buddhist country, or at least in the presence of five. After this request is repeated four times, full ordination occurs instantaneously. "In response to the question" refers to when Buddha asked Lekchin (Sudatta), "What is the sole state of ultimate bliss?" and Lekchin replied, "Liberation." The Buddha then asked, "What is the path that leads to this state?" "Faith," was the answer. At the moment that the Buddha felt pleased with this response, full ordination was received. "Taking the promise of the difficult dharmas" originated when Mahāprajāpatī (Sukyegui Dakmo) and five hundred women of the Śakya clan were asked by the Buddha to promise to accept the eight difficult dharmas.[29] "And so forth" refers to the occasion when Dre Zangde and a group of sixty disciples took the vows of refuge and became fully ordained as well.

Nine of these ten are independent of ritual, whereas "making the four requests" is dependent. The disciples of this time had few delusions, negative karma, or obscurations. They possessed wisdom, intelligence, and pure character. Furthermore, the abbots and preceptors were exclusively on the level of arhatship, which itself is the sublime characteristic of the preceptors, constituting the tenth way through which ordination was received in the past.

1.b.2 The present-day ritual, in three divisions:

1.b.2(a) The qualifications of the individual practitioner:

> In the present-day ritual one must be free from the five certain circumstances (as well as from the obstacle of birth, such as birth as a neuter and so forth), and of circumstances such as not receiving permission from the ruler and so forth; in particular, not having the potential to drive away a crow; and the obstacle of appearance, such as having blond hair and so forth. Those with excellent karma have developed renunciation.

According to the present-day ritual, the fully ordained and the novice in training must be free from five certain conflicting circumstances. The first is the erroneous view of believing that ordination can be maintained in the country in which it is taken, but that if one travels elsewhere it may not be possible to maintain the precepts in a different environment. The second, concerning the certainty of time, is to hold the view that ordination can be maintained for several years or months, but not necessarily for a lifetime. The third, concerning situations, is to take the vows with the view that they need not be maintained during times of war. The fourth, concerning sentient beings, is to believe that an enemy's life can be taken as long as one abstains from killing anyone or anything else. The fifth concerns the auxiliary precepts and the view that one does not need to uphold the minor precepts in the same way as the major ones.

In addition, there are four conflicting circumstances that cause obstacles to ordination, and so must be avoided. The obstacle of birth is to be born as a neuter, because even if one wishes to take vows there is then no basis for the birth of the vow. The obstacle of circumstance is to take vows without first receiving the ruler's or one's parents' permission. Although the vows will be born, this may result in a circumstance where one's personal freedom can be lost, in which case it may become impossible to maintain the vows. The particular obstacle referred to as "not having the potential to drive away a crow" means being too young, physically disabled, or in extreme pain. Although the vows will be born in the mind stream, they cannot be cultivated if these obstacles exist such that it becomes impossible to develop the higher qualities through training. The obstacle of appearance, such as "having blond hair and so forth," includes having severed limbs, birth in the caste of butchers, and so forth. In such cases, although the vows will be born and will develop, one's appearance (being either displeasing or extremely unpleasant), may create the condition that ordinary laymen are unable to develop faith toward the doctrine. It should be noted that blond hair was extremely rare in India during the time in history that the vinaya originated. Presently, this is no longer an obstacle in a world where men and women of all races are taking Buddhist ordination and wearing the robes of the saṅgha. Furthermore, in the case of these latter two—the particular obstacle and the obstacle of appearance—if there is some specific benefit to taking the vows, then the taking of the vows will not be restricted. In addition, to receive ordination one must not have any remaining broken vows from a previous ordination and must be twenty years of age, mentally sane, in possession of the three robes and begging bowl, and fully able to recognize the meaning of the symbolic indication given when ordination is received.

In short, it is not enough merely to wish to be protected from fear or to hope for better circumstances. One must have true renunciation and the wish to quickly reach any of the three states of nirvāṇa.[30] A fortunate aspirant with this motivation and all the qualifications mentioned above is considered a suitable vessel.

1.b.2(b) The qualifications of the preceptors, abbots, and others:

> The abbots and others must possess knowledge of the excellently spoken vast and perfectly complete vinaya and be well versed in all of the one hundred and twenty-one disciplines.

Those who qualify as preceptors of ordination must themselves embody the perfectly pure morality of honorable and noble qualities. They must not have even the slightest infraction of pure morality and should be knowledgeable in the Tripiṭaka, as well as accomplished in their own personal practice. There should be no doubt in the minds of others concerning their noble qualities. They must have been fully ordained for at least ten years in order to be qualified to bestow ordination upon others.

1.b.2(c) The manner of accomplishment:

> Full ordination is received in progressive stages. However, permission is granted in the sūtras to "receive without doing the former." At the conclusion of three repetitions, the vows are obtained.

The first line of the root text, "full ordination is received in progressive stages," refers to the usual step-by-step procedure whereby, ordinarily, one will take refuge, lay ordination, novice ordination, and full ordination in that order. However, even if lay or novice precepts have not been received, the Buddha clearly taught that the vows of full ordination can still be bestowed and received. At the time of receiving full ordination, all preceding vows are simultaneously embraced. The moment the vows are received is at the conclusion of the third repetition.

2. The methods that guard the vows from deterioration, in two subdivisions:
2.a Briefly revealed:

> In the interim, the obtained must be guarded from deterioration.

It is not enough simply to receive vows. Afterwards, one must guard and maintain them according to the corresponding advice. If vows are unguarded, the faults that arise can be very great, whereas if they are guarded and maintained the benefits are just as great. Recognizing this, one must then understand the methods by which to guard vows, which is the training of knowing what to accept and what to reject.

First, the training in what to reject will be explained in detail.

2.b An extensive explanation, in two subdivisions:

2.b.1 An extensive explanation of the actual training in what to reject and accept
2.b.2 Briefly revealing what is thereafter considered acceptable

2.b.1 An extensive explanation of the actual training in what to reject and accept, in two subdivisions:

2.b.1(a) Training for lay householders
2.b.1(b) Training for the fully renounced

2.b.1(a) The first, training for lay householders, in three categories:

2.b.1(a.1) The refuge vows
2.b.1(a.2) The twenty-four-hour vows
2.b.1(a.3) The lay householder vows

2.b.1(a.1) The refuge vows are twofold:

2.b.1(a.1.1) The uncommon training for each of the Three Jewels of Refuge:

> The three uncommon refuge precepts are to not search for refuge elsewhere, to abandon harming sentient beings, and to not accompany a heretic. Respect must be generated for each.

After taking refuge in the Buddha, one must discontinue searching for refuge elsewhere, such as from worldly gods and others. After taking refuge in the Dharma, one must abandon any harmful intention toward other living beings. After taking refuge in the Saṅgha, one must no longer accompany heretics, those who uphold and assert incorrect views. These three must be rejected. The three trainings to accept are the following: after taking refuge in the Buddha, one must respect any image or likeness of the Buddha; after taking refuge in the Dharma, one must respect all scriptures and syllables of the Dharma; after taking refuge in the Saṅgha, one must see the robes of ordination as symbolic of the Buddha himself. These three are to be recognized and respected as the Three Jewels of Refuge.

2.b.1(a.1.2) The common training for each of the Three Jewels of Refuge:

> To never forsake the Three Jewels, even for one's life or rewards; to not search elsewhere, regardless of how pressing the need may be; to not fail to make offerings at the correct time; to actively establish oneself and others in refuge; and, before traveling, to bow to the buddha of that direction: These are the five common precepts as taught by Lord Atīśa.

2.b.1(a.2) The twenty-four-hour vows, in two subdivisions:

2.b.1(a.2.1) An actual explanation of these vows, based on restriction of time:

> The abandonment of the four roots establishes morality. The abandonment of liquor establishes conscientiousness. To establish uncontrived conduct is to abandon three things: expensive and high beds, dancing and ornamentation, and eating after noon. These are the twenty-four-hour precepts. Because these eight branches do not remain permanently, they do not qualify as a prātimokṣa support for noble qualities. Only the seven precept categories qualify.

The "four roots" are the four root precepts: not to kill, steal, have sexual intercourse, or lie. Any action that even approaches these four must be abandoned. This assists in the establishment of stable morality. So that one may remain mindful, drinking liquor must be abandoned. To establish pure conduct, expensive or high beds, dancing, wearing ornaments to adorn the body, and eating after midday are all abandoned. These eight vows are taken for the duration of one day and night (twenty-four hours) only, so they do not qualify as a permanent discipline. Because they are not a permanent discipline, these vows are not a suitable support for the development of the noble qualities that arise from receiving permanent, lifetime vows in any of the seven prātimokṣa categories.

2.b.1(a.2.2) If taken as permanent vows, the manner in which they become known as *gomi* lay ordination:

> Although guarding these eight branches for the duration of one's life is goma lay ordination, according to the explanations of Vasubandhu in the *Sthavira* (*gNe-brTen sDe-pai*) tradition, this does not exist in the Sarvāstivāda tradition.

These eight precepts were embraced for the duration of his life by the great *ācārya* Candragomin. Thereafter, this became known as gomi lay ordination. This tradition was carried on by the Theravādan tradition according to Vasubandhu. However, gomi lay ordination does not exist in the Sarvāstivādā tradition.

2.b.1(a.3) The lay householder precepts, in three subdivisions:

2.b.1(a.3.1) Recognizing the five abandonments of lay ordination:

> The precepts of lay ordination are to abandon killing, stealing, lying, adultery, and all intoxicants.

One must guard against taking life, stealing, speaking an "unsurpassed" lie, and committing adultery. These are the four root precepts. For each, with the exception of stealing, it is necessary that the object be another human being. If the object is not a human being, then although there is fault, the action will not have the potency to completely damage the vow. The root precept to abandon adultery has taken the place of the abandonment of sexual intercourse in order to simplify the precept for lay householders. The branch precept to abandon all intoxicants is included because if intoxicants are allowed, the potential to guard against damaging other precepts is lost.

2.b.1(a.3.2) An explanation of the divisions of lay ordination based on enumeration in two divisions:

(1) The tradition of the Vaibhāṣika:

> To wish and promise according to enumeration is to maintain one vow, several vows, almost all, and complete training. This means the abandonment of either one, two, three, or five.

According to this system of lay ordination, one may decide to take only one or several of the four root precepts to qualify. For example, if one feels that the abandonment of killing is the only precept one is able to maintain, then by embracing that precept, the status of lay ordination is obtained. In addition, if one decides to take another precept, then several precepts are held. If yet one more is added, this is categorized as almost all of the four root precepts. If, in addition to these three, one decides to abandon adultery and intoxicants, this is the complete training of lay ordination.

(2) The tradition of the Sautrāntika:

> In addition, to abandon sexual intercourse is to hold "lay ordination of pure conduct." Scholars assert that both this and gomi lay ordination qualify as neither lay nor full ordination.

To hold the five root precepts of lay ordination and, in addition, to abandon sexual intercourse is to accept the lay ordination of pure conduct, *tsang chöd genyen* (*gsang spyod dgen bsyan*; *brahmacaryupāsaka*). For both this and gomi lay ordination, the aspirants have abandoned a spouse and the sexual conduct of laymen and so are no longer of the ranks of ordinary lay householders. On the other hand, they have not yet received the saffron robes or other signs of ordination for the fully renounced. Therefore, the wise agree that they qualify neither as lay nor as fully renounced and remain in a category of their own.

2.b.1(a.3.3) The corresponding training, in two subdivisions:

(1) The actual corresponding training:

> The six remaining nonvirtues and similar activity must be abandoned.

Of the four root precepts for lay ordination, three concern the nonvirtues that correspond to the body. Lying is one of the four nonvirtues corresponding to speech. This leaves six remaining nonvirtues that must also be abandoned. The three remaining that relate to speech are slander, harsh speech, and idle gossip, and the three that relate to the mind are craving, ill will, and incorrect view. In addition, one must also abandon killing animals or any living creature, including insects. Although failure to fully comply with this advice does not constitute the loss of one's root precepts or lay ordination, faults must be confessed and vows restored in turn.

(2) Instructions concerning the training of a tantric lay householder must follow:

> An upholder of lay ordination who is also a pure-awareness holder
> must, except for the signs and rituals of complete ordination, practice
> all that remains. This is explained in the *Subāhuparipṛcchā-sūtra.*

An upholder of lay Buddhist ordination who has entered mantra becomes known as a pure-awareness holder, or a vidyādhara. Although it is not necessary for such an individual to display the outer signs of full ordination such as robes, begging bowl, or shaved hair—which are the result of receiving the specific ritual—all remaining precepts in the vinaya system must be upheld and practiced.

This was clearly taught by Lord Buddha himself in the *Subāhuparipṛcchā-sūtra.*

2.b.1(b) Training for the fully renounced, in three divisions:
2.b.1(b.1) An explanation of novice precepts for male and female
2.b.1(b.2) An explanation of the precepts for the female novice in training
2.b.1(b.3) An explanation of full ordination precepts for male and female

2.b.1(b.1) The novice precepts, in three subdivisions:
2.b.1(b.1.1) The actual precepts of the novice
2.b.1(b.1.2) Corresponding practice to avoid deteriorations
2.b.1(b.1.3) Corresponding precepts received at the time of preparatory ordination

2.b.1(b.1.1) The actual precepts of the novice, in two subdivisions:

(1) The four root precepts:

> The abandonment of killing, stealing, lying, sexual intercourse,...

Taking the life of a human or a fetus in the womb qualifies as killing. Removing a valuable article[31] without permission qualifies as stealing. Having intercourse in any of the three orifices qualifies as sexual intercourse. Telling an "unsurpassed" lie qualifies as lying. Guarding against committing any of these four becomes the practice of morality. Failure to guard oneself tears morality apart, and this is termed a "root" defeat. If a root defeat occurs and is not concealed, the vow may be restored. However, if it is concealed, then as in the case of the fully ordained, the breach is irreparable.

(2) The six branch precepts:

> ...drinking alcohol, dancing, wearing ornaments and so forth, sleeping on expensive or high beds, eating after noon, and possessing gold and silver are the ten basic precepts (condensed as such to avoid discouragement).

Abandoning drinking alcoholic beverages, which have the power to intoxicate the mind; acting wildly and unconscientiously by dancing and singing; and blowing and playing musical instruments for enjoyment and so forth are the three precepts that correspond to entertainment. Abandoning trying to make oneself more attractive by wearing earrings, flowered and jeweled necklaces, and other ornamentation; anointing the body with perfumed scents; and applying makeup are the three that correspond to personal adornment. Abandoning sleeping on an expensive, ornate bed made of gold, silver, or brocade silk or on a bed that exceeds the height of a cubit and eating a meal after noon (according to the time of the country where one is residing) are the fourth and fifth precepts. Although touching gold and silver is permitted, the possession of it is not. Of these six branch precepts, the one concerning alcohol is the branch corresponding to conscientiousness, while the remaining five correspond to conduct. Because one may become discouraged if many precepts are imposed, and in order to reverse the tendency to refrain from taking vows altogether, the novice ordination has been condensed into these ten basic precepts. Otherwise, there are actually thirty-three precepts that the novice accepts. The three that correspond to killing are to refrain from killing animals, throwing grass containing living beings into water, and using water that has sentient beings in it. The vows that correspond to lying are the following: to refrain from baseless slander, slander based on an insubstantial reason, slandering the saṅgha, agreeing with and contributing to slander (thus causing laymen to lose faith), knowingly telling a lie, making fun of one's teacher, teasing the disciplinarian, making fun of another by claiming they are teaching only to receive food, accusing someone of committing a "remainder," ignoring or disregarding the precepts, and concealing food in order to receive more. These total fifteen. Adding the four root precepts to these fifteen totals nineteen. Adding the precepts against drinking alcohol, singing and dancing, playing music, wearing ornaments, wearing necklaces, applying makeup, using an expensive bed, using a high bed, eating after noon, and possessing gold and silver total thirty. If one includes the three rules that guard against these failures (mentioned below), this totals the thirty-three precepts of a novice male or female.

2.b.1(b.1.2) Corresponding practice to avoid deteriorations:

> Separating from the saffron robe and begging bowl, digging the earth, touching jewels and touching fire, eating after stopping, climbing trees, cutting trees, taking offerings, urinating or defecating upon grass, eating stored food, and destroying seeds are the thirteen exceptions permitted without fault. Otherwise, the practice of acceptance and abandonment is identical to that of the fully ordained.
>
> Similar to "owning," possessing unstitched fabric for thirty days; similar to "separating," separating in the monastery; similar to "harboring," harboring is permitted.

Abandoning owning an extra saffron robe, owning two begging bowls, being apart from one's saffron robe, digging in the soil, touching precious jewels, touching fire, eating after completing a meal, climbing a tree higher than a human, cutting grass or a growing tree or plant, eating food that has not been offered, urinating or defecating upon grass, eating stored or leftover food, and destroying seeds that are unsuitable for planting (but that have been blessed or offered) are the thirteen precepts that a novice is exempt from maintaining. Otherwise, a novice must accept all remaining precepts of the fully ordained. However, a novice may mentally confess a fault and purify it accordingly.

In addition, concerning the fully ordained category known as "owning," the novice is permitted to possess fabric longer than thirty days. In the category "separating," the novice may be separated from the saffron robe within the confines of the monastery. Concerning the fully ordained category known as "harboring," a novice may also harbor or store food if this is done for the purpose of health and physical sustenance.

2.b.1(b.1.3) Corresponding precepts received at the time of preparatory ordination:

> Failing to reject the sign of a layman, failing to maintain the sign of a renunciate, and disrespecting the abbot are the three downfalls. Renunciation is to train in the precepts of a novice.

A novice training to be fully ordained is called *barma rabjung* (*barma rab byung*). If such a novice wears long-sleeved or white or black-colored clothing for one full day with attachment, this constitutes the downfall of failing to abandon the sign of a lay householder. If a novice in training fails to wear the robes of ordination, this constitutes the downfall of failing to accept the sign of ordination. Disrespecting the preceptor abbot is the third downfall. These three downfalls cause the precepts of a novice in training to be lost. A novice must uphold these three precepts, as they are the final three of the thirty-three precepts outlined earlier.

2.b.1(b.2) The explanation of the precepts for the female novice in training in two divisions:

2.b.1(b.2.1) Briefly revealed:

> In addition to novice ordination,...

A female novice in training for full ordination must accept, in addition to her ten novice precepts, twelve additional precepts for the duration of two years. However, even if she does not lose the four root vows but damages any of the root precepts by committing a fault, she must then retake all the vows for the duration of another two years. She would not lose her status as a novice in training.

2.b.1(b.2.2) Extensively explained, in two subdivisions:

(1) The six root precepts:

> ...to refrain from traveling alone, swimming, touching a man, staying together, arranging a marriage, and concealing faults are the six root precepts.

To refrain from traveling on a road or path alone, swimming in water, touching the body of a male, sitting together with a male, arranging the union or marriage of a male and female, and concealing the faults of another female novice in training are the six root precepts.

(2) The six corresponding precepts:

> To abandon possessing gold, shaving pubic hair, digging in the earth, eating unoffered or harbored food, and cutting grass are the six corresponding precepts.

To refrain from possessing gold or other precious metals or jewels, shaving one's pubic hair, digging in the earth, eating unoffered food or harbored food, and cutting fresh grass are the six corresponding, additional precepts for the female novice in training.

2.b.1(b.3) The explanation of full-ordination precepts for male and female, in two subdivisions:
2.b.1(b.3.1) That which must be rejected
2.b.1(b.3.2) That which must be accomplished

2.b.1(b.3.1) That which must be rejected, in two subdivisions:

(1) Briefly revealed:

The bhikṣu precepts total two hundred and fifty-three.
The full-ordination precepts for a male total two hundred and fifty-three.

(2) Extensively explained in six categories:

The following six categories are the precept divisions for the fully ordained male:

(2.a) The category of root downfalls
(2.b The category of remainders
(2.c) The category of rejected downfalls
(2.d The category of solitary downfalls
(2.e) The category of individual confession
(2.f) The category of faults

(2.a) The category of root downfalls has three divisions:
(2.a.1) Revealing the basis in brief
(2.a.2) An extensive explanation of the basis
(2.a.3) Summing up

(2.a.1) Revealing the basis in brief:

The four root downfalls are known as the basis for all precepts.

To carefully maintain the vows that guard against these four is the very basis for all other vows, which identifies their status as "root" vows. If a root vow is damaged, it cannot be restored through a remedial force. The vow is thus destroyed, and this is termed a "defeat" of moral discipline.

(2.a.2) An extensive explanation of the four root defeats:

(a) The root downfall of sexual intercourse:

The basis is the body. All parts capable, in the birth canal, with a capable male organ, with an attached mind devoid of shame and fear, and engaging in the activity with the ultimate obtainment of satisfaction are the factors that comprise the total loss of pure conduct.

In the case of sexual intercourse, the basis is the body of a female (with all limbs intact) who has the potential to experience the feeling of intercourse. Intercourse consists of a healthy, capable male organ entering into any of the three orifices: the mouth, the anus, or the vagina. A shameless attitude, a desire with attachment to experience sexual bliss, a dependence upon the activity of joining into union with the object, and the ultimate completion of the act by experiencing physical bliss and satisfaction complete the four branches. If these four are complete with the object, intent, action, and result, the vow of pure conduct is completely lost, constituting a defeat.

(b) The root downfall of stealing:

> The basis of stealing is the wealth of another human being. The thought is to benefit oneself through the intention to steal. The object is one of value in its country of origin; and the activity is stealing with the ultimate thought to steal or to receive the object, even if another is engaged to obtain it.

The basis, the object to steal, must be wealth possessed by another human that is of substantial material value. One's own intention must be to steal in order to benefit oneself through possession of that object, no matter what it is. The object must be of significant value. To physically confiscate the object and experience the result of personal possession, thus acknowledging that object's separation from its original owner, constitutes the second defeat. In addition, if you employ someone else to steal for you or use your power or force to coerce someone to steal for you, this also constitutes the defeat of stealing.

(c) The root downfall of killing:

> The basis of killing is an unmistaken awareness of the object as another human being. The intention is to kill, with recognition of the object, and the activity is killing without hesitation or reversal, ultimately bringing about the cessation of life. This includes the condition of engaging another to kill, or expressing delight.

The basis for killing must be another human being, which includes an unborn fetus. There must be no mistake or confusion as to whether the object is someone other than oneself. The intention must be the certain conviction to take the life of that object. The physical activity of using a weapon, or some other means, to irreversibly end the life of the object is then effected so that ultimately the death of the object occurs before one's own death. In addition, the defeat occurs if you engage or employ a second party to carry out the act or if you are party to the encouragement of the act. In addition, if many monks were to confer and decide that someone's life should be taken, and only one monk carries out the act, all the monks together would accrue the same negativity.

(d) The root downfall of an "unsurpassed" lie:

> The basis for a lie is a human being with the ability to comprehend the meaning of words. The intention is to say something that will affect and change their understanding. The subject is one's own clairvoyance or noble qualities, which, although nonexistent, are promoted as an "unsurpassed" lie. Ultimately, if the object hears the lie, the vow is lost.

The basis for an unsurpassed lie is another human being with the potential to hear and understand the meaning of words being spoken. This means that the mentally impaired do not qualify; nor do neuters or hermaphrodites. The basis must be a human being who is free from these conditions. The intention must be to affect that individual's understanding so that he will come to believe that which you know to be untrue. The subject must be one's own spiritual status or level of development: for example, to claim to possess the five types of clairvoyance or to have transcended the desire realm, to have attained the first level of meditative absorption, to possess the noble qualities of the buddhas, and so forth, when you know this to be untrue. Ultimately, even if the object's mind does not change after hearing these words, if the meaning is understood, the defeat occurs. This qualifies as an unsurpassed lie of four characteristics. The four characteristics are that the speech is one's own, the words are unmistaken, their meaning is clear, and the words are heard directly by the object.

(2.a.3) Summing up:

> Since any of these four root downfalls will defeat a bhikṣu, they are known as the four root downfalls or defeats, as taught by the All-Knowing One.

This clearly indicates that the success of one's training and status as fully ordained is dependent upon the pure maintenance of these four root precepts. Therefore, one should create the outer condition of studying the vinaya with a fully qualified lama who can unmistakenly and clearly define the path of what to accept and what to reject. The inner condition is to practice this path with joyous fortitude, to become fully endowed with skillful means, to remain conscientiously patient during any onslaught of adversity, to examine one's mind to observe whether or not a fault has developed, and to immediately weed out such shortcomings with mindfulness and alertness unceasingly applied.

(2.b) The category of remainders, in two divisions:

(2.b.1) Briefly revealed:

The thirteen remainders of the saṅgha are the following:

A remainder is defined as a fault concerning what remains of what was once a pure vow. If one commits a remainder, then although one's vows are no longer perfectly pure, they are not completely lost. Nevertheless, the vow must be restored in the presence of the saṅgha. The thirteen remainders are divided as follows: five that correspond to attachment to other beings, two that correspond to desire for material objects, two that correspond to harm, and four that correspond to advice.

(2.b.2) Extensively explained:

> emitting seminal fluid apart from the previously mentioned orifices; holding any part of a woman's body with attachment; due to attachment to a female, openly discussing sex; encouraging a female to engage in sexual contact with oneself as a form of offering; encouraging sex in order to arrange a marriage between a male and a female; for personal welfare, constructing a dwelling place larger than the permitted size; building a large house; uttering baseless or factual slander about a bhikṣu; dividing the saṅgha; supporting a schism and opposing one's precepts; causing laymen to lose faith; ignoring expulsion; and disregarding advice given to restore downfalls.

The first remainder is to lose one's semen and experience physical bliss. The root text mentions "excluding the three orifices" (anus, mouth, or vagina), because these three orifices are mentioned already in the category of root downfalls. The remainder occurs if, through masturbation or contact with the body of another, one loses one's semen with a desirous mind and a capable male organ. The second is to experience bliss by touching, with an attached mind, the bare skin or hair of a woman. The third is to openly speak about sex with a female who has the ability to understand what is being said. The fourth is, out of attachment, to encourage a female to engage in sexual contact by convincing her that this is an offering or service. The fifth is to personally make arrangements to unite a male and female that lead to a sexual encounter. These are the five remainders that correspond to attachment to another sentient being.

The sixth is to beg—without permission from the saṅgha and for one's own welfare—for materials from others in order to build a house that is eighteen by eleven cubits in width and length on land that is disputed or that has an abundance of insects or dangerous conditions. Even if you contract with someone else to build for you, this constitutes a remainder when the construction is complete. The seventh is to construct a house larger than seventy-six by forty-four cubits, even if it is an offering to the Three Jewels, without the saṅgha's permission or on unsuitable land that is disputed, overrun by insects, or unsafe. Once the roof has been laid, the remainder occurs. These two correspond to attachment to material things.

The eighth occurs when the object is another fully ordained monk. If one slanders his conduct concerning the four defeats when one has not directly seen, heard, or known of such facts, and when the person spoken to understands what is said, the remainder occurs. With only the slightest proof as a support, and another fully ordained monk as your object of contempt, to slander him by saying he has committed a defeat so that another person hears it is the ninth remainder. These two remainders correspond to harmful intent.

Singling out two groups from among a group of the ordained with the intention to divide them and persisting after being told not to do this three times constitutes the tenth remainder. To agree with and support a monk who has caused a schism, knowing that this conduct contradicts the precepts but continuing nonetheless, is the eleventh remainder.

The twelfth is to involve oneself in conduct such as drinking liquor, accompanying women, and other activities that contradict the training, so that lay householders are caused to lose faith in the saṅgha. To be expelled from the ranks of the saṅgha due to this behavior and yet to ignore the expulsion and accuse the saṅgha of prejudice constitutes a remainder.

Further remainders are committed if a monk commits a downfall and is being punished by the saṅgha (so as to assist him to restore his vow), yet disregards this advice altogether, retaliates, and disregards the command of the saṅgha. These final four are the remainders that correspond to advice.

(2.c) The category of rejected downfalls, in two divisions:

(2.c.1) Briefly revealing the enumerations:

> The thirty abandoning downfalls are explained as:

The meaning of the term "downfall" implies that the cause of the downfall must be abandoned. After abandonment, the downfall must be confessed for the vow to be restored. If the vow remains unrestored, the ripening result will be a fall to lower states of rebirth. There are thirty corresponding precepts.

(2.c.2) An extensive explanation of the divisions has three categories. Each category has ten precepts:

(a) The category concerning clothing:

> keeping extra cloth for personal use for longer than ten days; separating from the saffron robe for the duration of one night; keeping unstitched robe fabric for longer than one month; allowing a bhikṣuṇī to wash the robes; receiving fabric from a bhikṣuṇī; asking for and receiving fabric from an unrelated lay householder; if offered,

> accepting more than one upper or lower garment; with the hope of receiving a saffron robe, enquiring as to measurements and value; begging for cloth by indirectly reminding others to offer; and receiving valuable jewels for the purchase of robes.

The first of the ten precepts that correspond to clothing is the abandoning downfall of keeping an unblessed cubit of fabric in one's own possession for more than ten days, even if one does not hope or expect to receive more. The second concerns the downfall of separation from one's Dharma robes for the duration of one night. The third is to retain cloth for a month. "Cloth" in this context refers to unblessed fabric that is larger than a cubit in size and that is kept specifically with the hope to receive more cloth in order to make one of the three robes. If thirty days pass while this fabric is in a monk's possession, then at sunrise on the thirty-first day the downfall occurs. The fourth abandoning downfall is to allow a fully ordained female who is not a family relation to wash one's ordination robes. The fifth is to receive fabric larger than a cubit in size from an unrelated, fully ordained female. The sixth is to ask for and receive fabric larger than a cubit from an unrelated lay householder when you already possess the three robes. The seventh is to receive more than an upper or lower garment from an unrelated lay householder (in the case of having an incomplete set of robes). The eighth is to enquire about the price and dimensions of fabric with the hope of having it offered to oneself. The ninth is to remind an unrelated lay householder to offer cloth, after hearing that it will be offered. The tenth is to personally receive precious metals or jewels, given by a sponsor to make robes, which must be given to the disciplinarian. To ask the disciplinarian three times to be given the new robes is permitted. It is further permitted to go to the disciplinarian three more times without asking. If the monk goes again after that, and receives the robes, the downfall occurs.

(b) The category concerning cushions and seats:

> Making a cushion with expensive silk; making a cushion solely composed of rare black wool; making over half of a cushion out of rare black wool; before six years of use, making a new seat cover; although owning a suitable cover, making a new one; accepting black wool and carrying it beyond three miles; allowing a fully ordained female to spin and wash wool; accepting gold or silver; receiving interest payments or profit; intentionally engaging in business.

The first abandoning downfall of this category is to make a cushion for oneself that is filled with the most expensive material. The second is to make oneself a cushion out of a rare and valuable substance, such as black wool. The third is to fill over one-half of one's cushion with a rare and valuable material. (Previously, in India, both silk and black wool were very rare and valuable.) The fourth is to make a new cushion for oneself without permission from the saṅgha or before one's old cushion has been used for six years' time. The fifth is to make a new seat cover that does not have a patch at least one and a half cubits in size; this patch must be taken from one's old suitable cover. The sixth is to carry, with attachment, a large load of black wool farther than three miles. If one has a helper who carries it more than five hundred human armspans, the downfall occurs. The seventh is to allow an unrelated, fully ordained female to spin or wash one's wool. The eighth is to own, or ask someone else to keep for oneself, unblessed gold, silver, or any precious metal or jewel without the saṅgha's permission. The ninth is to receive interest or profit from an unrelated layman as a result of doing business or selling goods. The tenth is to conduct a business transaction with an unrelated layman in order to gain profit.

(c) The category concerning the begging bowl and so forth:

> Keeping an unblessed begging bowl for longer than ten days; keeping a pair of begging bowls; asking others to weave cloth without payment or gift; extending the size of the loom; taking back cloth given to a bhikṣu; receiving cloth before the given time; remaining more than seven days in a secluded, frightful place without the three robes; keeping the rainguard for more than one month after *gagyei* (*dgag dbye*; *pravāraṇā*) [the ceremony that concludes the traditional rainy season retreat]; personally receiving and keeping offerings dedicated to the saṅgha; harboring medicine for longer than seven days.

The first of the two abandoning downfalls of holding and seeking a begging bowl is to possess a suitable but unblessed begging bowl for longer than ten days. At sunrise on the eleventh day, the downfall occurs. The second is to receive a pair of unblessed begging bowls from an unrelated lay householder and to keep them in one's possession for longer than ten days. The third and fourth abandoning downfalls are to engage an unrelated lay householder to weave cloth for oneself without payment and to extend the size of the loom (without permission from the owner) in order to weave the cloth given to one by an unrelated lay householder. The fifth is to take back cloth that one had previously given to another fully ordained monk. The sixth is to receive and possess cloth and other material before the second day of gagyei (Skt. *pravāraṇā*),[32] the conclusion of the rainy season retreat.

The seventh is to stay in an isolated place without the three robes of ordination for longer than six days. At sunrise on the seventh day, the downfall occurs. The eighth is to keep the rainguard, which is given to be worn during the summer season rainy retreat, one month before the retreat or fifteen days after gagyei. The ninth is to personally possess any article that has been dedicated by the sponsor to the saṅgha in general. The tenth abandoning downfall is to harbor medicine intended for illness for longer than seven days.

(2.d) The category of solitary downfalls, in two divisions:

(2.d.1) Briefly revealed:

The ninety solitary downfalls are:

Again, the term "downfall" is used because if its corresponding precept is damaged, this will cause one to fall to the lower realms. These particular downfalls are termed "solitary" because if the downfall occurs in the case of these ninety precepts, the corresponding vow is restored only through confession. Confession is the sole method to restore these vows.

(2.d.2) Extensively explained:

(a) The category of intentional action:

> knowingly lying; expressing the faults of a bhikṣu; slandering a bhikṣu in order to create a schism (although an intermediary has established harmony); reviving a quarrel; teaching Dharma to a laywoman; practicing Dharma with the unordained; verbalizing another bhikṣu's downfall (that leads to lower realms); truthfully expressing unsurpassed spiritual development; making accusations; ignoring the foundational training.

The first solitary downfall, to knowingly lie, does not refer to the type of lie that qualifies as a root downfall, a remainder, a transgression, or a fault. Here, one need only knowingly lie about any subject, and the object must clearly understand the lie. The second is taking as one's object a fully ordained monk and expressing the fact that he has committed some negativity, with the explicit intention of bringing harm to him. The third is to slander fully ordained monks who are harmonious in order to cause a division among them. If the object hears and understands this, the downfall occurs. The fourth concerns the circumstance of two fully ordained monks who have been quarrelling and who have been reprimanded by an intermediary (a senior disciplinarian). To again aggravate the situation so as to divide these two monks, and to have this understood by a third party, constitutes the downfall. The fifth is to speak more than five or six words of Dharma to an unaccompanied laywoman who wishes to hear and understand. The sixth is to speak about Dharma in the company of lay householders in an unruly or unconscientious manner. The seventh is to senselessly express the faults, defeats, or downfalls of another fully ordained monk to a layman so that the object hears and understands. The eighth is to describe to a lay householder, without a specific reason or purpose, one's own unsurpassed spiritual qualities so that the object hears and understands. The ninth is to accuse, out of favoritism, a monk who is working for the saṅgha of giving extra materials to another monk, and for the object to hear and understand this accusation. The tenth is to disrespect any aspect of the vinaya (for example, to say during sojong that the minor precepts can be disregarded and to have the object hear and understand this).

(b)The category of seeds and so forth:

> Destroying viable seeds; blaming to avoid personal abuse; not listening to instructions and responding incorrectly when one's downfalls are told; failing to put away the seats; leaving the cover spread out; expelling a bhikṣu; overpowering to harm; puncturing with the bed stand; tossing water and grass that contain living beings; knowingly constructing a temple with two layers of bricks.

The first in this second category of solitary downfalls is to destroy any seed that is not already ruined or to cut grass, trees, or any other growing or potentially growing plant. The second is to claim, though the disciplinarian is acting in accordance with the Dharma, that he has unfairly mistreated one, so as to take the blame or shame away from oneself and place it upon another. The third is to pretend to not hear or understand when told of one's downfall by another monk (who has the intention to benefit) and, in addition, to knowingly respond incorrectly. The fourth solitary downfall occurs if, after using a throne or seat of the saṅgha, one fails to put it away and walks beyond forty-nine armspans' length from that object. The fifth is to fail to gather up the monks' seat covers after use if there is grass growing nearby or if other conditions are present that potentially provide a habitat for insects. The downfall occurs if one fails to remove the mats, whether they are damaged or not, and then walks beyond forty-nine armspans' length from the mats. The sixth is, out of anger, to personally expel or engage another to expel a monk from the temple. The seventh is to have harmful thoughts toward and to physically or verbally suppress another monk previously admitted to the monastery. The eighth occurs if, while on the floor above the temple, one drops forcefully onto a bed that has pointed legs, causing the legs to puncture holes in the temple ceiling. The ninth occurs if one throws water that is known to contain insects or living beings so that they die, or throws water on grass or trees where insects may die. The tenth occurs if one personally engages in, or employs another to begin, constructing a temple on land that is geographically unstable and dangerous. If there is a potential for the temple to collapse due to conditions, yet one knowingly begins the building, the downfall occurs after two or three levels of bricks go up.

(c) The category of unauthorization and so forth:

> What follows pertains to relationships with fully ordained females. Teaching Dharma without authorization; although authorized, teaching after sunset; teaching Dharma for food; having cloth sewn; giving

> away the saffron robe; traveling together for the same purpose; traveling here and there, together, in a boat; sitting together in solitude; standing together in solitude; and eating food requested to be made. These are the actions to abandon.

The downfalls in this category pertain to a fully ordained male's relationship with a fully ordained female.

The first is for a fully ordained male to teach Dharma to a fully ordained female without permission, and for it to be heard and understood. The second is, with permission to teach, to do so in a fearful place after sunset so that the ordained female hears and understands the teaching.

The third is to accuse another fully ordained monk of teaching to a fully ordained female in order to acquire food, and for the accusation to be heard by another monk and understood.

The fourth is to allow an unrelated, fully ordained female to sew and complete an article of clothing for oneself. The fifth is to give away one's own suitable saffron robe to an unrelated fully ordained female who is simply an acquaintance. The sixth is to travel together for the same reason with an unrelated, fully ordained female farther than the distance of five hundred armspans. Each distance of five hundred armspans qualifies as a downfall. If the distance reaches two-hundred-fifty armspans only, this constitutes a fault. The seventh is to enter into the same boat with an unrelated, fully ordained female and to travel here and there, with no particular goal, beyond five hundred armspans' distance. Each additional five hundred armspans constitutes an additional downfall.

The eighth is to sit together in an isolated place with an unrelated female whose companion is not present, even if the distance between the two of you is an armspan's length. The ninth is to stand together in an isolated place with any female, and in particular with a fully ordained female. The tenth downfall occurs if an unrelated, fully ordained female has previously boasted about one's noble, exalted qualities to a family and made arrangements for food to be prepared and offered at an appropriate time, and to then partake of the food.

(d) The category of repetitive behavior and so forth:

> Eating repeatedly; staying and eating with a heretic for longer than one day; eating the contents of two full begging bowls; eating after completing a meal; intentionally lying concerning a downfall about rejected food; without permission, gathering and eating at the incorrect time; untimely eating in the afternoon; eating harbored food; swallowing any of the four medicines of unoffered food; and begging to receive delicacies.

The first downfall of eating repeatedly is, after begging for the noon meal from an unrelated layman, to partake of that meal and again go out to beg for food at two or three more households and to receive and partake of it. However, a downfall does not occur in the case of illness, famine, or strenuous labour performed for the saṅgha, such as building *stūpas*, temples, and so forth.

The second downfall occurs if, while in the house of an unrelated layman where there are heretics and without a specific invitation, one stays more than one day and partakes of the noon meal on the second day. The third occurs when, begging at the house of an unrelated layman at the appropriate time, one receives more food than the contents of a large begging bowl, two full medium-sized bowls, or three small bowls and carries it elsewhere to eat it.

The fourth occurs if, at the appropriate time and when not suffering from illness or famine, one partakes of the noon meal and claims to be finished and later takes more food and eats again. The fifth is to state that another monk has completed eating his meal (when he has not) and uses this untruth to claim that the monk has therefore committed the downfall of eating repeatedly.

The sixth is for more than three fully ordained monks to gather separately without permission to eat food at the appropriate time. The seventh is to eat food at an inappropriate time if one is not suffering from an illness or another specific condition that permits an exception. (The appropriate time to eat is from dawn to midday, according to the time in one's country of residence.) Even if one is suffering from an illness, the appropriate time to eat must still be considered.

The eighth downfall occurs if, when one is ill or suffering, one harbors any of the four medicines beyond the designated time for consumption, fails to discard them, and partakes of them. The ninth downfall occurs if, when one is not sick or starving, one helps oneself to any of the four medicines without their being offered, and allows just one swallow to enter one's system. Each additional swallow constitutes an additional downfall.

The tenth occurs if, while free from illness or other adverse conditions, one specifically begs for delicious food, such as milk, from unrelated lay householders. To receive and partake of this food constitutes the downfall. The "four medicines" referred to in precepts eight and nine are food allowed to be eaten during the appropriate time because they are recognized as medicine meant to sustain the body; beverages that are taken at specific intervals throughout the day for sustenance; medicine that is designated for use for a period of seven days, such as medicine for the wind humor (for example, butter); and medicines that are permitted for use for the duration of one's life to improve health in general.

(e) The category corresponding to water and so forth:

> Utilizing water containing living beings; sleeping close to cohabitation; standing in isolation; naked dwellers; watching the military; staying more than two days in a military camp; making arrangements for the military; beating a bhikṣu; attempting to strike another; concealing downfalls leading to lower rebirth.

The first downfall is to use water for bathing, washing, drinking, or any other use which contains living beings without first carefully examining it. The second is to enter, stay, or sleep close to a dwelling where a male and female are cohabitating.

The third is to stand in an isolated place where a male and female are cohabitating. The fourth is to give food to an ordained naked dweller[33] and for it to be received. The exception here would be if the individual is a relative or is physically ill, or if you are able to lead the individual to the path of virtue. The fifth is to venture away from the proximity of one's residence in order to watch the military without first receiving an invitation or order from the ruler or officer in charge. The sixth is, without circumstance or reason, to spend more than one or two nights with the military. The seventh downfall occurs if, due to some circumstance, one stays with the military for a specific purpose and, while doing this, touches any weapon or makes any strategic arrangements. The eighth is to beat or strike another fully ordained monk out of anger or to engage someone else to do so.

The ninth is to attempt to strike another monk out of anger. The tenth occurs if, amongst a gathering of the saṅgha, one knows beyond a trace of doubt that another monk has committed a defeat or a remainder and, without an important reason, one conceals this knowledge. If you know the monk has committed a downfall and conceal that fact, you acquire a fault.

(f) The category corresponding to dwelling places and so forth:

> Obstructing a bhikṣu from receiving food; causing (oneself or another monk) to touch fire; speaking incorrectly about affiliation with the saṅgha's activities; sleeping more than the duration of two nights with the unordained; failing to reject the views of negative traditions; making friendly conversation; sleeping near a novice who has failed to reject negative views; wearing cloth of an unsuitable color; touching jewels, weapons, and musical instruments; unnecessarily bathing.

The first downfall of this category occurs when, begging together for food at a layman's house at the appropriate time, one speaks in such a way as to stop the family from offering food to the other monk. The downfall occurs when your words are heard. The second is, due to unconscientious behavior and attitude, to touch fire or to cause another monk to touch fire (other than at the time of a specific religious ceremony). The third is, if while meeting with the saṅgha, one agrees with their position and later changes one's mind and expresses contrary ideas that are heard by another. The fourth is to sleep three nights in the same house with a layman without a specific reason. At sunrise on the fourth morning, the downfall occurs. The exception is if one's sleeping place is eight-and-one-half cubits away from the layman.

The fifth is to claim that drinking liquor, eating after noon, and other breaches of precepts are harmless so that you are actually maintaining the spiritual views of negative traditions and refusing to give them up. The sixth is to exchange friendly conversation and stories with an excommunicated monk and, out of friendship, to stay together with him for more than one night. The seventh is to stay for more than one night with a novice who has failed to reject negative views, and to become overly friendly.

The eighth is to willingly wear white fabric, with the exception of muslin cloth (natural fabric), larger than a cubit's width and length. To wear such cloth that is black or of a mixed color also qualifies as a fault. The ninth downfall occurs if one touches precious jewels, weapons, or musical instruments or tells another fully ordained monk that he may do so. The exception is if this is done to protect another, for the welfare of the sponsor, or as an offering for teaching Dharma. The tenth is to unnecessarily bathe or submerge more than half of one's body in water (for example, when it is not the summer season or when one is not suffering from a physical illness).

(g) The category corresponding to intention and so forth:

> Taking the life of animals; causing a bhikṣu to develop regret toward ordination; tickling; playing with water; sleeping in the same area as a woman; frightening a bhikṣu; hiding a bhikṣu's possessions; with uncertainty, again using previously given objects; baseless abuse; traveling with a female who is unaccompanied by her spouse.

The first downfall here is, with the intention to kill, to take the life of any animal or insect or to engage another to do so. Each life taken qualifies as an individual downfall. The second is to tell another fully ordained monk that his vows were never really received or that they have deteriorated, so that he develops regret upon hearing this. The third occurs if, in order to make contact with another monk's body, one touches under the arms or elsewhere and tickles.

The fourth is, with an undisciplined, uncontrolled mind, to submerge half of one's body in water to play, or to encourage another to do so. The fifth is to sleep near a female who is unaccompanied by her husband and to allow the entire night to pass.

The sixth is to intentionally frighten another monk or to engage someone else to do so. The seventh occurs when, with the intention to steal and devoid of any beneficial motive, one takes articles that belong to another monk, such as his begging bowl, robes, and so forth, and hides them or engages someone else to do so.

The eighth is, if having previously given another monk some article, one reclaims it and uses it without being absolutely certain that it was the monk's intention to give it back. (This does not mean having the intention to steal the article.)

The ninth occurs if, without the basis of having actually seen, heard, or unmistakenly knowing it to be true, one slanders one monk to another by accusing him of committing any of the thirteen remainders, and to have this be heard.

The tenth is to travel together with an unrelated female, whose husband is not present, for a distance of five hundred yards. Two hundred and fifty yards qualifies as a fault.

(h) The category corresponding to visitors, thieves, and so forth:

> Similarly, accompanying a thief; bestowing full ordination before age twenty; digging the earth; although invited, staying and eating more than four months; claiming not to know; listening to discord; leaving without saying one has committed no harm; disrespectfully contradicting; drinking liquor; and, during the incorrect time of afternoon, going to town.

The first of these downfalls occurs if one travels five hundred *krośa* (4,500 armspans equal one krośa) without paying the required toll tax or if one travels that same distance in the company of a thief.

The second is to give full ordination to someone who has not yet reached twenty years of age (including the time spent in the womb). At the conclusion of the third repetition, the preceptor abbot acquires the downfall. In addition, for the spiritual mentor and other monks present, this qualifies as a fault.

The third occurs if, without specific reason, one digs more than four finger widths into the earth or engages someone else to do so. The fourth is to stay longer than previously invited by a sponsor or to stay longer than four months without having established a definite time frame. The fifth is, while being given valid spiritual advice by another monk, to interrupt and tell that monk he doesn't know what he's talking about or to chastise him as to why he didn't consult someone else about the matter first (so as to imply that he doesn't know what he's talking about).

The sixth is to intentionally listen to two or more monks' conversation, because of one's adverse relationship with one of them, with the intention to continue quarrelling. Hearing the conversation qualifies as the downfall. The seventh is, while attending the purification ceremony, to suddenly leave without telling one's associates and companions the reason for leaving and, specifically, failing to mention that no faults have been accrued prior to leaving.

The eighth is to disrespect, contradict, or claim that someone is incapable of accomplishing the words of the Buddha, the saṅgha, or the disciplinarian without any explanation.

The ninth is to drink or eat any substance that has the power to intoxicate the mind, whether it is made from grain and yeast (beer), fermented fruit (wine), or any other substance. There is no fault if the substance has been boiled so that the potency is lost or if one takes it for medicinal reasons or as a body salve. The tenth occurs according to the time of one's location and involves going to the town or marketplace in the afternoon, or at any time before the sun rises the next morning, unless one has a specific reason for doing so. Walking out the door without telling anyone and going beyond one's own dwelling place qualifies as the downfall.

(i) The category of teaching Dharma and so forth:

> Accepting food in the afternoon from more than three families; sleeping in the palace of the king and queen; during sÒtra recitation, claiming to understand; making an expensive needle-sheath; making a seat higher than the required measurement; with a harmful intent, spreading cotton on a cushion; making a seat cover, undergarment, rainguard, or saffron robe larger than the required measurement.

The first downfall occurs if one goes to more than three patrons to beg for the noon meal, or to more than three households in the afternoon to beg for food.

The second occurs if, without a specific reason (such as being summoned for a religious service) one goes to the palace of the king and queen at night or stays for the duration of the night. The third occurs if, after two repetitions during the time in which the prātimokṣa-vinaya is being recited, one claims to know the meaning, as though one has complete understanding of the vinaya, showing disrespect. When this is heard by another, the downfall occurs.

The fourth is to make oneself a needle-sheath out of an expensive material, such as ivory, or to engage someone else to do so. The fifth is to personally build oneself a seat or throne higher than a cubit's length or to engage someone else to do so.

The sixth is, with a negative intention, to knowingly spread cotton on another monk's cushion, seat, or throne. The seventh is to make oneself a seat cover that is larger than three cubits' length by two cubits and six finger widths.

The eighth is to make oneself an undergarment larger than six cubits' length by three cubits' width. The ninth is to make oneself a rainguard larger than nine cubits' length by three cubits' and eighteen finger widths. The tenth is to make a saffron robe for oneself of the same size as the Buddha's body or larger.[34]

If any of these downfalls occurs, one must confess it and eliminate the cause for its development. For example, if the robes and so forth are larger than the required measurements, they must be cut down to meet the requirements. The expensive needle-sheath must be destroyed. While in the presence of the object to whom one is confessing, when asked if this downfall has occurred, one must be able to confirm it in order to complete the confession. If not, this qualifies as a fault.

(2.e) The category of individual confession, in two divisions:

(2.e.1) Briefly revealed:

> In the category of individual confession, there are four:

In this category, a broken or damaged precept is repaired by confessing with strong mental remorse.

(2.e.2) Extensively explained:

in town, receiving and eating food received from a bhikṣuṇī in a household; eating without reversing a bhikṣuṇī's order; receiving and partaking of unfit food (according to the precept training); receiving and eating food in the monastery, rather than guarding the forest. These are the four.

The first occurs if, while in town begging for food at the appropriate time, one receives food from an unrelated fully ordained female that was intended for her own consumption. The second occurs if, when by invitation from the patron, one partakes of the food prepared and served according to the orders given by a fully ordained female without first reversing her order. The order for partaking of the food must be given by the seniormost monk, and no fully ordained female must be allowed to interfere. To ignore her interference and to go ahead and eat creates the need for an individual confession.

The third occurs if, when the saṅgha has agreed that a particular food is unsuitable to be received from a householder and makes a rule that it is to be avoided, one then ignores the rule, receives the food, and partakes of it. The fourth occurs when a monk who has been appointed to stay away from the monastery in order to guard the forest returns in order to receive food from a patron in the monastery and then partakes of it. These are the four precepts restored through individual confession.

(2.f) The category of faults has two divisions:

(2.f.1) Briefly revealed:

The one hundred and twelve faults are known as:

The meaning of "fault" is that it is a minor failure of morality, producing minor harm, thus qualifying as a personal fault rather than as a breach of a vow. Faults do, however, lead to an eventual breach of the vows when accumulated and, although they are initially less weighty than the downfalls, must be guarded against diligently and with mindfulness. The extensive explanation of the one hundred and twelve faults is divided into nine categories.

(2.f.2) Extensively revealed:

(a) The one hundred and twelve faults are divided into nine categories. The first category concerns the wearing of clothing:

wearing the lower garment unevenly, too high, too low, like an elephant's trunk, with uneven folding, with bulging, and unnecessarily protruding. These are the seven corresponding to the lower garment. Uneven, too long, and too short are the three corresponding to the upper garment. These total ten.

The first seven precepts of this category relate to the lower garment worn by a monk. When worn, it must not hang unevenly so that one side is higher than the other and must not be worn as high as the knees or as low as the ankles. The top of the garment must not be folded down over the belt and must not bulge out from under the belt. The top of the belt must not protrude or stick out unnecessarily. These are the seven.

The precepts that correspond to the upper garment are that the two robes (symbolic of full ordination) must not be worn unevenly so that they hang in a manner that is not symmetrical. They must not be allowed to hang too long or too short. These three bring the total to ten precepts concerning how the fully ordained wear the robes of ordination, and demonstrate the emphasis placed upon the proper representation of the saṅgha.

(b) The category concerning conduct while traveling:

> Undisciplined, improperly dressed, chattering, gazing distractedly, gazing at a distance, covering the head, hiking up the garments, hanging over shoulders, clasping hands behind one's head, clasping hands at the nape of the neck, jumping, striding, walking on the balls of the feet, walking on the heels, embracing the hips, twisting the body, tossing the arms, twisting the head, embracing the shoulders, and holding hands. These comprise the twenty behaviors to avoid when going to a layman's home.

The first is to lack awareness of one's body and speech while traveling to, and remaining in, the households of laymen. The second is to travel without wearing both the upper and lower robes or wearing them carelessly.

The third is to chatter or be unnecessarily noisy. The fourth is to distractedly look from side to side while walking. The fifth is to look ahead in the distance (in other words, farther than the length of an ox's yoke). The sixth is to cover one's head while traveling. The seventh is to hike up one's robes in such a way that the genitals are exposed. The eighth is to allow the upper robe to hang over both shoulders. The ninth is to clasp one's hands behind one's head. The tenth is to clasp the nape of one's neck while walking. The eleventh is to jump around. The twelfth is to take large strides while walking. The thirteenth is to walk on the balls of one's feet. The fourteenth is to walk on one's heels. The fifteenth is to place one's hands on one's hips and then walk with one's elbows extended out. The sixteenth is to twist one's body around. The seventeenth is to toss one's arms while walking. The eighteenth is to twist one's head from right to left while walking. The nineteenth is to embrace another monk around the shoulders while walking. And the twentieth is to hold hands with another monk while walking.

(c) The category concerning sitting on cushions or seats:

> Sitting without permission; sitting without checking; dropping forcefully; stretching with legs crossed; crossing legs at the thighs; placing one ankle upon the other; hanging legs below the seat; sitting with legs spread; exposing the genitals. These are the nine to abandon while sitting.

This category concerns the nine actions to avoid while sitting. The correct position for a monk to assume is to sit with legs crossed in full or half-lotus position or tucked under the body. The first action to avoid is, while visiting a household, to sit without being asked or without receiving the patron's permission. The second is to sit down before checking to see if there are any living beings on the seat or cushion. The third is to sit down forcefully, allowing the full weight of the body to drop. The fourth is, while sitting, to stretch one's legs out and cross them. The fifth is to sit with one leg hanging over the other thigh. The sixth is to sit with one ankle upon the other. The seventh occurs if, while on a throne, one's legs hang down in front. The eighth is to sit with legs spread apart. And the ninth is to expose one's genitals while sitting.

(d) The category concerning receiving food:

> Receiving improperly; receiving to the brim; receiving together; not receiving in order; glancing sideways at the begging bowl; opening the bowl too early; hiding the received and reopening; opening over another's bowl. These are the eight to abandon when receiving food.

In this category there are eight faults. The first is to receive food in a way that disrespects the vinaya. The second is to receive so much that the begging bowl is filled to the brim. The third is, if two or more dishes are offered, to discriminate about the quantity of a certain type of food over another (for example, if only rice is being offered, not accepting it because of wanting to receive vegetables or another dish instead). The fourth is to receive food out of the proper order of distribution. The fifth is to glance out of the corner of one's eye rather than concentrating on one's own begging bowl. The sixth is to uncover the begging bowl before the sponsor has arrived to offer the food. The seventh is to receive additional portions (out of desire) or to hide the food already received in order to receive more. And the eighth is to place the bowl over another vessel or bowl while receiving food.

(e) The category concerning partaking of food:

> Eating inappropriately, too much, too little, improperly, with an open mouth, or while talking; swishing; snapping; sucking; blowing; licking; eating individual grains; complaining about the food; shifting a mouthful around; smacking the lips; regurgitating; licking the hand; licking; shaking the hand; swirling; shaping the food like stūpas. These are the twenty-one to abandon while eating.

The following explains the twenty-one precepts concerning conduct while partaking of food. The first is to refrain from any manners that contradict or disrespect the vinaya. The second is to refrain from eating very large amounts of food. The third is to refrain from eating very small amounts of food. The fourth is to refrain from eating with poor manners according to worldly etiquette. The fifth is to refrain from opening the mouth before the food is brought up to it. The sixth is to refrain from eating while speaking to others. The seventh is to refrain from making swishing sounds with food in the mouth. The eighth is to refrain from snapping one's tongue in delight. The ninth is to refrain from sucking in with food in the mouth if the food is too cold. The tenth is to refrain from blowing out if the food is too hot. The eleventh is to refrain from eating while extending the tongue from the mouth. The twelfth is to refrain from eating grains individually (for example, picking at individual grains of popcorn or puffed grain). The thirteenth is to refrain, while eating, from finding fault with the food. The fourteenth is to refrain from swishing the food around in the mouth from one side to the other. The fifteenth is to refrain from smacking the lips while eating. The sixteenth is to refrain from regurgitating and then re-eating the food like an animal. The seventeenth is to refrain from licking food off one's hand with the tongue. The eighteenth is to refrain from licking clean the begging bowl or one's plate after eating. The nineteenth is to refrain from shaking the hands with food on them. The twentieth is to refrain from swirling food or drink around in the begging bowl. And, lastly, the twenty-first is to refrain from playing with the food by forming it into shapes, such as stūpas and so forth.

(f) The category concerning begging bowls:

> Looking at a begging bowl so as to poke fun; touching a water vessel with food stuck to the hand; sprinkling water; throwing dirty water without permission; keeping leftover food; placing the bowl on the bare earth, an edge, a steep hill, or steps; washing the bowl at an edge, a precipice, a steep hill, while standing, or in a strong current. These are the fourteen to abandon.

The first corresponding precept is to refrain from looking at another monk's begging bowl in such a way as to poke fun or show disrespect. The second is to refrain from touching the water vessel if food is stuck to one's hand. The third is to refrain from sprinkling water that has food in it on other monks sitting close to you. The fourth is to refrain from throwing out the dirty dish water without first asking the owner of the house for permission to do so at a suitable place. The fifth is to refrain from storing leftover food in one's begging bowl. The sixth is to refrain from placing one's bowl on the ground without its stand, so that it may tip over. The seventh is to refrain from carelessly placing the bowl by an edge. The eighth is to refrain from placing it on a steep hill or incline. The ninth is to refrain from placing it on steps where it may fall. The tenth is to refrain from washing the bowl by the edge of a cliff, where there is a danger of the bowl falling over. The eleventh is to refrain from placing it by a precipice. The twelfth is to refrain from placing one's bowl on a steep hill. The thirteenth is to refrain from washing the bowl while standing in the middle of the road. The fourteenth and final precept in this category is that one must not get water from a strong waterfall or current of rushing water, where there is a danger that the bowl may slip from one's hands and be carried away.

(g) The category concerning teaching the Dharma:

> Teaching Dharma while standing or (while listeners are) lying down; while sitting too low; while following behind others; at the path's edge; with a listener's head covered or with clothing hiked up; with cloth hanging; with hands crossed at the neck or behind the head; with hair tied up; while wearing a hat, a diadem, or a *mālā* on the head; on an elephant; while riding a horse or in a palanquin or carriage; while wearing shoes; while carrying a staff, umbrella, weapon, sword, fighting materials, or arrows; or while wearing armor. These are the twenty-six to abandon while teaching.

This category explains the twenty-six precepts to uphold while teaching or discussing the Dharma. The first precept is to refrain from teaching the Dharma while standing up, if the listeners are seated. The second is to refrain from teaching if the listeners are lying down on a bed. The third is to refrain from sitting lower than the listeners. The fourth is to refrain from teaching if the disciples are walking in front of you. The fifth is to refrain from teaching while walking on either side of the listeners. The sixth is to refrain from teaching if any listener has his head covered by cloth when he is not ill. The seventh is to refrain from teaching Dharma if a listener's robes or garments are hiked up too high. The eighth is to refrain from teaching if a listener has cloth hanging over his shoulders. The ninth is to refrain from teaching if a listener's hands are crossed at the neck. The tenth is to refrain from teaching if a listener's hands are behind his head. The eleventh is to refrain from teaching if a listener's hair is worn tied in a knot at the top of his head. The twelfth is to refrain from teaching if a listener is wearing a hat. The thirteenth is to refrain from teaching Dharma if a listener is wearing a diadem or crown. The fourteenth is to refrain from teaching if a listener's head is adorned with a flower lei or wrapped with a rosary of beads. The fifteenth is to refrain from teaching if a listener's head is wrapped in cloth (like a turban of white cloth). The sixteenth and seventeenth are to refrain from teaching if a listener is riding an elephant or a horse. The eighteenth is to refrain from teaching Dharma if a listener is in a palanquin. The nineteenth is to refrain from teaching if a listener is in a carriage. The twentieth is to refrain from teaching if a listener is wearing shoes. The twenty-first is to refrain if a listener is holding a staff. The twenty-second is to refrain if a listener is holding an umbrella. The twenty-third is to refrain if a listener is holding a spear or any weapon. The twenty-fourth is to refrain if a listener is carrying a sword. The twenty-fifth is to refrain if a listener is carrying a bow and arrow, and the twenty-sixth is to refrain from teaching Dharma if a listener is wearing any type of armor. Dharma should not be taught in any of the above cases except, of course, in the case of illness.

(h) The category concerning etiquette to establish:

> The three manners to accomplish are to avoid the emission of feces and urine while standing; to avoid the emission of feces, urine, or mucus in water; and to avoid emission on grass.

The first manner to establish is explained as the avoidance of eliminating feces or urine while in a standing position. The exception is if one is ill or if there is a particular necessity. The second precept is to avoid eliminating in water. The third is to avoid eliminating upon grass. This also includes mucus or sputum. If there is no other place to eliminate one's waste, it is permitted.

(i) The single precept concerning movement:

> To avoid climbing a tree higher than a human is the single vow pertaining to movement.

If there is no danger from wild animals or others, one must avoid climbing a tree higher than the length of a normal human body. This is the sole precept in the fault category that is unrelated to any other category.

This completes the explanation of the one hundred and twelve precepts regarding faults.

2.b.1(b.3.1) The explanation of what a fully ordained female must train to abandon:

> A fully ordained female has eight root downfalls, twenty additional remainders, thirty-three rejected downfalls, one hundred and eighty downfalls, eleven individual confessions, and one hundred and twelve faults. The total, therefore, is three hundred and sixty-four.

The precepts for a fully ordained female are categorized in the same way as those for a fully ordained male. However, a female has three hundred and sixty-four precepts as compared with a male's two hundred and fifty-three. In the category of root downfalls, the female has the same four root downfalls as the male, with four added. These are the following: touching a male's body, sleeping on one's back, concealing a root downfall of another fully ordained female, and using one's body and speech to refuse another female reentry into the saṅgha (after a proper confession has been made).

A fully ordained female has twenty remainders as compared with a male's thirteen. Seven of these are the same as those in the male's category and are therefore considered common, whereas the thirteen additional remainders are considered uncommon.

In the category of rejected downfalls, the fully ordained female must observe thirty-three precepts. The first nineteen of these concern the owning of, separation from, and storage of possessions. These precepts are the same as those for fully ordained males. There are fourteen remaining precepts (beginning with keeping an additional begging bowl for more than twenty-four hours and so forth). The fully ordained female has one hundred and eighty downfalls, seventy-two of which are the same as those for males. There are one hundred and eight additional precepts, the first of which is not being allowed to become an abbess of a monastery or saṅgha unless one has been fully ordained for twelve years.

In the category of individual confession, a female observes eleven precepts. Of these, the precepts common to both males and females relate to the breaking of rules established by the saṅgha and to entering a layman's house in order to partake of food. There are ten remaining precepts (which include not begging for milk or yogurt, etc.) that belong only to the categories for fully ordained females.

As for the fault category, both males and females have one hundred and twelve precepts. Two of these one hundred and twelve (to not be seated without permission in the sponsor's home and to not defecate or urinate upon grass) are already included in other categories for females. The remaining one hundred and ten are the same as those for males. The additional two are that a female must not wear her robe in such a way as to expose her waist, nor should she enter a layman's house with a sense of attachment. These precepts for fully ordained females, which total three hundred and sixty-four, were not propagated in Tibet, and it is for this reason that they are not elaborated upon in the root text.

2.b.1(b.3.2) The corresponding training to accomplish is in three divisions:

(1) The three foundations for all training:

> The manner through which to purify all lapses in discipline is sojong (*so sbyong*; *uposatha*) [confessional ceremony], yarney (*g. yar gnas*; *vārṣika*) [rainy season retreat], and gagyei (*dgag dbye*; *pravāraṇā*) [the ceremony that concludes the rainy season retreat].

Sojong means to purify the faults in one's precept training so that the pure nature of that training can develop and increase. In addition, sojong is the method through which to restore any deterioration of vows so that the "unwanted object to abandon" as well as any negativity can be fully eliminated. There are two ways to practice sojong. The first is foundational sojong (*upoṣadha*), which is practiced by an individual who is able to uphold moral discipline, whose desires are few, and who is easily satisfied. While on the path, by listening to teachings on the Tripiṭaka and by contemplating its meaning and meditating, conflicting circumstances are avoided and conducive conditions are produced. For such an individual, the main meditation methods employed on the path are quiescence (*śamatha*) and heightened awareness (*vipaśyanā*).[35] By applying antidotes to mental afflictions and delusions, the individual trains on the five paths[36] and in the thirty-seven limbs of enlightenment.[37] The result is the achievement of the fourfold accomplishment of the śrāvakas.[38]

The second method of practicing sojong is specifically to reconcile one's faults. Here, there are five different types of formal sojong purification practice. The first is the sojong of the fourteenth day of the waning moon. This is practiced six times in one year on the twenty-ninth day of the second, fourth, sixth, eighth, tenth, and twelfth lunar months. The second is the sojong of the fifteenth day, which is practiced eighteen times per year. This sojong is performed on the full-moon day of all twelve months in the year, as well as on the thirtieth day of the month on the first, third, fifth, seventh, ninth, and eleventh months.

The third is the sojong of good fortune, which is practiced in order to consecrate a ceremony or any other Dharma activity so as to bring blessings and auspicious conditions. The fourth is the sojong practice that reverses harm, which is practiced in order to remove or avert illness, war, or other calamities and potential disasters. The fifth is the sojong to consolidate the saṅgha, which is practiced to bring unity and conformity to the congregation. These final three types of sojong practice are performed whenever necessary.

The second training is the foundational yarney practice, better known as the three-month rainy season retreat. Yarney is practiced primarily to enhance one's spiritual practice by cloistering with the saṅgha and by maintaining certain restrictions for a duration of time. The yarney practice was begun because many of the non-Buddhists of that time would ridicule Buddhist monks for being active during the summer season. In Asia, the summer season is a time of abundant rainfall, many insects abound, and it is easy inadvertently to kill an insect by just walking around outside. Such a lack of mindfulness appeared to contradict a monk's principal precept not to kill. To correct such views and to avoid harm to living beings, yarney was established. There are two time frames for yarney. The first begins on the full-moon day of the sixth lunar month and ends on the full-moon day of the ninth. The second begins and ends one month later.

After commencement on the morning of the sixteenth day, the monks assemble to consecrate the environment by the repetition of certain mantras. During the following ninety-day period, the monks must remain cloistered within the confines of specifically defined boundaries. They spend the majority of this time hearing, contemplating, and meditating according to the vinaya and bodhisattva precepts and training.

The third foundational training is gagyei, the ceremony that concludes the yarney retreat. Gagyei means to "lift the restrictions," referring specifically to the restrictions and limitations imposed during yarney. There are two types of gagyei, one that is time-determined and one that is not. Seven days before the concluding gagyei ceremony, the monks must be informed as to where the ceremony will be held so that preparations can be made. All yarney participants must then leave the boundaries of the retreat in order to perform gagyei in a different location. If any monk is unable to attend because of illness or some other unfortunate circumstance, he must let it be known that he is in agreement with the gagyei location. During the several-hour ceremony, kuśa grass is distributed to the monks, and mantras are recited. Many sūtras are also recited, including the *Triskandhaka* (*Treatise on the Three Aggregates*).[39]

The second type of gagyei is of undetermined timing. For example, if yarney has been conducted for only one and a half months and is disturbed because of war or the necessity of abandoning the retreat's location, the gagyei must still be performed as the concluding ceremony.

(2) The five foundational conditions for staying comfortable:

> The foundations of cloth, dwelling places, medicine, and so forth are taught elsewhere.

Although these five conditions are not elaborated upon in detail, they are briefly mentioned here. All clothing must be worn in accordance with the vinaya. The thirteen necessities for a monk include the following: the patched yellow robe of the fully ordained (or another robe for the novice), an undergarment, a sweat shawl, a shawl to be worn over the sweat shawl, a lower robe, a shawl for the lower robe, a protective cloth for shaving the head, a face towel, a regular towel, a mat, a bandage, a rainguard, and a cloth bag. These possessions are allowed for the necessity of basic comfort.

The use of leather or fur is permitted if one is in a very cold climate. Otherwise, the ordained must not wear leather even as shoes. If, when visiting a household or temple the only place to sit is upon leather, it is permitted to sit but not to sleep upon it. A monk suffering from an eye or cold disease is permitted to wear the hide of a bear, as this is considered to be of medicinal value. In an extremely cold environment one may wear a fur hat, boots, or other articles of clothing in order to keep warm.

Concerning dwelling places, a monk should make use only of places where pure discipline is maintained. He must always take care of his surroundings, and if they are loaned to him to use he must return them in excellent condition.

The four types of medicine that a monk is allowed to utilize were elaborated upon earlier. These include food taken for sustenance and medicines necessary to maintain good health.

(3) A concise, indirect revelation of what is permitted and conducive:

> In brief, originally there were no sanctions or prohibitions. If something is suitable, it is permitted. If it is unsuitable, it is prohibited. If it corresponds to the unsuitable and contradicts what is right, it is taught to completely reject it.

At the time that Lord Buddha Śākyamuni was passing into parinirvāṇa, he gave this final advice to the fully ordained monks who had gathered: "I have revealed the training of the vinaya to all of you in great detail. Listen now, though, to the essence of this training. Originally, there were no sanctions or restrictions. If there is ever any question as to whether a deed is close to that which is prohibited, then it must be rejected. If a deed is conducive to that which is permitted, then it should be accepted. This is a matter of intelligent discrimination."

3. An explanation of the physical support necessary for the vows to take birth:

> With the exception of heretics, committers of heinous crimes, human inhabitants of the northern continent, nymphs, hermaphrodites, the five classes of neuters, those who change sex three times, and manifestations, the desirable supports for the vows to take birth include all male and female human inhabitants of the three continents.

The exceptions are, first, those beings who, because of their obscurations, are not suitable physical supports for the development of the precepts. These include heretics (defined as those who maintain incorrect views) and those who have accrued the weightiest negative karma possible by killing their own father or mother or an arhat, spilling the blood of a realized being with a negative intention, or causing a schism in the saṅgha. Other exceptions include those born as inhabitants of the northern continent Uttarakuru, where, due to karmic propensities, the obscuration of delusion is particularly heavy; those born as neuters or spontaneously arisen hermaphrodites of any of the five types;[40] those who experience spontaneous sex transformation more than twice; or nonhumans manifesting in the form of humans (spirits who temporarily assume a human form). Concerning such cases, even if the vows are given there would be no basis for development.

Otherwise all male and female inhabitants of the eastern continent Videha, the southern continent Jambudvīpa, and the western continent Avaragodānīya are suitable supports for the birth of the prātimokṣa vows.

4. An explanation of the restoration of vows in the case of deterioration, in two divisions:

4.a Briefly revealed:

> Afterwards, in case of damage, the explanation of precept restoration follows:

After a suitable support for the development of the precepts receives them, they must be guarded accordingly. However, if, due to an abundance of delusion or other causes, the precepts are allowed to deteriorate, these methods are revealed in order to restore them.

4.b Extensively explained:

4.b.1 The causes for losing precepts
4.b.2 The actual restoration

4.b.1 The causes for losing precepts, in two subdivisions:

4.b.1(a) The common causes:

> For the precepts to be lost, they are offered back, death occurs, two sex organs simultaneously develop, or sex change occurs three times. The weightiest cause of all, severing the vows from their root, is to hold the view that there is no cause and result.

There are four causes that completely eliminate the prātimokṣa precepts. First, one must approach an individual who possesses the ability to understand one's intention to offer back the precepts. The person returning the vows must do so from the depths of his or her heart. Then, in the presence of that individual, the vows are offered back, at which time they terminate. The second cause is death, wherein they automatically terminate since they were taken only for the duration of a lifetime. The third cause is if two sex organs develop simultaneously or one experiences a sex change more than twice. Finally, the weightiest cause of all is to develop incorrect view, such as disbelieving in the infallible law of cause and result. In each of these cases, since the root of virtue has been severed, there is no longer any foundation or basis to support the precepts. The twenty-four-hour precepts are an exception in that they automatically terminate when that time expires. This was explained earlier.

4.b.1(b) The uncommon causes, in three categories:

4.b.1(b.1) Specific individual causes for the loss of the precepts:

> Receiving ordination before age twenty and learning of it later terminates the vows of full ordination. A female novice in training who transgresses her promise in order to serve (beyond one night) loses her precepts. Each of these is uncommon.

There are three specific cases that also cause the precepts to terminate. The first concerns a male who has received full ordination and later learns of the age requirement of twenty years. If his age does not total twenty years (including the time spent in the mother's womb), the vows automatically terminate. The second concerns the female novice in training for full ordination. Although one of her defeats is sexual intercourse, if she so much as promises to engage in sexual intercourse and yet doesn't actually perform the act, the vows still terminate after the passing of a night. The third concerns the observance of the twenty-four-hour vow. After the passing of a night, the vows automatically terminate.

4.b.1(b.2) The specific differences of opinion concerning the loss of precepts:

> If a root downfall occurs or the Dharma vanishes, the precepts are lost. According to the Vaibhāṣika of Kaśmīr, a vow-holder who commits a root downfall "possesses two," like having both wealth and debts. Some say that all vows deteriorate if one root downfall is committed.

According to the Sautrāntika school of Buddhist philosophy, if a root defeat occurs and is concealed, all the precepts are lost. In the second moment after the vow is broken, if there is no sense of shame and the damaged precept is not immediately recognized and openly confessed, it becomes irreparable.

According to the Tāmraśātīya school of the śrāvakas, when the transmission tradition of the Buddhist Dharma declines to the point that it no longer exists, the vows will also cease to exist and will naturally terminate. This would mean that a valid description of the vinaya training (in other words, of what to accept or reject) will no longer be available. However, according to the teachings of Asaṅga and Vasubandhu, if vows were previously received, even though the Dharma vanishes, those vows will not be lost. This is because the realization already achieved will not vanish due only to external circumstances. However, if vows were not previously received, after the Dharma vanishes they will not develop, because of the nonexistence of the precept-granting rituals and guidelines.

According to the Vaibhāṣika school as it came to be practiced in Kaśmīr, if a root defeat occurs the other vows are still not entirely lost. The individual concerned would then qualify as one who has committed a root defeat and yet still possesses the other vows. This is likened to the situation of one who owes a large debt yet still has some wealth.

Other schools assert that all vows deteriorate when any one of the four root defeats occurs. The vows do not terminate, though, because the remaining vows are still possessed. However, the deterioration affects the potency of the other vows and postpones accomplishment and realization. If a root defeat occurs and, in the second moment, the individual feels shame and remorse, the other vows do not deteriorate and the vow may be restored. If there is no sense of shame, and the defeat is concealed, the individual loses all other precepts and may no longer join the ranks of the saṅgha, accept offerings, or wear the robes of ordination.[41]

4.b.1(b.3) An explanation of the causes that disqualify the development of a precept in order to discern whether or not this qualifies as a root defeat:

> Beginners, mental instability, intense illness, and inability to accomplish are without fault.

The term "beginners" refers to the original monks at the time of Lord Buddha Śākyamuni's life. It has already been stated that initially there were no restrictions or rules. Then, as time passed and different mistakes were made, the Buddha established the rules of pure morality according to each specific situation and the capabilities of the ordained. For example, when the monk Zangchin had sexual intercourse, this did not constitute a root downfall because the corresponding precept had not yet been established. It did, however, become the cause for the establishment of that precept. Because of Zangchin's status as a beginner and, in a sense, a "pioneer," there was no foundation for the fault to develop. Similarly, an individual whose mental state is unstable due to intense pain and suffering does not have the basis for a fault to arise. In addition, even if one has tremendous respect for the precepts and a sincere wish to maintain them, if one lacks the potency to actually accomplish them, there is also no basis for fault. This is like having a dream in which one experiences sexual intercourse; because one is powerless in a dream, the act does not qualify as a defeat. All of these are exceptions that disqualify conduct as root downfalls.

4.b.2 The actual restoration, in three subdivisions:

4.b.2(a) An explanation of the restoration divisions
4.b.2(b) Revealing the manner in which all methods of purification are condensed into the four powers
4.b.2(c) Instructions on how to carefully guard the precepts by recognition of faults

4.b.2(a) An explanation of the restoration divisions, in two subdivisions:

4.b.2(a.1) Recognizing the fault of concealment:

> Concealment is defined as not expressing a secret.

Concealment means to wish to keep a downfall or broken precept secret from another and to then intentionally fail to mention it. In addition, it means to carry out one's actions in such a way so as to conceal any wrongdoing or fault. If one commits a defeat, and if there is even one moment's intention to hide it, this constitutes concealment.

4.b.2(a.2) An explanation of the actual distinctions, in two subdivisions:

4.b.2(a.2.1) Restoration of vows pertaining to root downfalls

4.b.2(a.2.2) Restoration of vows pertaining to remainders and so forth

4.b.2(a.2.1) Restoration of vows pertaining to root downfalls, in two subdivisions:

(1) A concealed root downfall cannot be made good:

It is not possible to make good a concealed root downfall in this life.

If one fails to offer one's vows back if any of the four defeats occurs, and intends to conceal this from others for even a moment, this becomes a concealed defeat, which cannot be restored again in this lifetime. Such an individual must be expelled from the ranks of the ordained saṅgha. However, if that individual confesses the concealed root downfall with heartfelt remorse and makes a vow to never repeat the action, the fully ripening karma of lower rebirth may be averted and transformed. Confession is therefore extremely important. If there is no remorseful confession because of an individual's failure to realize the gravity of his fault, that individual must experience rebirth in the hell realms for fourteen million fourteen thousand years. If, after an individual has been expelled from the saṅgha, he maintains the discipline of training in the scriptures by way of hearing, contemplation, and meditation, the saṅgha must relocate him and maintain his support. He is not allowed, however, to stay with and enjoy the benefits of the saṅgha. If he has requested forbearance, and the saṅgha refuses, from then onward if his share of sustenance reaches considerable value and is kept by the saṅgha rather than being distributed to him, all of the saṅgha members accrue a root downfall.

(2) If not concealed, it can be made good:

> If there is no concealment and the act is openly revealed through confession to the saṅgha, recognition of the fault, and a vow not to repeat it, the fault is purified and the vow is retaken.

If any of the four defeats occurs, but the individual develops instant remorse without even a moment's thought to conceal it and immediately verbalizes the defeat in the presence of a fully qualified member of the saṅgha, if he is then asked whether or not he recognizes this fault, he must reply in the affirmative. If he tells the truth with heartfelt recognition of his failure, openly reveals it, and promises he will not repeat the act in the future even at the cost of his life, it is then considered to be confessed. Then, for the duration of his life, that individual must maintain a humble status by performing the five lower behaviors and abstaining from the five higher behaviors of fully ordained monks. The five lower behaviors to perform are, first, to arise before the other monks to open, clean, and prepare the temple; second, during teachings, to fan the room in order to make it comfortable for the others; third, if there is an assembly, to prepare the seats and cushions and to ring the gong to call the saṅgha to gather; fourth, to prepare incense and other offerings; and fifth, during the evening, to prepare water and wash the feet of the senior monks. At all times and in all situations, the individual must never do anything that even inclines toward nonvirtue, and he must always remain at the perimeter of the saṅgha with an attitude of humility and respect.

The five higher behaviors to abstain from are, first, to receive respect and veneration together with other fully ordained monks; second, to place one's sleeping mat together with those of other fully ordained monks; third, to discuss downfalls with the fully ordained; fourth, to penalize or punish monks; and fifth, to travel together with the fully ordained. This tradition is practiced by the Cittamātra, Madhyamaka, and Vajrayāna schools.

4.b.2(a.2.2) Restoration of the vows pertaining to the thirteen remainders:

> The vows pertaining to the thirteen remainders and others are gradually restored through confession according to their weight.

If any of the thirteen remainders occurs, and if, without allowing one day to pass, the individual confesses this in the presence of the saṅgha, the corresponding precept is restored. If the individual allows several days or more to pass without confession, he must step down in his rank and position within the saṅgha for an equivalent number of days. Thereafter, he must also perform actions to please and serve the saṅgha, such as cleaning the monastery and so forth. If the individual feels shame and truly upholds the Vinaya, Sūtra, and Abhidharma Piṭakas, he may confess in the presence of one saṅgha member. The vow is restored according to the weight of the failure. For example, if the fault is a defeat, this must be confessed before five or six fully ordained monks. If it is a remainder, a major transgression, or a weighty fault, this must be confessed in the presence of four (or at least one) fully ordained monks. It is extremely important to confess and make good any deterioration of precepts so that at the time of one's death there is no remaining fault. If death does arrive and the fault remains, then, although it is no longer possible to confess through verbal or physical means, the fault must be mentally confessed and restored. If heartfelt remorse accompanies the confession, the fault is removed. If one is unable to meet with the necessary object before which to confess, the confession will not be complete. In such a case, a blessing ceremony must be performed so that the downfall does not increase, and as soon as possible one must find an object before which to complete the confession. Otherwise, to confess by merely mouthing words and to claim that the weight of one's nonvirtue has thereby been purified is considered to be equivalent to a "great" lie, and carries with it the corresponding negativity.

4.b.2(b) Restoration through the application of the four powers:

> In brief, without bringing together the four powers there can be no confession. The power of remorse consists of a remorseful confession of previous deeds: a regret from one's heart, as though one had taken poison. The power of the antidote, like a medicine for poison, consists of an intensive activation of virtue in order to purify the fault. The power of restoration consists of the strength of the conviction never to repeat the fault, like never drinking poison again. Like reliance on a doctor, taking refuge and making confession (and so forth) with intense faith comprise the power of the support. These are the four to apply.

In case of any accumulation of negativity or downfall of morality, all remedial forces and methods are condensed into the four powers, without which there can be no confession. The first power, the way in which to remorsefully confess a previously committed downfall, is likened to mistakenly drinking poison and then experiencing the intensity of that pain as well as the threat to one's life. At such a time it is certain that one will feel extreme remorse and attempt to expel the poison from one's system. This experience of heartfelt remorse, which is not merely a mouthing of words, is the experience of the power of remorse.

Just as it would be necessary to rely upon a skilled physician to cure an illness caused by poison, in order to purify one's faults one must engage the full attention of body, speech, and mind to diligently train in the antidote, virtue. This is the experience of the second power, the power of the antidote. Just as one would never intentionally drink poison again, once a downfall has been fully acknowledged, the vow that one takes to never repeat this kind of behavior is the power of restoration. The purging of poison from one's system is a process that takes time and is dependent upon the support and guidance of one's physician. In the same way, in order to restore one's mind stream as a suitable vessel for the precious Dharma, one should depend entirely on the lama and the Three Precious Jewels. Going for refuge, generating the supreme bodhicitta, and reciting the sūtras of confession in the presence of a suitable support for one's refuge—and doing this with confidence and determined faith—is the power of the support.

According to this tradition, one must be certain that all powers are present in confession. If they are not, then not only does one lose the potency to recover from the downfall, but the effects of the fully ripening karma accrued from the downfall will be particularly intense. Maintaining awareness of the infallible ripening effect of karma and of the need for always applying all four powers in confession are the most important points to keep in mind.

4.b.2(c) Instructions on how to guard the precepts through recognition of faults:

> However, if even one powerful negative downfall occurs, the obtainment of a bhūmi is indefinitely postponed. The precepts must be guarded like one's eyes!

Although it is considered that faults may be purified by effecting confession accordingly, and that even a root downfall may be made good if it is unconcealed and confessed, until one achieves the level of arhatship the imprint of a defeat cannot be fully purified. In addition, because of that very imprint, it becomes even more difficult to achieve arhatship. This is due to the obscuration impressed upon one's mind stream as a result of the accumulation of negativity. Although one may diligently persevere in the remedial forces required to remove this negative karma, the ability to actualize the noble qualities of the stages of higher realization will certainly be impaired, thus delaying one's accomplishments. Thus, the need to guard even minor precepts and subtle thoughts and deeds must never be underestimated. Just as one's eyes are guarded at all cost, all vows, large or small, must be protected! Even though a fault may seem small, it possesses the potency to contribute to the production of a much greater fully ripening result.

If one attempts to conceal or hide faults from others, this becomes known to the spiritual guides and deities. In addition, one's bad reputation will spread everywhere, and one will become an object of ridicule and disregard by worldly gods, as well as an embarrassment in the company of the *khenpo* (*mkhan po*) or vajra teacher. One will also feel uneasy among the saṅgha, despondent, and guilty about receiving offerings from patrons. The virtuous local deities and protectors will no longer look after one. Negative spirits and the various classes of demons will be attracted to one, and all that is nonconducive will come one's way in that very life. Noble qualities will fail to develop, previous knowledge will be forgotten, and at the time of one's death strong regret will arise with no escape but the inevitable experience of unbearable suffering in the lower realms.

In brief, if one desires bliss and happiness in this and future lifetimes, extreme care should be taken in the practice of guarding morality and restoring deteriorations with a sincere and complete confession.

5. The benefits of guarding the precepts have three divisions:

5.a The benefits of morality alone:

> Receiving precepts in order to cure an illness or escape punishment, although clearing these conditions, is the morality of protection from fear. Receiving precepts for the sake of future lifetimes is the morality of excellent aspiration. Although the result—the bliss of gods and humans—is obtained, liberation is not.

The benefits of protecting precepts from deterioration accrue in accordance with one's motivation. If one does this in order to be free from illness, to escape punishment, or to experience conducive circumstances in this life, this is the practice of morality to protect oneself from fear. In essence, it is a morality that is practiced in order to receive protection. To practice morality with the intention of escaping the fears of lower rebirth and of achieving the bliss of rebirth as a god or human being is the practice of morality with an excellent aspiration. Although the result that is wished for may be obtained, unless cyclic existence itself is fully renounced there can be no hope of obtaining liberation.

5.b The benefits of the prātimokṣa precepts:

> If the vows are held with the morality of full renunciation, arhatship[42] is obtained, as in the life story of Nanda.

If pure morality is practiced together with a true renunciation of cyclic existence and the wish to achieve nirvāṇa, then by embracing one of the eight categories of prātimokṣa training and guarding those precepts from deterioration (according to one's aspiration), the corresponding level of arhatship will be obtained.

For example, when the Lord Buddha Śākyamuni's younger brother, Nanda, first took ordination, he was forced to do so by the Buddha. Later, by his miraculous powers, the Buddha led his brother to a god realm, where he developed a strong wish to be reborn among the beautiful goddesses in that wondrous place. After returning to the human realm he diligently practiced morality with this aspiration for a higher rebirth. Later, the Buddha led him to the hell realms to show him their sufferings, and the thought of total renunciation then developed in his mind. Thereafter, Nanda's observance of the prātimokṣa precepts became pure and fully empowered to produce the result of arhatship, which he did indeed obtain. Other temporary benefits include becoming an object of the veneration of all practitioners of pure morality and all wise ones; having a peaceful and stable mind at the time of death; and in future lifetimes taking rebirth in higher god realms such as Paranirmitavaśavartin, Nirmāṇarati, Tuṣita, and Yāma, where extreme enjoyment and miraculous powers prevail. Ultimately, through the practice of pure morality alone, single-pointed meditative absorption is accomplished. In dependence upon that, the innate wisdom, free from conceptualization, develops to sever the root of existence, grasping at a "self," which results in the realization of nirvāṇa "without traces."[43]

5.c The benefit of how the precepts are the basis for all noble qualities:

> The noble qualities of refuge in the Three Jewels and others are supreme in the latter (precepts). Since the initial precepts are the foundation of the later ones, the aspirants of bodhicitta and mantra must follow them accordingly. Thus, they are the basis for all noble qualities.

As is stated in the *Nirvāṇa-sūtra*, "Whoever takes refuge in the Three (Jewels) will swiftly become a buddha." The benefits of refuge ordination, though profound, are multiplied as one embraces the higher categories of prātimokṣa training. The benefits of full lay ordination are one hundred times greater than refuge alone. The benefits of novice ordination are one hundred times greater than lay. The benefits of full ordination are one hundred times greater than novice. The first categories become common disciplines of the following categories, and so serve as steps on the path to the latter. Likewise, the prātimokṣa precepts serve as support for the bodhisattva vows. Both serve as the basis of support for secret mantra. Thus it should be clear that practitioners of secret mantra must have the foundation of having established and ascended the two preceding paths.

In the past, when the Buddha's doctrine was all-pervasive, there was time to practice pure morality and to perform all the various aspects of training. Now, at the time of the doctrine's decline, to maintain pure discipline for even one day is considered to be of even greater benefit. As is stated in the *Samādhirāja-sūtra,* "For as many grains of sand exist on the banks of the river Ganges for ten million eons of time: if you make, with a sincere heart, that many offerings of food, drink, incense, flowers, and light to the millions of buddhas who come and go, and if you compare this to the practice of pure morality during the time of the decline of the doctrine of the sugatas, the merit accumulated in one day of pure morality is far more sublime."

Having completed this subject, the conclusion of the chapter follows:

> This explanation of the stages of the prātimokṣa-vinaya completes the second chapter.

Of the five chapters of this commentary, the principal subject of the second chapter—the common training of the śrāvakas, the prātimokṣa, and the categories of vinaya training for male and female practitioners—is now complete. This is taken from the Buddha's teachings of the four great scriptures of vinaya: the *Vinayavastu, Vinayavibhāga, Vinayāgama,* and *Vinayottama.*

CHAPTER THREE: THE BODHISATTVA VOWS

B. Chapter Three: The Bodhisattva Vows, in three divisions:

1. The manner in which the Buddha taught the Pāramitā Piṭaka:

> Mahā Muni, the guide of sentient beings in this fortunate eon, at Vulture's Peak and elsewhere, boundlessly taught the extremely extensive piṭaka to those of the class of Mahāyāna.

Although Lord Buddha Śākyamuni achieved full awakening as a buddha many countless eons prior to his life as Śākyamuni, for the purpose of alleviating the suffering of cyclic confusion and guiding all beings to permanent peace, he reentered this world to demonstrate the twelve miraculous deeds[44] and, specifically, to reveal the path to freedom from suffering. Through this intentional manifestation he was able to reveal the manner in which all beings may achieve the great, unsurpassed state of full awakening. In the previous chapter on the prātimokṣa, explanations were given on the manner in which the Buddha first introduced the Vinaya Piṭaka and how it was compiled, propagated, taught, and practiced. This chapter explains the bodhisattva vows and conduct, the principal subject of the second and third turnings of the Dharma wheel. The path of bodhisattvahood was revealed within the extraordinary context of the five states of perfect certainty. The "certainty of the teacher" was the fourth Buddha of this eon, Śākyamuni. The "certainty of the place" was Vulture's Peak, India, and elsewhere. The "certainty of the assembly" was the gathering of those of the class of Mahāyāna, including gods, *nāgas,* humans, demigods, spirits, and others of the common assembly. The uncommon assembly was composed of countless bodhisattvas. The "certainty of the Dharma" was the extremely extensive discourse focusing upon mental development within the context of the Sūtra Piṭaka, with emphasis on each of the three piṭakas respectively. The vinaya aspect of the sūtra teaching includes a description of the bodhisattva vows. The sūtra aspect reveals the extensive profundity of meditative absorption. The abhidharma aspect of sūtra reveals the divisions of the stages and paths, as well as the distinctions between *dhyāna* and *samādhi,* or mindfulness and meditative absorption.

During the third turning of the wheel, the meaning of ultimate truth was revealed so extensively that it was beyond ordinary conception. Here, the "certainty of the time" was experienced according to the aspiration of the recipients. Some understood instantaneously, while others comprehended gradually, according to their own level of understanding.

It is agreed by all Buddhist schools that the first turning of the wheel primarily revealed the teachings according to relative truth. Although the second and third turnings revealed both relative and ultimate explanations, there is much disagreement concerning this. In the Nyingma tradition, we assert that the second turning revealed the nature of both relative and ultimate truth, but with an emphasis on the temporary ultimate, whereas the third turning revealed the ultimate, absolute truth.

2. After it was compiled, the manner in which it was taught and practiced:

> The *Gambhīradarśanaparamparā* (*Tradition of the Profound View*) was compiled by Mañjuśrī, elaborated upon by Nāgārjuna and others, and propagated by Śāntideva. The *Udāracaryāparamparā* (*Tradition of Extremely Vast Conduct*) was compiled by Maitreya, elaborated upon by Asaṅga and his brother, and propagated by Atīsá. Our tradition of Padmasambhava follows that of Nāgārjuna.

The common teachings presented during the first turning of the wheel were compiled on three separate occasions. The teachings of the second turning were compiled through uncommon and extraordinary means. According to the uncommon tradition of Mahāyāna, in the southern direction of Rājagṛha, India, on the peak of Bimasambhava, one million bodhisattvas gathered to receive the teachings of the Tripiṭaka, which were then compiled by Maitreya, Mañjuśrī, and Vajrapāṇi. These teachings are found in the two great traditions of Ārya Nāgārjuna and Ārya Asaṅga.

According to the tradition of Nāgārjuna, the teachings on the profound nature of emptiness were compiled by Ārya Mañjuśrī. Following this, and in accordance with the Buddha's prophecy, the great spiritual master Nāgārjuna composed the six categories of explanations concerning the Middle Way, based on the second turning of the wheel, which established *svaśūnyatā,* the reality that all phenomena are empty of any inherent nature.[45] Nāgārjuna then composed the *Vigrahavyāvartanīkārikā* and other texts (based upon the third turning) that serve to establish *paraśūnyatā,* the view that although all phenomena are not empty of their own nature or reality, they are asserted as being empty according to conventional reality. With this, the Tradition of the Profound View, Gambhīradarśanaparamparā, came into existence. Following Nāgārjuna, the great propagators of this tradition include such highly realized masters as Candrakīrti, Āryadeva, and others. (The great Śāntideva and Jetāri were responsible primarily for propagating the teachings on the generation of the awakened mind, bodhicitta.)

According to the tradition of Ārya Asaṅga, known as the Tradition of Great Extensive Conduct, Udāracaryāparamparā, the teachings were originally compiled by Maitreya. These teachings, which are contained in the Five Great Commentaries of Maitreya, essentially elucidate the empty nature of objective appearances.[46] Later, Ārya Asaṅga elaborated upon these works by composing his own commentaries, which were then further elaborated upon by such celebrated masters as the supreme scholar Vasubandhu, who composed the eight categories of the *Prakaraṇa.*[47] These teachings were further propagated by the great Dignāga, Dharmakīrti, Candragomin, and Dīpaṃkara Śrījñāna *(*Atīśa), who was responsible for bringing this lineage of bodhisattva vows into Tibet.

In our Nyingma tradition, which follows the lineage of Ācārya Padmasambhava and the earlier translation school, the bodhisattva vows and rituals are received and practiced primarily according to the tradition of Nāgārjuna. The view, however, is maintained in accordance with both traditions.

3. The principal subject, in two subdivisions:
a. A general explanation of the nature and distinctions of the vows to be received
b. A specific explanation of how to receive the vows

a. A general explanation of the nature and distinctions of the vows to be received, in two further subdivisions:

   1. The nature of the vows:

> The nature is a mind moist with love and compassion that wishes to obtain full awakening for the sake of others, together with the intention to abandon all faults of the three doors.

The essence of the principal subject concerns the nature of bodhicitta, the spirit of "awakening." Here, love is defined as the kind of unconditional love a mother has for her only child, directed toward all living beings by viewing them all with loving-kindness joined with the strong desire to see them established in true, permanent happiness. A "mind moist with compassion" refers to the undiminishing wish to see that all beings are set free from suffering and the causes of suffering. The desire to achieve full awakening is the wish to engage in activities solely for the purpose of benefitting others. With this attitude, one desires to unite method and wisdom in the practice of aspirational and practical bodhicitta and to actualize the nature of the six transcendent virtues.[48] In addition, this desire includes the intention to abandon all nonconducive circumstances that obstruct one from accomplishing the purpose of others, as well as all faults of the three doors (body, speech, and mind) that produce obstacles to one's accomplishment of full awakening.

According to Ārya Vimuktasena and Ācārya Haribhadra, in terms of the primary consciousness, the awakened mind is the consciousness of mental activity. According to Ārya Asaṅga and his brother Vasubandhu, the awakened mind arises as a mental event (secondary consciousness). As it says in Ārya Asaṅga's *Bodhisattvabhūmi* (*Stages of Awakening*), the aspiration of the bodhisattvas is the supreme intention, explained as the secondary consciousness that strives after virtue. It is stated in Vasubandhu's *Alaṅkaṭīkā* that "the awakened mind is the mind that maintains as its focus the two purposes."

The Nyingma school asserts that when the mind performs the activity of developing within itself the awakened attitude, this becomes the principal mind. Secondary mental events are also considered to be part of the awakened mind, as they arise from the principal mind. Both are called the awakened mind.

2. The distinctions of the vows, in three subdivisions:
   - 2.a Briefly revealed
   - 2.b Extensively explained
   - 2.c Summing up

2.a Briefly revealed:

> The distinctions are well known as the two traditions of Nāgārjuna and Asaṅga. Each has from one to six, with two each.

The two general distinctions are the well-known traditions of Nāgārjuna and Asaṅga. The specific distinctions include the six categories that exist in each of these two traditions. In addition, each tradition has the two categories of the development of awakened mind: aspirational and practical.

2.b The extensive explanation, in two subdivisions:

2.b.1 The divisions ranging from one to six:

> First, compassion as the essence of emptiness; second, training in the two accumulations of merit, relative and absolute; third, the three trainings of morality, meditative equipoise, and wisdom, the motivation engaged in the aspiration of accumulation and preparation; and fourth, the seven impure stages with residual purity, full maturation of the three pure stages, and great loving-kindness as the complete abandonment of obscurations, the awakened mind of the state of buddha. These constitute four. The fifth is the five paths, and the sixth is the six transcendent virtues.

These six categorize the different divisions of the awakened mind. The awakened mind arises at the moment that the nature of emptiness is realized. The innate compassion that spontaneously arises from within is the awakened mind of the essential nature of emptiness. The second distinction occurs during the training and development of the two accumulations of merit, relative and absolute. The awakened mind that develops from external elaborations, such as the vow-receiving ritual, is known as relative awakened mind. The subtle awakened mind that arises from awareness of the nature of truth is known as the ultimate awakened mind. The third level occurs while training in pure morality, single-pointed meditative absorption, and self-liberating wisdom. These three levels of training are known as the awakened mind of abstaining from harm, amassing virtue, and accomplishing the purpose of others.

The fourth distinction occurs on the paths of accumulation and preparation, where one engages in conduct with the aspiration to realize the nature of emptiness free from limitation. The result of this is the development of the awakened mind that concentrates solely upon the purpose of others. While one ascends the first seven bodhisattva stages of impure development, one realizes the total equality of self and others by developing the extraordinarily pure awakened mind. Then, on the three pure levels of bodhisattvahood, one spontaneously gives rise to primordial wisdom free from conceptualization and, by means of this, accomplishes the purpose of others. This is called the fully ripened awakened mind. When nonconceptual, great loving-kindness develops by one's having completely removed the two obscurations and all habitual propensities, this is called the awakened mind of the status of buddha. These are the four initial distinctions of the awakened mind.

The fifth distinction includes all five paths of Mahāyāna practice and the various levels of awakened mind that develop respective to them. The initial awakened mind arises when one enters the first of the five paths, the path of accumulation. Then, as one continues on to the second, the path of preparation, the awakened mind continues to develop. On the path of seeing, the meaning of the nature of truth is directly perceived, and on the path of meditation one is fully liberated from all coemergent obscurations. Upon reaching the path of no more learning, uncompounded primordial wisdom is actualized in its place. Within this ultimate state of fruition, one possesses the ability to spontaneously accomplish the purpose of others. This potential is not actualized on the preceding levels. This, the highest level of awakened mind, is termed "inconceivable awakened mind." These are the five progressive levels developed in dependence upon the five paths.

The sixth distinction includes the levels of development in conjunction with the progressive development of the six transcendent virtues.

2.b.2 The analogies that exemplify the stages of awakened mind:

> Earth, gold, the moon, fire, and so forth are the twenty-two examples of the levels of accomplishment within the ten bhūmis.

The aspiration of awakened mind is likened to the earth, for it is the very basis of all virtue, particularly the state of full awakening. The undiminishing, ever-constant aspiration of awakened mind is likened to gold in that it remains strong and unwavering until full awakening is reached. The ever-increasing virtue that continues to manifest and develop as the awakened mind itself develops is like the moon. These three stages of the development of awakened mind are experienced during the first of the five paths, the path of accumulation. Then, on the path of preparation, when the six transcendent virtues are actualized, awakened mind is likened to fire because it burns away the gross, coarse obscurations in the same way that fire burns dry wood. As one embarks upon the path of seeing, the spontaneity of the awakened mind is like a treasure that satisfies the needs and desires of sentient beings. This is the awakened mind of generosity, which is experienced on the path of seeing. This awakened mind is the very source of pure morality, from which all precious and noble qualities arise. Thus, it is likened to a precious jewel. This gives rise to innate patience so that undesirable circumstances cannot disturb the mind. This awakened mind of patience is likened to a lake.

The enthusiastic effort that arises from this awakened mind averts all demonic, negative forces. Thus, it is likened to a vajra. This unmovable state of concentration is likened to a mountain. The wisdom nature of this awakened mind is like a medicine that pacifies the illness of the two obscurations. The skillful application of method combined with wisdom to accomplish the purpose of others is likened to a virtuous mentor who demonstrates that the root of virtue is inexhaustible. This awakened mind completely fulfills all the aspirations, hopes, and prayers of oneself and others and so is likened to a wish-fulfilling jewel. Like the sun, this awakened mind has the power to cause the crops of virtue to fully ripen in the minds of the faithful. Finally, the awakened mind is like a melodious song because it reveals the primordial wisdom nature of truth to aspirants striving on the path of virtue. These nine perfections, from morality to primordial wisdom, are all levels of the accomplishment of awakened mind that occur on the path of meditation. The final, fifth, path is that of no more learning. On this path, initially there are five pure levels of awakened mind development, which correspond to the eighth, ninth, and tenth bodhisattva stages. The first level is likened to a king because on this level clairvoyance arises, giving one the power to unimpededly accomplish the purpose of others. The second level is likened to a storehouse of treasures because this awakened mind inexhaustibly gathers the two accumulations of ordinary and wisdom merit. The third level is like a great highway because the thirty-seven wings of awakening are perfected as the very path that the noble ones of the three times follow. The fourth is like an excellent courier because, here, the accomplishment of śamatha and vipaśyanā together lead one on the perfectly pure path that is free from the two extremes of eternalism and nihilism. The fifth level is likened to a deep well of water, which refers to one's ability to fully retain the original purity and understanding of words and to unobstructedly teach the path to others.

The final three levels are the ultimate three levels of the realization of awakened mind. They can be understood in terms of preparation, the actual path, and completion. Preparation is like a pleasing musical instrument, which symbolizes the great pleasure garden that allows all aspirants who desire liberation to hear the words of truth. Actual practice on this level is likened to a river that leads to the great ocean of all-encompassing omniscience. This is the very source from which one accomplishes the purpose of others without any effort. Finally, a great lofty cloud symbolizes the ultimate completion or fruition, which is the dharmakāya. From this embodiment of absolute reality, all beings whose minds are untame are brought to maturity.

These are the twenty-two analogies that exemplify the levels and qualities of the development of the supreme awakened mind in terms of one's progression on the five great paths to omniscience.

In addition, there are other distinctions that exist on the bodhisattva levels of progression. There are three levels of striving toward virtue on the path of preparation: common, average, and superior. To strive toward virtue with superior intention in conduct is to practice on the level of the path of preparation. The transcendent virtue of generosity is the path of seeing. Morality, patience, enthusiastic effort, concentration, wisdom, method, aspiration, strength, and primordial wisdom are the nine levels accomplished within the path of meditation. Extraperceptive abilities, common and transcendent primordial wisdom merit, the thirty-seven limbs of enlightenment, quiescence and heightened awareness, and retention and teaching are the five specific levels that arise on the three pure bodhisattva levels (the eighth, ninth, and tenth bhūmis). The festival of the Dharma, the sole path that leads to awakening and the dharmakāya, is accomplished on the level of buddhahood itself. These are the ten stages of progression of the Mahāyāna conquerors, which include the preparatory state, the actual practice, and the conclusion. Once the path is entered, one continues until the ultimate fruition is realized: the status of buddhahood itself.

2.c Summing up:

> All are condensed into the two categories of aspirational and practical awakened mind, within which the wish and action are complete, like wishing to go and actually embarking.

Since all distinctions of the levels of development of awakened mind can be condensed into the aspirational and practical, the distinction between the two should be clearly understood. The wish to obtain full awakening for the sole purpose of benefitting and liberating others is aspirational awakened mind. To actualize that wish, and to directly engage in the corresponding conduct of the practice of the six transcendent virtues, is practical awakened mind. Within the context of this practical application, one must understand that all six transcendent virtues are maintained in the perfection of any one transcendent virtue. For example, if one practices the transcendent virtue of generosity by giving material aid to another, by giving protection from fear, or by giving the gift of Dharma, then the act of giving with the four immeasurables (love, compassion, joy, and equanimity) as one's driving force constitutes the transcendent virtue of generosity. The transcendent virtue of morality is engaged by performing this act of generosity with mindful attentiveness and with pure morality of body, speech, and mind. The transcendent virtue of patience is practiced by maintaining patience at the onset of any adversity surrounding one's practice of generosity. The transcendent virtue of enthusiastic perseverance consists of maintaining this generosity with irreversible effort and joy. The transcendent virtue of concentration consists of single-pointedly focusing upon one's training, free from mental distraction. The transcendent virtue of wisdom consists of maintaining awareness of the empty nature of the subject, object, and activity of the practice.

The two awakened minds are likened to wishing to travel to a particular place and actually embarking on that journey. As is stated in the *Bodhicaryāvatāra*, "This awakened mind is understood, in brief, as the understanding of the two distinctions, namely the aspirational awakened mind and the practical awakened mind. This is like the wish to go and actually embarking. Just as this distinction explains, those who are wise must discern the distinction between these two levels."

b. A specific explanation of how to receive the vows, in five subdivisions:
   1. How to receive unobtained vows
   2. Guarding obtained vows from deterioration
   3. The physical support for the generation of the vows
   4. If they deteriorate, the method of restoration
   5. The benefits of guarding the vows

1. How to receive unobtained vows is taught in two subdivisions:
   - 1.a An explanation of the ritual for developing relative awakened mind
   - 1.b An explanation of how it is not necessary to perform a ritual to develop ultimate awakened mind

1.a An explanation of the ritual for developing relative awakened mind, in two further subdivisions:

1.a.1 Briefly revealed:

Initially, the manner in which to receive unobtained vows is...

In order to naturally establish the awakened mind, initially one must understand the manner in which to obtain the vows.

1.a.2 Extensively explained:

...from a virtuous, vow-upholding spiritual mentor,...

Relative awakened mind is developed in dependence upon external conditions, which include the strength of the presence of a virtuous spiritual mentor or friend, the strength of one's own inner awakening, the strength of the root of one's virtue, the strength of having heard the Mahāyāna teachings, and, finally, the inner experience of meditation. The awakened mind that develops in dependence upon a spiritual friend is considered to be unstable, because one cannot be certain about the spiritual friend's stability. The remaining four conditions are considered to be stable because they will not deteriorate in the face of adversity. The principal point is that relative awakened mind arises in dependence upon external forces. Accordingly, there are four ways to give rise to it: first, the obtaining of a qualified spiritual preceptor; second, the actual mode of receiving relative awakened mind; third, the exception of receiving it from a mental support, if necessary; and, finally, recognition of the moment that constitutes the obtainment of the bodhisattva vows.

With regard to the first, a qualified teacher means one who purely upholds either or both traditions of the bodhisattva vows and who possesses loving-kindness and compassion. As it says in the *Bodhicaryāvatāra*, "The spiritual teacher must be one who is learned in the meaning of the Mahāyāna, who has supreme uncontrived conduct based on the awakened mind, and who at the cost of life itself would never abandon the awakened mind."

1.a.2(a) The manner in which to receive the vows is explained according to the two traditions:
1.a.2(a.1) The tradition of Nāgārjuna
1.a.2(a.2) The tradition of Asaṅga

1.a.2(a.1) The tradition of Nāgārjuna, in two subdivisions:

1.a.2(a.1.1) The type of individual qualified to receive the vows:

...a disciple who is a suitable vessel for the Mahāyāna, inspired by faith.

According to Ārya Nāgārjuna's tradition, if a disciple has the sincere wish to receive the vows and the ability to understand the ritual, it is not essential to possess a human body as the sole support. The sūtras clearly document countless examples of gods and nāgas who developed the supreme awakened mind. Thus, whoever has the wish and the ability to receive these vows automatically qualifies as a suitable vessel for Mahāyāna practice.

1.a.2(a.1.2) The vow-receiving ritual:

> After the seven-branch offering, both aspirational and practical awakened mind are simultaneously received. Then, the meditation upon joy for oneself and others follows, in the tradition of Nāgārjuna.

The vow-receiving ritual includes the preparation, the actual ritual, and the conclusion. First, for the preparation, one must specifically reject an extreme feeling of despair toward the predicament of cyclic existence and should reject a strong attraction toward the state of permanent peace. Instead, one must develop great joy in the thought and development of the awakened mind. Examining one's mind and checking to see if these three methods are established is the preparation. Then, in the presence of a fully qualified preceptor, a maṇḍala offering and supplications must be made. Following that, refuge is taken in the Three Jewels, and the specific method of reciting the seven-branch offering prayer is performed. One is then ready for the ritual through which the bodhisattva vows are received.

While generating intense, heartfelt compassion for all parent sentient beings—those who have shown us tremendous, irrepayable kindness in the past and who are suffering such pain in the present—one intends to take the vow to both temporarily and ultimately offer all of one's own happiness and bliss to benefit to all beings. Further, one prays to take upon oneself all of their suffering and discontent, regardless of the difficulties involved. This is the way to train one's mind. Then, requesting forbearance, one begins the recitation: "O buddhas, bodhisattvas, and gurus, please listen to what I now say from the depth of my heart. Just as all buddhas of the past developed the thought of enlightenment, the spirit of awakening, and then practiced the stages of gradual development by following the training of all the Buddha's sons and daughters, so may I too, for the sake of all beings, develop the awakened mind and follow the training exactly as all bodhisattvas have done in the past."

In taking the vow and repeating this verse, one recalls the manner in which the buddhas and bodhisattvas of the past generated the awakened mind. One then makes the promise to practice exactly in accordance with their example by fully embracing the vow to develop both aspirational and practical awakened mind. After one repeats these verses three times, the actual bodhisattva vows are received.

In conclusion, one rejoices in one's own virtue, as well as in the virtue of others. To rejoice in one's own virtue, the following verses are repeated: "At this moment my life has become truly fruitful, for, having attained a fully endowed human body, today I have developed the true essence of the buddhas, the awakened mind, and thus have become a member of the family of all the buddhas."

Then, to rejoice in the virtue of others, repeat these verses taken from the *Bodhicaryāvatāra*: "Today, in the presence of all the objects of refuge, I invite the world to be guests at this festival of ultimate and temporary delight. May gods, demigods, and all be joyful!"

Finally, to express one's gratitude, benediction prayers and offerings are made. A brief explanation of the vows is then given, which concludes the vow-receiving ritual in the tradition of Nāgārjuna.

1.a.2(a.2) The tradition of Asaṅga, in two subdivisions:

1.a.2(a.2.1) An explanation of the type of individual who qualifies to receive the vows:

> Asaṅga's tradition is explained in this way: Although it is not necessary to have prātimokṣa ordination in order to receive the vow of the aspirational awakened mind, in order to fully receive all the vows, one of the seven categories of prātimokṣa must be received first.

According to the tradition of Ārya Asaṅga, one may receive the aspirational awakened mind vow without the prātimokṣa precepts as a basis. However, in order to receive the practical awakened mind vow, one must hold at least one of the seven precept categories of prātimokṣa.

1.a.2(a.2.2) The vow-receiving ritual:

> By enquiring about obstacles, promising to train, and so forth, aspirational and practical awakened mind are received through their individual rituals.

The preliminaries for Ārya Asaṅga's tradition are identical to those of Nāgārjuna's. The ritual itself involves receiving the aspirational awakened mind vow and then the practical awakened mind vows. After inviting all the buddhas and bodhisattvas to bear witness, one repeats the verses in the ritual after the presiding preceptor. First, state your name and repeat: "From this moment on, until I am enlightened, may I never give up, though my life be at stake, the attitude of wishing to gain full enlightenment for the sake of all sentient beings in order to free them from the fears of saṃsāra and nirvāṇa's calm apathy. Buddhas, bodhisattvas, and gurus, please listen to what I now say from the depth of my heart! Just as all buddhas of the past developed the thought of enlightenment, true awakened mind, and then practised its stages of gradual development by following the training of all the Buddha's sons and daughters, so may I too, for the sake of all beings, develop awakened mind and follow the training exactly as all bodhisattvas have done." These verses are repeated three times, and the vows are perfectly received at the conclusion of the third repetition. At the conclusion of the ritual one generates joy, the vows are revealed, and offerings and auspicious prayers are made to express gratitude. Following this, in order to receive the practical awakened mind vow, as stated earlier, one must first hold one of the seven prātimokṣa precept categories. Then, if one fully intends to train in the bodhisattva way of life according to the teachings in the Bodhisattva Piṭaka, one must faithfully generate the strength to accomplish this. The preliminary to this ritual begins with supplication, examination of intention, prayers for the swift accomplishment of the awakened mind, enquiries as to one's ability to overcome obstacles, and enquiries as to one's enthusiasm for the training. Following this, the actual ritual begins with the spiritual preceptor calling you by name and enquiring three times as to whether you consider yourself a suitable vessel to accomplish the purpose of this discipline. When one replies in the affirmative by proclaiming this promise three times, the vows are received. In conclusion, one offers prayers to the noble ones, the benefits of the vows are explained, the vows themselves are revealed, and gratitude is expressed by the making of offerings and prayers.

1.a.2(b) The explanation of receiving vows from a support (as an exception):

> Both traditions agree that it is appropriate to use the conquerors as a support.

Usually the vows are taken in the presence of a qualified preceptor toward whom one has respect and faith. If one is unable to meet with such a qualified mentor, the vows may be received before an image of the Buddha as a support. Both traditions agree that this is permissible. One may also receive the vows by visualizing the presence of buddhas and bodhisattvas in the space in front of oneself. This method is clearly stated in Paṇḍita Atīśa's *Bodhipathapradīpa* (*The Light that Illuminates the Path to Awakening*).

1.a.2(c) Recognizing the margin that indicates that the vows have been received:

> The vows are received at the conclusion of the third repetition.

Both traditions agree that the vows are received through the symbolic indication of repeating the verses three times. At the conclusion of the third repetition, the vows are instantaneously received.

1.b An explanation of how it is not necessary to perform a ritual to develop absolute awakened mind:

> The development of ultimate awakened mind through ritual occurs in the tradition of secret mantra. If explained according to sūtra, it is the nature of the promise that develops through the force of meditation.

Ultimate awakened mind is defined as the primordial wisdom of the nonconceptual, direct perception of the nature of truth. It is the actual meditative equipoise of the bodhisattvas and arhats, as well as the nondual nature of the equipoise and post-meditational experience of the state of buddha. To define this for the sake of understanding, within the context of *pāramitā* practice it is the sphere of truth, the *dharmadhātu,* as well as the primordial wisdom that actually realizes the sphere of truth. In order to realize this, one must meet a qualified spiritual teacher who has the power to reveal the path to liberation. One must also have a great accumulation of ordinary and primordial wisdom merit, as well as some personal realization of the nature of truth. These are the three causes for the realization of ultimate awakened mind.

The vehicles of secret mantra define ultimate awakened mind as the foundational primordial wisdom of sheer lucency, free from grasping and clinging. As is stated in the *Māyājāla* (*Net of Illusory Manifestations*) and root *Guhyasamāja* (*Secret Assembly*) *Tantras,* "Free from all substantiality and having fully abandoned all aggregates, elements, sense fields, and grasping or clinging to subjective and objective appearances, the equality of the identitylessness of phenomena, the nature of one's own mind, originally unborn, is the very nature of emptiness." According to the secret mantra vehicle, this ultimate awakened mind as just defined can be received through a vow-bestowing ritual. This is clearly documented in the *Māyājāla, Abhisaṃbodhi,* and other tantras.

It is believed that the development of the resultant state of primordial wisdom is dependent upon the path of relative practice and development. Just as the bodhisattva qualifies to enter the path of secret mantra, similarly, by giving rise to the aspirational awakened mind, the strength to develop and meditate upon the ultimate awakened mind is developed. In the secret mantra tradition it is necessary to practice meditation after receiving initiation and words of honor. The ritual alone does not have the power to bring about results. The results are totally dependent upon one's own effort applied to practice.

According to the sūtra tradition, ultimate awakened mind is born from the very nature of one's commitment and wish to give rise to it. It is the characteristic of ultimate awakened mind that it will develop through the strength and force of meditation.

According to the *Saṃdhinirmocana-sūtra,* "Ultimate awakened mind transcends this world, is free from all boundaries and limitations, and is exceedingly luminous, ultimately true, stainless, and unmoving, like a still candle burning in motionless space. It is accomplished through the ongoing meditation practices of quiescence and heightened awareness."

2. Guarding the obtained vows from deterioration, in three subdivisions:
   2.a Briefly revealed
   2.b Extensively explained
   2.c Summing up

2.a Briefly revealed:

> After receiving the vows, the methods for guarding them from deterioration are the three moralities of the bodhisattvas: namely, refraining from harm, amassing virtue, and fulfilling the purpose of sentient beings.

Initially one must penetrate the inner meaning of how to guard the precepts from deterioration. As a basis, the necessary personal condition is to meet with and never abandon a virtuous spiritual guide of the Mahāyāna. One must then establish the conditions through which to study, learn, and sever all doubt about the truth of the great ocean of sūtras and the stainless commentaries written upon them. Scholarship alone being insufficient, the teachings must be enthusiastically internalized and brought to fruition according to one's own potential. All conflicting circumstances that may bring the result of damaged vows must be abandoned. All conducive causes that fortify the precepts must be utilized and increased.

Nonconducive causes include having no interest to listen, mental distraction, and slothful meditation. These are the three obstacles to accomplishing one's own purpose. Great laxity in action, conduct that causes others to lose faith, a motivation lacking compassion, and mistaken actions are the four faults that obstruct one's ability to accomplish the purpose of others. Since these seven causes bring deterioration and failure to accomplish one's own purpose and that of others, they must certainly be rejected.

As for establishing the necessary causes, one must first recall the benefits of developing the awakened mind, then the fault of allowing vows to deteriorate, and finally the difficulty of obtaining the precious human rebirth. These are the three recollections. Upon this basis one must establish the firm conviction to never allow the precepts to deteriorate in this lifetime. In addition, one should always practice the seven-branch offering prayer, make regular supplication prayers to the buddhas and bodhisattvas, and abandon all negativity that contradicts true Dharma practice. These are three methods to unmistakenly ensure that the vows will not deteriorate in the future.

In addition, there are "five ways to cherish," which ensure that in the present and future one's vows will remain pure: to cherish sentient beings more than oneself, to cherish one's Dharma practice more than the greatest wealth, to cherish the awakened mind more than one's heart, to cherish the spiritual mentor more than one's parents, and to cherish the obtainment of buddhahood more than any enjoyment. These twelve causes should be regarded as additional vows that give rise to conducive circumstances so that one may purely guard the bodhisattva vows.

To increase these conditions, one must view mindfulness as one's own eyesight, enthusiastic effort as the riding of an excellent horse, renunciation as the reins and whip, and the citadel of liberation as the goal or destination. As the great, omniscient Longchenpa said, "With constant mindfulness, alertness, and conscientiousness, abandon nonvirtue and accomplish the great ocean of goodness."

Except for certain practices that beginners do not yet possess the capacity to perform, it is necessary to perform all other training that is within one's potential. Once the vows have been purely received, to then allow them to deteriorate is to deceive all sentient beings and to accumulate extremely negative karma. On the other hand, to guard and maintain them is to accumulate positive karma, bringing about great benefit for others.

In general, the morality of bodhisattvas is described as the practice of the three moralities. The first is to refrain from all harmful conduct of the three doors that may impair one's bodhisattva training. The second is to accomplish the practice of the six transcendent virtues, amassing only virtue and merit. The third is to fulfill and accomplish the purpose of others through the four means of assembling disciples.[49] These three are actually of one nature, just as the nature of a wish-fulfilling jewel is threefold in that it illuminates darkness, amasses all desirable wealth, and cures disease and illness. By training in and perfecting these three moralities, at the time of obtaining buddhahood the first two moralities become the total endowment of abandonment and realization, whereas the third becomes the obtainment of fully endowed concerned activity.

2.b Extensively explained as the three divisions of morality:
2.b.1 The morality of refraining from harm
2.b.2 The morality of amassing virtue
2.b.3 The morality of accomplishing the purpose of others

2.b.1 An explanation of the morality of refraining from harm is given first and is explained according to the two traditions of Nāgārjuna and Asaṅga.

The sūtra tradition of Nāgārjuna follows the *Ākāśagarbha* and *Mahāguhya-upāyakauśalya* and the distinction of precepts elaborated upon in the *Śikṣāsamuccaya* (*Compendium of Precepts*) by Śāntideva. The tradition of Asaṅga follows the *Bodhisattvabhūmi* and the *Saṃvaraviṃśika* (*Bodhisattva Vows in Twenty Verses*) as taught by the master Candragomin.

2.b.1(a) Nāgārjuna's tradition, in two subdivisions:
2.b.1(a.1) An explanation of the root downfalls
2.b.1(a.2) The auxiliary faults are explained elsewhere

2.b.1(a.1) An explanation of the root downfalls, in three further subdivisions:
2.b.1(a.1.1) An explanation of the actual root downfalls

2.b.1(a.1.2) A concise categorization of the supports for the vows and of their downfalls

2.b.1(a.1.3) Revealing how the abandonment of common aspirational and practical awakened mind qualifies as a root downfall

2.b.1(a.1.1) There are three divisions of actual root downfalls:

(1) The first division, the five that are closely related to rulers:

> To embezzle the property of the Three Jewels, to abandon the Dharma, to punish or expel a moral or immoral bhikṣu, to commit a heinous nonvirtue, and to hold incorrect views are the five pertaining to rulers.

These first five root downfalls are categorized as closely relating to rulers or heads of state because they are easily committed by an individual of that stature in such a position of authority. However, this is merely a way of categorizing and should not be interpreted as pertaining exclusively to rulers. These are root downfalls for all practitioners who have taken bodhisattva vows according to Nāgārjuna's tradition.

To embezzle the property of the Three Jewels means to steal or embezzle images of the Buddha, articles that belong to stūpas, Dharma books, facilities and articles that belong to the spiritual teacher, or any articles that belong to or are meant to be utilized by the saṅgha (such as their property or the property of others, whether it is considered to be of value or not). Stealing these properties oneself, or engaging another to do so, constitutes the root downfall. Second, the abandonment of Dharma is to claim that any of the teachings that constitute the three vehicles of the Buddhist path—or any corresponding training, precepts, or methods—are invalid and therefore do not lead to permanent happiness and liberation. To then personally reject a practice based on this view, or to directly cause someone else to do so, constitutes the second root downfall.

The third root downfall is, out of anger and aggression, to disrobe, expel, strike, punish, or imprison a monk, whether he is a pure upholder of morality or not. To cause the monk to be reduced to lay status, or to instigate others to do this, constitutes the downfall.

The fourth is to kill one's own father or mother or an arhat; to cause a schism in the saṅgha; or, with ill intention, to spill the blood of a buddha. These are the five heinous nonvirtues. To commit any one of them constitutes the fourth root downfall.

The fifth, to hold incorrect view, is to disbelieve in the infallible truth of the law of cause and result and to claim that virtue and nonvirtue do not produce the results of happiness and suffering respectively. To commit even a minor unwholesome deed with an incorrect view such as this accumulates extremely heavy negative karma.

(2) The second division, the five that are closely related to administrators:

> The destruction of a dwelling, village, city, metropolis, or nation are the five that pertain to administrators.

The first downfall is to destroy a dwelling place, defined as an abode where only one family lives. The second is to destroy a village, defined as a place where four or more families live. The third is to destroy a city, which means a place where at least eighteen different businesses are being carried out. A metropolis is a place where more than eighteen businesses are being practiced, and a nation is an entire country or race of people. The destruction of any of these five constitutes a root downfall. Like the first category of five that relates to kings, these five are easiest for administrators or people in specific positions of authority to commit (for example, a minister of defense). However, they pertain to all practitioners on the bodhisattva path.

(3) The third division, the eight that closely relate to ordinary people:

> Prematurely talking about emptiness to the untrained, thus causing them to take interest in the śrāvaka path; turning from full awakening in order to develop the Hīnayāna motivation; abandoning the prātimokṣa in order to train in Mahāyāna; as a śrāvaka, failing to reverse attachment and so forth and reversing, yet bringing no results; overpowered by jealousy, praising oneself and disparaging others; promoting oneself for the sake of gain and respect; instigating the punishment of a bhikṣu; taking the possessions of a renunciate and giving them to someone merely reciting prayers, thus causing someone to give up śamatha practice. These are the eight root downfalls that relate to common people.

The first of these eight root downfalls is to speak to someone about the fundamental view of the nature of emptiness, which is free from all limitations of ordinary mind, without first examining to see if that individual has received any preparatory training, or to speak of emptiness to those whose sensibilities are only capable of the views that correspond to Hīnayāna training. If, as a direct result of one's words, the listener then seeks the views of the lesser spiritual pursuit, this constitutes a root downfall.

The second is to tell someone who has already entered the Mahāyāna path that this path does not have the potential to result in full awakening, thereby encouraging them to practice the Hīnayāna path instead. If this causes an individual to reject the Mahāyāna in order to enter the Hīnayāna, this constitutes a root downfall.

The third is to cause someone to abandon their Hīnayāna practice (whether they are ordained or not) by saying it is useless, thereby influencing them to enter the Mahāyāna path instead.

The fourth is to tell a Hīnayāna practitioner that this path will not reverse attachment or other delusions and, with the specific intention of turning their mind from this path, to claim that it does not lead to permanent peace.

The fifth is, due to jealousy and the wish to receive profit and praise from others, to boast of one's own qualities and to belittle other bodhisattva practitioners by telling lies.

The sixth is, with the motive to achieve profit and praise from others, to publicly claim that one has realized the profound meaning of the nature of emptiness when, in fact, this claim is an unsurpassed lie.

The seventh is to intentionally slander a monk in order to impose some financial punishment upon him and to take his property or share of the saṅgha's offerings and give it to someone else to use or use it oneself.

The eighth is to steal any possessions used by a practitioner of meditative concentration and to give these articles to someone who is merely engaged in prayer-recitation ceremonies. When the meditator's practice becomes disrupted because of this action, the downfall occurs.

2.b.1(a.1.2) A concise categorization of the supports for the vows and of their downfalls:

> Although the vows are specifically categorized, they pertain to everyone. They are mentioned as eighteen and classified as fourteen.

These three categories of root downfalls that are closely related to rulers, administrators, and laymen total eighteen. These eighteen are vows that all bodhisattva vow upholders must guard. Though counted as eighteen, four of the vows that pertain to ministers can also be counted as one, making the total fourteen.

2.b.1(a.1.3) Revealing how the abandonment of common aspirational and practical awakened mind constitutes a root downfall:

> To forsake the aspirational and practical mind constitutes a root downfall.

The motivation of the lesser spiritual pursuit, or the abandonment of the mind to be of benefit to other sentient beings, is to give up the aspiration of awakened mind. As it states in the *Mahāguhya-upāyakauśalya*, "Oh, sons and daughters of the family, the attitude of śrāvakas and pratyekas is a heavy root downfall for a bodhisattva." Therefore, giving up one's aspiration becomes the nineteenth root downfall. To then abandon the practical application and to fail to engage in specific virtuous actions for the benefit of others becomes the twentieth. Each of these twenty is a root failure in the practice of the morality of bodhisattvas.

Since bodhisattva practitioners are clearly delineated with regard to the different levels of practice, it should be understood that those of superior sensibility will guard themselves perfectly and not commit any of these twenty root downfalls. Those of middling sensibility should at least refrain from completely abandoning the awakened mind, feeling ill-will toward others, striking or physically harming others out of anger, or giving incorrect or erroneous teachings out of delusion. Those of inferior sensibility, whose minds are unruly and far more difficult to tame, must solely concentrate upon never losing the aspirational awakened mind. If the aspirational vow is allowed to deteriorate, then the practical vow will also be lost, creating even heavier harm and negativity.

2.b.1(a.2) The auxiliary faults are explained elsewhere:

> The eighty auxiliary faults and others are minor in comparison and are not explained here. Refer to the *Śikṣāsamuccaya* (*Compendium of Precepts*).

There are eighty remaining auxiliary faults in this tradition of bodhisattva training. Since the results are minor if the faults are committed, they have not been elaborated upon in Ngari Panchen's root text. Reference is made to Śāntideva's *Compendium of Precepts*, where an extensive explanation is offered. They are listed here in brief for the reader's information.

The auxiliary faults are as follows: The first is, in spite of knowing that someone is suffering or mentally distressed, failing to alleviate their suffering when you have the potential to do so. The second is failing to help others to develop bliss and mental peace. To fail to comfort others physically and mentally in the first two instances constitutes four faults. Further, making a distinction of time of present or future with each of these four brings the total to eight. In addition, making no effort to create the causes and conditions of benefit for others, and ignoring the application of antidotes for each of the eight faults, totals twenty-four.

Ignoring the methods that establish happiness and the methods that uproot suffering in order to avoid great suffering; failing to apply the antidotes for minor suffering to oneself or others; failing to experience great bliss and mental peace and allowing minor vows to deteriorate; and including the present and future times for each of these, as well as applying them to self and others, totals sixteen. If you then consider the two distinctions of "temporarily" and "permanently" for each, the total comes to eighty. In addition to these minor offenses, one must refrain from the ten nonvirtues, the eight worldly dharmas, the five wrong livelihoods,[50] and all other activities that fall in the direction of nonvirtue.

2.b.1(b) The tradition of Asaṅga is explained in two subdivisions:
2.b.1(b.1) Training in aspirational awakened mind
2.b.1(b.2) Training in practical awakened mind

2.b.1(b.1) Aspirational training is explained in two further subdivisions:

2.b.1(b.1.1) A general explanation:

> Aspirational training according to the tradition of Asaṅga is to never mentally forsake any sentient being, to recall the benefits of the awakened mind, to accumulate merit and persevere in purifying the mind, and to aspire to correctly accept and reject the eight white and black dharmas.

According to the tradition of the great bodhisattva Asaṅga, methods of practice are employed so that one never loses the root training of the development of aspirational awakened mind. Thus, one should never ignore or forsake any sentient being who is unhappy and who can be uplifted or benefitted through one's own efforts. Whether that being is a suitable vessel for Mahāyāna practice or not, one must never abandon the mind of compassion, even if one is unable to render actual support, assistance, or benefit.

The method to guard bodhicitta from deterioration is to recall its benefits. In the *Gaṇḍavyūha-sūtra*, an explanation of the unsurpassed benefits of the awakened mind is given in two hundred and thirty examples. If one is unable to study this, one should at least be perpetually aware of the benefits as mentioned in the well-known prayer of Maitreya Buddha.

The methods to develop the strength of the awakened mind include having the wish to accomplish virtue and then bringing that wish into action that accumulates merit, such as generosity and so forth, and simultaneously accumulating primordial wisdom merit through awareness of the empty nature of subject, object, and activity. One should be diligent in bringing these two levels of accumulation into union.

The methods to increase the awakened mind include cleansing one's continuum by meditating upon love and compassion, training the mind by giving rise to the awakened mind during the six times of day and night, and training in conduct by dedicating one's own happiness and virtue to others and taking on the negativities and suffering of others through the practice of taking and sending. These three trainings should be practiced regularly.

Finally, the basis of aspirational training for never forgetting the awakened mind is to unmistakenly practice the four white dharmas and abandon the four black dharmas.

2.b.1(b.1.2) A specific explanation of the eight white and black dharmas:

> To deceive an object of veneration, to develop unnecessary regret, to abuse the exalted, and to behave with an ulterior motive toward sentient beings are the four black dharmas to abandon. The opposite are the four white dharmas to fully accept.

The four black dharmas are the following: to intentionally lie to one's object of veneration, such as the spiritual teacher, abbot, and others; to develop, with a negative attitude, regret toward any deed or action that is actually positive in nature; to blatantly disrespect, with verbal criticism or negative thought, a bodhisattva or another truly spiritual being who possesses the awakened mind; and to deceive other sentient beings through one's negative behavior. These four black dharmas must be abandoned. The four white dharmas are the opposite: to intentionally refrain from speaking falsely, to attempt to place all beings on the pure path of the greater pursuit, to recognize and respect all bodhisattvas as buddhas, and to have even more compassion for sentient beings who are poor, needy, or lacking material wealth.

2.b.1(b.2) The training in practical awakened mind, in two subdivisions:

2.b.1(b.2.1) An explanation of the root downfalls:

> Out of attachment to personal gain and respect, to praise oneself and belittle others; out of avarice, to not give ordinary material wealth and Dharma; out of anger, to harm others and fail to reverse the harm; and to teach impurely, fabricating the Dharma. These are the four root downfalls of practical training.

All conduct that is not conducive to the pure practice of practical awakened mind qualifies as a root downfall according to this tradition of Asaṅga. The first root downfall is, out of personal attachment, to receive profit, gain, or respect from others as a result of praising oneself and blaming or belittling others. The second downfall is, out of avarice, to fail to give material assistance that one is capable of giving to those who are suffering, alone, or downcast, or failing to give Dharma teachings or spiritual assistance to those who are sincerely interested and who are suitable vessels when one has the potential to help them. The third downfall is, out of intense anger or aversion, to not only speak harshly to others but to also physically harm or strike them and to then fail to develop any regret or remorse over one's conduct. The final downfall is to claim, out of delusion, that true Mahāyāna scriptures are not actually the Buddha's direct utterance, disrespectfully rejecting them, and then creating one's own version of the teaching by fabricating the Dharma and proclaiming this to be the actual Dharma. These four are root downfalls of practical awakened mind training because, if any one of them occurs, it has the negative strength to completely eliminate all the other bodhisattva vows.

The most important training according to both traditions is as follows: Those inferior bodhisattvas, as well as laymen, who are still developing their training must never forsake or abandon a single sentient being. This alone must be practiced. In the same way that if there is no surface there will be nothing for a drawing to remain on, if there is no aspirational awakened mind there will be no method through which to guard the bodhisattva training. However, if one were to think that the abandonment of sentient beings constitutes the abandonment of all trainings, it would be impossible to carry on any further. Śrāvakas, pratyekas, and even hawks and wolves have concern for the living beings that they care about, such as their offspring and others. Bodhisattvas of middling sensibility, as well as the ordained, must definitely abandon the four black dharmas, but those of superior sensibility must never forsake even a single sentient being, in addition to guarding all eighteen root precepts as taught by the *Ākāśagarbha-sūtra.* These variations of requirements do not present any conflict, as they correspond to the abilities of the aspirant. Simply put, whatever one is capable of doing must be done.

2.b.1(b.2.2) The auxiliary faults are mentioned elsewhere:

> The forty-six minor auxiliary faults are explained elsewhere.

Although the root text does not explain the forty-six minor vows, they are mentioned in brief in the explanation of the *Bodhisattva Vows in Twenty Verses.* Thirty-two of these vows relate to the morality of amassing virtue, and twelve relate to the morality of accomplishing the purpose of others. The forty-six auxiliary faults are further divided into six categories: seven that contradict generosity, nine that contradict morality, four that contradict patience, three that contradict enthusiastic effort, three that contradict concentration, and eight that contradict wisdom. The seven that contradict generosity are the following: failing to make offerings each day to the Three Jewels of Refuge with one's body, speech, and mind by offering prostrations and praise and by meditating upon their positive qualities in order to develop respectful belief and confidence in them; out of discontent, following and acting upon thoughts through which you desire to grasp and possess things; not showing respect to older monks who may be bodhisattvas; not answering questions you are capable of answering; not accepting invitations from others because of your own anger or because of wanting to hurt the other person's feelings or, out of pride, considering yourself of too exalted a rank to be with more humble people, or thinking that other people of more respected rank will look down on you if you are seen with humble people; not accepting gifts of money and so forth from others because of anger, pride, or jealousy; and not teaching the Dharma to those who wish to learn it.

The nine that contradict morality are the following: ignoring, not forgiving, and not helping those who have broken their discipline of moral self-control; not teaching someone an aspect of the Dharma that he wishes to learn and that you are qualified to teach, but which is not your own personal practice or interest; not committing, if circumstances deem it necessary, one of the seven nonvirtuous actions of body and speech with an awakened-mind motivation by saying that to do so would be against the vowed rules of moral conduct; again, though circumstances require it, not committing one of the seven nonvirtuous actions of body and speech with an awakened-mind motivation because of a lack of compassion; accepting things from others who have obtained them by one of the five wrong livelihoods—namely, flattery, extortion or blackmail, contrivance, bribery, or deceit; being interested mainly in frivolous activities such as entertainment, sports, drinking, and being silly and so forth, causing your mind to wander and your time, which you could be using more constructively for the practice of Dharma, to be limitlessly wasted; holding an attitude of wishing to escape from saṃsāra by yourself alone; not keeping these awakened-mind vows because you think this will make you unpopular; and if you have broken one of your vows because of defilements, not doing the opposing virtuous actions assigned to you.

The four that contradict patience are the following: while you are practising virtue, still becoming angry and retaliating if you are hit, scolded, called a derogatory name, or are the object of someone's anger; neglecting to help those who are angry with you; refusing to accept the apology of others who admit they have wronged you; and following and acting out thoughts of anger.

The three that contradict enthusiastic effort are the following: gathering a circle of disciples and followers because you wish to obtain such things as profit, praise, love, and security from them; not eliminating from yourself such obstacles as laziness, procrastination, and delusions of incapability, as well as wasting your time and energy on the trivial matters of saṃsāra; and being addicted to frivolous talk and gossip about sex, drink, drugs, sectarianism, and so forth because of your attachment and desire for them.

The three that contradict concentration are the following: not making an effort to study the means for attaining single-minded concentration; not eliminating the distractions that block your meditation; and seeing the exhilaratingly good feelings and other benefits you obtain from meditation as being ends in themselves and being attached to them.

The eight that contradict wisdom are the following: neglecting to study the Hīnayāna teachings; turning to another means of practice when you already are following an effective means for yourself, for this would be like changing teachers and vehicles in midstream when you are already on a steady and sure course to enlightenment; spending all your time and energy on reading non-Buddhist teachings which, though permitted and even beneficial for enabling you to understand and help others, should not be pursued to the neglect of studying the Dharma; favoring and becoming attached to non-Buddhist teachings, even when merely reading about them; rejecting the Mahāyāna teachings; praising yourself and belittling others due to personal arrogance or anger; not attending religious discourses, meetings, ceremonies, and so forth; and despising your guru and not relying upon his words.

The twelve remaining auxiliary faults oppose the morality of accomplishing the purpose of others. The first four arise from allowing the purpose of others to deteriorate. These are the following: not giving help to those who need it; avoiding taking care of sick people; not working to alleviate the physical suffering of others; and not showing the teachings of the Dharma to those who are unaware of them and who therefore work only for this life.

The next six faults arise by failing to be of benefit to others. These six are the following: not repaying the kindness that others have shown you; not working to relieve the grief of others; not giving material aid to the poor and needy; not taking care of your circle of disciples, relatives, attendants, and friends by refusing to give them teachings or material aid; not encouraging and supporting the practice of Dharma and the virtuous actions of others; and not praising and encouraging others who deserve praise.

The final two are faults arising from failure to put an end to negativity. They are, first, not preventing those who are committing harmful actions in general—and specifically those who are a menace to the Dharma—from continuing their harm by whatever means are deemed necessary by the circumstances and, second, if you possess extraphysical powers, not using them at a time of need.

Concerning that which opposes the morality of abstaining from harm, if the prātimokṣa support for the bodhisattva vows is that of full ordination, then the occurrence of any of the four root downfalls constitutes a root bodhisattva downfall and the loss of all vows. Otherwise, all other downfalls would constitute the loss of the auxiliary bodhisattva vows. The same holds true for all vow-holders of the prātimokṣa categories. For example, if a lay Buddhist commits a root downfall, he in turn loses the root bodhisattva vows.

2.b.2 An explanation of the morality of amassing virtue, in two subdivisions:

2.b.2(a) Briefly revealed:

> The amassing of virtue is the training in the six transcendent virtues.

To amass the profound accumulations of virtue and merit for the sake of oneself and others, one must purely train in the actual practice of each of the six transcendent virtues.

2.b.2(b) Extensively explained, in six subdivisions:

2.b.2(b.1) The transcendent virtue of generosity (*dāna-pāramitā*):

> In order to alleviate poverty, give wealth, Dharma, and protection from fear.

The essence of generosity is the giving mind of the four qualities motivated by the seed of virtue. In Sanskrit, generosity is *dāna*, defined as that which meets the needs of another. The different types of generosity include giving the gift of Dharma teaching or instructive assistance to those whom one has carefully examined to determine if they are suitable recipients. Motivated by compassion, one then offers them the best explanations one is capable of giving. The giving of material aid means to give others ordinary possessions, such as food, clothing, shelter, and animals. The "great" giving of material aid would be to give away one's own son, daughter, spouse, or kingdom. The most difficult act of generosity would be to give a part of one's own body, such as an organ or a limb. Here it is considered unsuitable to give away one's parents, one's three ordination robes, or one's body if the intent is impure. It is taught that laymen should primarily focus upon giving material aid, whereas the ordained must give the gift of Dharma. The giving of protection from fear is to temporarily relieve others from illness, disease, possession by malevolent spirits, or distress arising from thieves, robbers, wild animals, hierarchical punishment, or the unknown and so forth. Ultimate protection is to grant others protection from the fears of cyclic existence, including the lower realms.

2.b.2(b.2) The transcendent virtue of morality (*śīla-pāramitā*):

With a renounced mind, train in the three moralities.

The essence of morality is a renounced mind that possesses the four specific qualities and that wishes to abstain from all harm, motivated by the seed of virtue. The original Sanskrit word is *śīla*, defined as cooling relief from the heat of discontent.

The different distinctions of morality include abstaining from harm while maintaining the awakened-mind attitude, amassing virtue so that the Dharma may ripen in one's mind stream, and, finally, accomplishing the purpose of others so as to bring all sentient beings to maturity. These three moralities must be practiced with skill so that one does not confuse what to accept with what to reject and so that—with the purest intention and practical application—one is able to carry out the sole purpose of truly benefitting others.

The first morality constitutes the common path of acceptance and rejection according to the seven categories of prātimokṣa training. (The uncommon training is to never allow one's root and branch bodhisattva precepts to deteriorate.) The second morality is to cause virtue that has not previously arisen to develop in one's mind stream. This is done by amassing the two accumulations and by developing the wisdom of hearing, contemplating, and meditating, including the six transcendent virtues and so forth. To increase the development of virtue, one must ensure the complete rejection of all that is nonconducive and detrimental to practice. The third morality is the skillful means of equalizing one's intention and actions so that they are directed solely for the purpose of others. In order to avoid any personal liabilities, one must constantly examine the three doors of body, speech, and mind by applying mindfulness and mental alertness.

2.b.2(b.3) The transcendent virtue of patience (*kṣānti-pāramitā*):

Patience is the endurance of anger, suffering, and the profound.

The essence of patience is a mind that disengages itself from conflict while maintaining the four specific qualities, still motivated by the seed of virtue. In Sanskrit, *kṣānti* is defined as the ability to disengage from conflict when presented with an object that imposes suffering or presents that which is undesirable. The three types of patience are the forbearance to not retaliate when harmed by an object, the ability to willingly endure suffering, and the ability to remain patient concerning difficulties involved in understanding the meaning of absolute truth.

Tolerance is necessary as a practice when oneself or one's colleague, compatriot, or loved one is the object of another's aggression and is being abused or physically harmed. In such a circumstance one must consider the faults of anger and retaliation and must strive to maintain a peaceful mind that does not wish or need to retaliate. In addition, not only must one not bear a grudge or hold a bad feeling toward this object of patience, one must also cultivate compassion and mercy as the antidote.

The ability to willingly endure suffering is necessary during the difficulties and hardships of Dharma practice. If one has an illness and needs surgery in order to be cured, one will endure the temporary suffering of surgery in order to receive the result.

The third type of patience is the dauntless ability to maintain faith in the Dharma of absolute truth, and particularly the explanations on the nature of emptiness, when one has not yet realized this. One must never become discouraged and lose enthusiasm to accomplish the purpose of others due to one's own inability to personally realize the view of emptiness. To realize that, in achieving the ultimate state of unsurpassed great bliss, difficulties and suffering are a necessary aspect of the Dharma path, one should be willing to accept them with a tolerant attitude until the goal is achieved. One should never become discouraged while facing these difficulties.

2.b.2(b.4) The transcendent virtue of ceaseless effort (*vīrya-pāramitā*):

> Bring together the ceaseless effort that is armor-like, that amasses virtue, and that benefits others.

The essence of ceaseless effort is the mind that takes great joy, with the four specific qualities, in the accumulation of virtue and goodness. In Sanskrit, *vīrya* is defined as undiminishing courage directed toward the supreme goal. The distinctions are armor-like ceaseless effort, the ceaseless effort of amassing virtue, and the ceaseless effort that benefits others.

"Armor-like" connotes the irreversible conviction to never give up until all sentient beings are established in the state of liberation, without allowing any obstacle to intervene. In order to accomplish the state of great awakening—liberation—and to do this without concern for one's own body or life, one must enthusiastically amass all accumulations of virtue without ever becoming discouraged or distracted by adversity, and must constantly persevere toward this goal. The third aspect of ceaseless effort is to be motivated by the joy that arises from aspiring to accomplish the two purposes (of self and others).

2.b.2(b.5) The transcendent virtue of concentration (*dhyāna-pāramitā*):

> Practice meditative concentration that is both worldly and transcendental.

The essence of concentration is the mind of the four specific qualities single-pointedly directed and motivated by the seed of virtue. In Sanskrit, *dhyāna* is defined as the mental continuum that maintains a point of focus without distraction. The distinctions are both mundane and transcendental. The mundane distinction is practiced by non-Buddhists as well as being a common practice on the Buddhist path. The four types of worldly concentration include the four levels of concentrations of the form realm, which are four successive levels of development, and the four types of formless meditative absorption, which include the meditation of infinite space, infinite consciousness, nothingness, and neither discrimination nor nondiscrimination. The three vehicles of the śrāvakas, pratyekas, and bodhisattvas each have their own methods of meditative concentration, all of which are transcendental. According to the teachings in the *Laṅkāvatāra-sūtra*, they can be placed in three categories: first, the ordinary practice of meditative concentration that does not enter the path; second, the meditative concentration of the two paths of accumulation and preparation; and third, the meditative concentration of the path of meditation and that which transcends meditation practiced by the arhats and all who have passed beyond cyclic existence.

2.b.2(b.6) The transcendent virtue of wisdom (*prajñā-pāramitā*):

> Maintain the profound wisdom of hearing, contemplation, and meditation.

The essence of supreme cognition is a mind with the four specific qualities possessing unmistaken knowledge, motivated by the seed of virtue. In Sanskrit, *prajñā* is defined as the most excellent realization or actualization of wisdom. The distinctions of wisdom are the wisdom of hearing, contemplation, and meditation. The wisdom of hearing arises from the study of the scriptures and commentaries as a basis for inner knowledge. In addition, in order to be of assistance to others, one also studies the branch sciences, such as the mechanical arts, healing or medicine, the science of language (grammar and so forth), and dialectics (philosophical reasoning). The spiritual knowledge of the Tripiṭaka forms the higher science of study.

The *Sūtrālaṃkāra* states: "If one is not knowledgeable in the five sciences, although one may become a supreme bodhisattva, the two states of omniscience will not develop. Therefore, to annihilate negativity, to teach and guide others, and to realize all that there is to know, one must persevere in hearing."

This is especially important to the penetration of the inner meaning of the three aspects of the sūtras: relative understanding, definitive understanding, and indirect analysis. In the case of indirect analysis, it is stated in the sūtras that one should kill one's father and mother, which means to eliminate the principal delusions from the mind stream. There are many such passages in the sūtras that cannot be taken literally.

In order to develop the wisdom that realizes the fundamental nature of reality as it is, one must investigate this reality in order to sever the cord of doubt and misunderstanding concerning the actual nature of phenomena, thereby setting the mind free from holding on to the concept of true inherent existence. In addition, one must examine the cause of this misconception, as well as the result, in order to eradicate attachment to the dogmas of existence, nonexistence, neither existence nor nonexistence, or both conjointly. Just as profound explanations were presented by Lord Buddha Śākyamuni in the second turning of the Dharma wheel in order to sever grasping at the concept of existence or nonexistence, the great interdependent origination of the play of relative activity is established and ascertained as the state of absolute inactivity.

The final turning of the wheel revealed the sheer luminosity of the primordial wisdom of the ultimate nature of truth, beyond the conceptualizing intellect. This causes one to discover if this primordial truth is empty of self-inherent being or not and to realize the inconceivable essential nature, which is far removed from mental investigation. The tantras necessitate the internal realization of this nature. The type of wisdom that arises from concentration occurs through the thorough mental investigation of what one has heard and understood. It is important to note here that this investigative wisdom allows one's outer faith to develop as fully convinced, irreversible faith. This is an essential step on the path, a step that is brought about through one's own efforts and through the severing of all doubts. The meaning of ultimate truth is realized through elimination and acceptance. In particular, when one experiences the wisdom of extraperception (the primordial wisdom free from conceptualization as taught in the second and third turnings and on the path of secret mantra), one must establish the view accordingly by severing all mental constructions and fabrications. As is stated in the *Prajñāpāramitā-sūtra,* "The perfection of wisdom is without word, thought, or expression. It is unborn, unobstructed, of the nature of space, the activity of one's own primordial-wisdom intrinsic awareness. I bow down to this, the mother of the buddhas of the three times."

Just as the luminous maṇḍala of the sun is omnipresent beneath the layers of clouds, in meditative equipoise upon the nature of mind, without attempting to accomplish anything, primordial wisdom—free from the intellect, a naked freshness of its own—will naturally arise as sheer luminosity. The force of the continuity of this meditation will give rise to great compassion for all beings who fail to realize their own primordial wisdom nature. This is the nature of truth. This union of the nature of emptiness and compassion is the very basis of the Mahāyāna path of sūtra and tantra and must be established through the development of threefold wisdom. The "three pure recollections" should also be inherent in all practice. The first pure recollection is the preparation for all practice, the development of the awakened mind; the second pure recollection is the actual practice joined with nonconceptual awareness; and the third pure recollection is the concluding dedication of merit for the benefit and liberation of all beings.

2.b.3 The morality of accomplishing the purpose of sentient beings, in two subdivisions:

2.b.3(a) The actual practice

2.b.3(b) An explanation of the vows that correspond to the three moralities

2.b.3(a) The actual practice, in two further subdivisions:

2.b.3(a.1) Briefly revealed:

> The morality of accomplishing the purpose of sentient beings is the practice of the four means of gathering.

The morality of accomplishing the purpose of sentient beings is the active practice and application of the six transcendent virtues, as well as the ability to selflessly serve all others impartially. Through the four means of gathering, one continues to establish this purpose.

2.b.3(a.2) Extensively explained:

> Initially, through generosity, the objects to tame are brought together.
> Then, through pleasing speech, their attentiveness is captured. They
> are then led through the nine vehicles, and their purpose is fulfilled.
> In order to guide them, one's own discipline is upheld.

This bodhisattva's practice of the four means of gathering is performed when one's mind is already mature and is therefore able to bring others' minds to the same level of maturity. First, through generosity, one brings together those whose minds are difficult to tame and who are difficult to attract. After attracting them, one teaches Dharma in a pleasing way, using rhetoric to further attract and stimulate their interest. Gradually, by introducing them to the precious Dharma through skillful means, their confidence is established, and their interest develops with regard to practice.

In that it is not possible for all beings to be able to begin practice on the same level, one must discern the three distinctions of common, average, and superior sensibilities. Those of common sensibility will relate to one of three paths: those of the śrāvaka, pratyeka, or bodhisattva. Those of average scope will relate to the three outer tantras of kriyā, upa, and yogatantra. Those of superior scope will relate to the three inner tantric paths of mahā, anu, and ati. One must know how to skillfully lead such disciples onto the progressive stages of the nine vehicles. In order to guide beings whose minds are untamed, it is absolutely necessary that one's own mind be tamed and one's own conduct be in accordance with what one propagates. In this way, one's own accomplishment will be a great inspiration to the field of disciples. If one has no personal accomplishment and one's actions contradict one's words, disciples will become disillusioned with listening and practicing.

2.b.3(b) An explanation of the vows relating to all three moralities:

> Train in all that is wholesome. Completely abandon all that is contrary. Continually rely upon mindfulness, alertness, and conscientiousness in the four activities of moving about, remaining still, eating, and sleeping. Purify all conduct in accordance with the sūtras, and pray to accomplish all that is conducive.

The method to obtain the state of full awakening is to develop and accumulate all virtue that has not yet been developed and to increase all that has been. Therefore, one should never allow even the slightest nonvirtue to develop, and one should uproot and fully abandon all negativities. In addition, constant mindfulness of one's vows is necessary so that they are always guarded from deterioration. One should be mentally alert as to whether a negativity has arisen in one's mind stream or not. Conscientiousness is necessary so as to not confuse what to accept and what to reject. If mindfulness, alertness, and conscientiousness are constantly present, daily life easily becomes the path of virtue.

For example, when eating, the first portion of food should be offered to the Three Jewels. One then consumes the food as nourishment for all the parasites and living creatures within one's body. The food is eaten without craving or attachment. At the conclusion of the meal, one dedicates the merit accumulated through this expression of generosity. While sitting, one should sit straight and carefully focus the mind. When sleeping, one should lie down on the right side with the head pointed to the north. Then fall asleep while recalling the noble qualities of the Three Jewels of Refuge. In these ways, virtue and merit are continually amassed.

2.c Summing up, in two divisions:

2.c.1 Repeating what other scholars assert:

> According to the sovereign of supreme knowledge, Longchenpa (*Klong chenpa*), the vows for aspirational awakened mind are the meditation of the four immeasurables, and the vows for the practical awakened mind are the practice of the six transcendent virtues. In brief, it is taught that these are condensed into the eight white and black dharmas.

The great, omniscient Longchen Rabjam possessed supreme knowledge and became the sovereign realized master of the words and meaning of all scriptures and the commentaries upon them. He possessed the wealth of all noble qualities that arise from hearing, contemplation, and meditation upon the Tripiṭaka, as well as the practice of the three trainings. According to this great master, the essential instructions for training in aspirational awakened mind are condensed into the practice of the four immeasurables, because this ensures that the depth and quality of one's commitment to all sentient beings will never dissipate. These four are immeasurable equanimity, love, compassion, and joy. Practical training is, in actuality, the six transcendent virtues, the practice of all bodhisattvas who have gone before. To further condense this, it is the practice of abandoning the four black dharmas and practicing the four white, as mentioned earlier.

2.c.2 Establishing our own assertion:

> Here, practicing all activities that bring benefit and bliss and rejecting everything that is nonbeneficial and harmful is the essence of the training of both traditions that disregards nothing.

If one has developed immeasurable love, all one's endeavors will qualify as practice because one will be striving to be of true benefit to oneself and others in this life, as well as working toward the establishment of ultimate bliss in the future. Whenever there is conflict between two parties, or whenever someone is expressing anger or aggression toward another, one must realize at that very moment that to retaliate is to become involved in negativity, to establish causes for lower rebirth, and to defile all of one's previously established virtue. All such negative involvement must be abandoned from the base. This advice is the heart practice of all the buddhas and bodhisattvas and is the essence of the sūtra teachings of the Mahāyāna path. The two methods for this training are the two great chariots of Nāgārjuna and Asaṅga. There is nothing that is not condensed into these two traditions.

3. The suitable support for the development of the vows:

> The support for development includes gods, nāgas, spirits, and others. Nāgārjuna taught that development occurs even in great sinners. Asaṅga taught that the prātimokṣa is a necessary support. In general, it is taught in the *Ratnolkānāmadhāraṇī* that, with faith in the Buddha and the Dharma and belief in the resultant unsurpassed awakening as well as the ocean-like pure conduct of the bodhisattvas, the awakened mind will be born.

The root support for the development of these bodhisattva vows is one who can understand the indications and implications of the vow-bestowing ceremony:

that is, one who can comprehend the meaning of these vows and who wishes to receive them. Gods, nāgas, and the various types of cannibal demons are not considered suitable supports for the prātimokṣa precepts. However, according to this tradition of Nāgārjuna, all of the above, including even those who commit the most heinous nonvirtue, may receive the bodhisattva vows if they aspire to do so. The sole prerequisite is that they must have the aspiration to develop the awakened mind.

According to the tradition of Asaṅga, in order to receive the practical awakened mind vow it is necessary to be a human being of one of the three world systems (other than the northern continent of Uttarakuru) and to have the mental capacity to understand the meaning of the vow. In addition, one must hold one of the seven categories of the prātimokṣa precepts as a support. Although one of the two traditions is more open than the other concerning requirements, the essential meaning is the same. If an individual has no interest in abandoning even one negativity, the awakened mind will not develop.

For example, the bodhisattva vows will never develop if there is harmful intent toward others. One must embrace the bodhisattva vows and way of life until enlightenment itself is reached. After passing from this life, it is not necessary to again meet with a compassionate spiritual guide and retake the vows. However, one must approach the path of practice according to one's own capacity and sensibility, be it small, medium, or great.

If by chance the vows are not maintained with mindfulness and alertness, and so are allowed to deteriorate, one should recall that such faults have the strength to destroy one's progress, purpose, and status as a bodhisattva in this life, and that in the future this may cause one to fall to the lowest hell realm. The fault is particularly heavy if one returns the bodhisattva vows. As it says in the *Bodhicaryāvatāra*, "To this state of unsurpassed great bliss I have invited all sentient beings as my guests. If I then deceive and disappoint them, just where can I expect to go?"

4. If the vows deteriorate, the manner in which to restore them, in two subdivisions:

4.a Briefly revealed:

> If the vows deteriorate after they are received, this will explain how to restore them:

Initially, instructions were given on how to receive the bodhisattva vows. Afterwards, how to guard the precepts from deteriorating and the methods of restoration, if they have deteriorated, will be taught.

4.b Extensively explained in three subdivisions:

4.b.1 The description of a downfall is given by revealing the "four dogmas."

> Whoever fails to examine what is correct or incorrect, whether to do something or not, or whether to be indifferent contradicts what is correct and commits a downfall. In order to accomplish a greater purpose, the lesser may be forsaken. This is a reflection.
>
> If there is no potential, there are no downfalls. To apply effort when there is no potential is also a reflection.

The four dogmas are practical guidelines for evaluating one's own behavior to determine whether or not the vows are being damaged. First, one must check to see if one has the potential to actually uphold these vows and training. Then, one must check to see if something is correct or not. After knowing something is correct, to then contradict it, fail to accomplish it, or remain indifferent to it is to reverse the activity of acceptance and rejection. Each one of these shortcomings constitutes a downfall.

As it says in the *Ratnakūṭa-sūtra*, "If one were to compare the making of offerings with great joy and pleasure for one hundred years to the maintenance of pure discipline for just one day, the latter is far more sublime." This quote clearly reveals the power of maintaining pure morality.

The greater purpose of training and guarding pure morality at the expense of forsaking a small act of generosity does not constitute a downfall. Although from the outer point of view it may appear to be a downfall, it really does not qualify as such and is therefore termed "a mere reflection." In addition, if a beginner who has not developed the potential to perform certain acts of generosity then fails to do so, this also does not constitute a downfall. On the other hand, if one offers, for example, the parts of one's body without the potential to really do this or with a negative, impure motivation, then although this may appear to be an astonishing act of generosity, it actually constitutes a downfall.

4.b.2 Revealing how the seven nonvirtues of body and speech are permitted if they accomplish the purpose of others:

> If they benefit others, the seven nonvirtues of body and speech are permitted because the purpose is virtue.

If, for the purpose of benefitting others, it is deemed necessary to commit any of the nonvirtues of body or speech, it is then permitted to do so. It is the higher conduct of bodhisattvas to consider the essential needs of sentient beings over everything else. For example, killing is permitted if it is done in order to protect many lives which would otherwise definitely be lost. It is permitted to steal if this helps beings who are poor and needy and who are truly suffering from hunger and thirst in a way that threatens their lives. In this circumstance, one may steal from the wealthy to give to the poor and needy. It is permitted to commit adultery if a woman or man is suffering tremendously from desire and claiming they will surely die if they do not have such sexual contact. In order to temporarily alleviate their suffering and ultimately lead them to the path of virtue, adultery is permitted as an act of compassion. Lying is permitted to save a life. For example, if a killer is pursuing someone with the intention to kill or harm them, and you intervene, lying about their whereabouts, this does not qualify as a nonvirtue. Slander is permitted if you know that someone who is a Dharma practitioner is associating with a negative friend who will eventually lead the practitioner to the lower realms. To intentionally divide them by slandering one against the other is permissible. Harsh speech is permitted if it is spoken to reverse nonvirtue. If someone is suffering intensely or experiencing mental depression, one may engage in idle chatter, storytelling, or gossip in order skillfully to lead them to the path of Dharma and the establishment of virtue. These nonvirtues of body and speech are permitted temporarily to help others avoid the accumulation of heavy nonvirtue. They are truly virtuous practices if done with the purest bodhicitta intention.

4.b.3 The general way to restore damaged vows, in two divisions:

4.b.3(a) The tradition of Nāgārjuna:

> If vows are allowed to deteriorate beyond a session, make prayers to Ākāśagarbha in the predawn. Confess all downfalls that occur in dreams. To purify remainders, recite the *Triskandhakanāmamahāyānasūtra* three times in the day and in the night. This is the tradition of Nāgārjuna.

The conditions for the deterioration and loss of vows are these: to lose the foundational support of the aspirational mind, to contradict the vows by allowing a root downfall to occur, and to reject the vows by offering them back. If the first or last of these occurs, then, at that very moment, the vows are uprooted and must be completely retaken in order to be restored. In the case of a root downfall that occurs during one of the three sessions in the day or night, to allow the session to end before confession is rendered constitutes a downfall. If such a deterioration occurs, one of middling sensibility must confess it before their meditation deity. In general, it is advised to make strong prayers to Ākāśagarbha and to unceasingly practice cleanliness and reliance upon external purity throughout the day and night. One should call out the name of Ākāśagarbha, make prostrations, and beseech him to reveal his presence and acknowledge the purification of your negativities. Pray to be purified of all negativity associated with a downfall that has actually occurred or that has occurred in the dream state.

If a sign of purification does not arise (acknowledgement from the buddhas, auspicious dreams, and so forth), then, in the predawn hours, praying as before, beseech Ākāśagarbha to arise with the first light of dawn to fill this entire world with the greatness of his loving-kindness and compassion. With these pure words of invocation, the signs that one's downfalls are cleared will then swiftly arise.

Those of inferior sensibility should confess through the application of the four powers. The power of the support is found in a virtuous Mahāyāna preceptor and the inner support of refuge and awakened mind. Those of superior sensibility may invoke the presence and awareness of the buddhas and bodhisattvas abiding throughout space, like an illusion or dream, and then repeat words of confession followed by meditative equipoise upon the ultimate purpose.

Otherwise, if one has committed a remainder, the repetition of the *Triskandhaka-sūtra* three times in the day and three times at night will purify. Retaking the bodhisattva vow is not like the prātimokṣa system. One may retake the vow each and every day, which also causes the vows to continue and to increase. Even if a root downfall occurs, if it is caught before the conclusion of the session it occurs in, then through confession alone the vow is restored.

Although the mode of restoration is uncertain and dependent upon the circumstance, whenever a fault does occur there is a remedial force that may be applied to restore it. This is a brief explanation of the restoration tradition of Ārya Nāgārjuna.

4.b.3(b) The tradition of Asaṅga, in two divisions:

4.b.3(b.1) Recognizing what constitutes the loss of a vow:

> The causes for losing aspirational awakened mind are the four black dharmas and the heartfelt abandonment of any sentient being. With unceasing shameless conduct and joy regarding the deed, to think that it is positive is a great delusion that destroys the vow. This is known as a defeat. It is not so if small or medium.

The causes for losing the bodhisattva vows include the conduct of the four black dharmas, and especially the abandonment of a sentient being from one's heart. This would also diminish one's practical aspiration. The four black dharmas of praising oneself and belittling others and so forth, with the four branches intact, constitute a defeat. The four branches are the following: repetitive conduct, no sense of shame, respect for and joy taken in the action, and believing the action has good, noble qualities or attributes. If these four branches are complete with the action, it is a great delusion, which constitutes a downfall. Because it has the power to destroy the vows, it is also called a defeat. If at the time the action occurs the four branches are complete, but afterwards one feels shame and the wish to quickly reverse it, it is only a minor delusion. If the action occurs with the four branches and one feels some sense of shame about it, then, after being reprimanded by another and reversing the action, it is a middling delusion. Neither of these latter two constitutes a downfall.

4.b.3(b.2) Restoration of a downfall:

> If a defeat occurs, the vow must be received again. State and confess the fault in front of three if medium, one if small. If there is no suitable

> person, confess with the mind. This is the incomparable tradition of *Udāracaryāparamparā* (*Extremely Vast Conduct*).

If aspirational awakened mind is abandoned, a great deluded defeat or root downfall occurs. In the presence of four qualified Mahāyāna preceptors, one must confess and then persevere in the practices of purification and accumulation. The vows must be retaken by repeating them three times. If it is a middling delusion that has occurred (similar to that of a defeat) it is confessed in the presence of three preceptors. If it is a minor delusion (for example, breaking one of the forty-six auxiliary precepts or a breakdown in one's motivation), then all such faults may be confessed in the presence of just one preceptor. If one is truly unable to find a qualified Mahāyāna vow upholder to confess before, then one may mentally imagine being in the presence of all of the buddhas and bodhi-sattvas and confess accordingly. This tradition, which requires a stricter conformation to the rules and more difficult steps of restoration, was especially created by the enlightened ones in order to suit the needs of beginners on the bodhisattva path. Because of this, it is unequaled by any other for the needs of beginners.

5. The benefits of guarding the bodhisattva vows, in three divisions:

5.a The benefit of the development of unceasing merit:

> If the awakened mind is maintained accordingly, even while sleeping and during unconscientious behavior, the strength of merit unceasingly arises.

By the power of purely generating the awakened mind aspiration, the result of temporary rebirth as a *cakravartin* ruler[51] may occur. Other results include rebirth in the higher realms and as powerful gods of the highest realms. As the *Bodhicaryāvatāra* states, "If this type of awakened mind aspiration is coupled with the practical application, it will bear the fruit of unceasing merit even during times when one is not intentionally practicing virtue, such as while sleeping or acting inattentively."

5.b The benefit of the transformation of name and purpose:

> One becomes a bodhisattva, and...

At the very moment that the awakened mind takes birth in one's mind, one's ordinary identity bcomes that of a bodhisattva, and one becomes an object of the veneration of gods and humans. Thereafter, if a small fault occurs but one's aspiration is not forsaken, one's identity as a son or daughter of the buddhas will not decline. In addition, the power and blessing of the bodhisattva's aspiration splendidly suppresses all the qualities of the śrāvakas and pratyekas. This alone will save one from all the suffering and pitfalls of cyclic existence.

5.c The benefit of attaining the unsurpassed status of awakening:

> ...in three, seven, or thirty-three countless eons, enlightenment is obtained.

The manner in which to obtain the ultimate result is explained as follows: By practicing the four mindfulnesses, the four perfect abandonments, and the four legs of miraculous transformation, one obtains the five types of clairvoyance as well as the stable continuity of deeper meditative absorption. This is the path of accumulation. From this, the four levels of the path of preparation arise, beginning with heat, the peak, forbearance, and the supramundane.[52] On the first two levels, the five powers are achieved, and on the final two levels, by meditation on the four strengths, all discursive grasping and clinging cease. One's noble qualities then develop beyond those of the path of accumulation.

Upon one's first direct perception of the nature of truth or, dharmatā, the two obscurations that arise from grasping at inherent existence are abandoned, and all one thousand two hundred noble qualities are obtained. At this point, one enters the nine stages of the path of meditation, and through the direct perception of the nature of truth, one maintains omnipresent awareness of primordial wisdom. Through this accumulated strength, the simultaneously arising obscurations are gradually abandoned.

On the three pure bodhisattva stages, all obscuration-based afflictions are exhausted, and even the subtlest underlying obscurities gradually fade away. It is on this level that all twelve thousand relative qualities are increased and expanded. Ultimately, on the tenth and final level, the vajra-like meditative absorption destroys all remaining and extremely subtle habitual propensities, and the state of fully perfected enlightenment occurs. Here there are differences in the progress of bodhisattvas of common, average, and superior sensibilities.

Those of sharpest scope and capability are like sheepherders who have previously vowed to first place all parent sentient beings in the state of perfect enlightenment and only then achieve liberation for themselves. For such individuals, enlightenment will occur after three countless eons of time. In the first eon, they will pass through the first two paths of accumulation and preparation. In the second eon, they will attain the seven impure bodhisattva stages. In the third eon, they will ascend the three pure stages to achieve the state of perfect buddhahood. Those of average sensibility are like oarsmen who have the aspiration that they and all other parent sentient beings may become enlightened simultaneously. For them, enlightenment will occur after seven countless eons. The first two paths will take two eons each. The path of seeing will take one, and the path of meditation two eons of time.The aspirant of common sensibility is like a king who, at the time of generating the awakened mind, aspires to achieve liberation first and then to liberate all others. For such individuals, it will take thirty-three countless eons to achieve enlightenment. The paths of accumulation and preparation will take three eons each, and after that each of the ten bodhisattva stages will take three eons of time each to accomplish.

Having completed the principal subject, the chapter is complete.

> This completes the third chapter, the explanation of the bodhisattva's training in the awakened mind.

In dependence upon relative methods and indications, and in order to meet the needs of all beings, the manner of developing, maintaining, guarding, and restoring both the aspirational and practical awakened mind has been taught according to the two great traditions of practice.

CHAPTER FOUR: SECRET MANTRA

C. Chapter Four: Secret Mantra, an explanation of the third root, the vajra vehicle of secret mantra, the training of all the vidyādharas, and the progressive stages of the samaya words of honor.

The vajra vehicle is taught in three divisions.

1. An explanation of how the doctrine of the vajra vehicle originated:

> The sovereign teacher, the vajra-holder Samantabhadra, taught the ocean-like classes of tantra in the great Akaniṣṭha. Later, at Dhānyakaṭaka and elsewhere, the teachings were once again revealed...

Originally, the Buddha revealed the tantras through the mode of the five fully endowed circumstances. The fully endowed teacher, our own Lord Buddha Śākyamuni, has remained from beginningless time as the foundational, originally pure sphere of the primordial wisdom of intrinsic awareness. In this state of actual awakening, spontaneous presence and primordial wisdom are one. From within this, the one taste of the enlightened intentionality of all the buddhas of the three times remains as the appearance of the embodiment of complete enjoyment, the sambhogakāya.

All objective appearances are in actual nature the self-expression of primordial wisdom, the pure primordial buddha (Samantabhadra). The nonconceptual state, free from grasping and clinging, is the "vajra." The indivisibility of the sphere of truth and primordial wisdom is the "holder." The pure sovereign ruler of all maṇḍalas is the teacher. Thus, the fully endowed teacher is the vajra-holder, Samantabhadra.

The fully endowed place is self-awareness, exceedingly pure and understood as the Akaniṣṭha pure realm.[53] The fully endowed assembly, one's own self-projection, appears as the immeasurable maṇḍalas of peaceful and wrathful deities. The fully endowed Dharma is the inexpressible nature of the lucid radiance of primordial wisdom's enlightened intentionality. The fully endowed time is the unchanging sphere of spontaneous, self-originating purity.

Within these five endowments, the ocean-like classes of tantra were unceasingly taught through symbolic indication in the Akaniṣṭha pure realm. Accordingly, only bodhisattvas on the eighth and ninth levels were able to hear the teaching. At this same time, for the benefit of extremely unruly beings, the Buddha manifested as the glorious Heruka (in wrathful aspect) and displayed the entire supporting maṇḍala of wrathful deities in the five pure realms of manifestation, nirmāṇakāya, and in the pure and impure ordinary worldly realms in order to tame the minds of sentient beings. Similarly, Buddha Vajradhara sent many mind-emanations to the realms of gods, nāgas, *yakṣas*, and others to reveal and propagate the tantras. Specifically in our human realm, the supreme emanation Lord Buddha Śākyamuni, while meditating for six years in austerity, sent his mind-emanations to the peak of Mount Meru and beneath the ocean in order to reveal the doctrine of secret mantra. Again returning to his body, he completed his display of the twelve miraculous deeds. In general, all of the secret mantra tantras were compiled by Vajrapāṇi and transcribed primarily into the languages of Sanskrit, Prākrit, Apabhraṃśa, Ḍākiṇī, those of barbarians, and others.

When the king of Oḍḍiyāna,[54] Indrabhūti, saw the Buddha and his assembly of śrāvakas flying in space, unsure of what he was seeing he called his ministers to observe the phenomenon and asked them if it was a flock of red-colored birds. They replied that it was the Buddha and his disciples. The king, wishing very much to see the Buddha, prayed to him to come down. The Buddha then appeared to him and asked him this question: "Can you firmly maintain the three precepts of total renunciation?" King Indrabhūti replied, "In this pleasure grove of the southern continent it is easy for me to take rebirth as a lowly fox if need be. However, to abandon desirable objects in order to achieve liberation—this, Lord Gautama, I cannot do." At these words, the assembly of śrāvakas disappeared. Then a voice was heard from space, saying, "What appeared to be śrāvakas and pratyekas was actually the great miraculous display of bodhisattvas." After this, the Buddha revealed the primordial wisdom maṇḍala and bestowed empowerment upon King Indrabhūti, who later accomplished the kāya of nonduality.

The Buddha manifested to reveal the Vajrayāna maṇḍalas at other power spots, such as in eastern China at Parvata Pakkhipāda, in central India at the Śmaśāna Śītavana charnel ground, and in Śrī Laṇkā at Dakpo Dradrok, and so forth. In addition, Lord Buddha taught many of the tantras in unknown places at uncertain times. At times, Lord Buddha himself manifested as the principal deity, and at other times he bestowed empowerment as the Buddha himself. After revealing all three vehicles in this world, the Buddha then manifested at Dhānyakaṭaka Caitya, where he opened the great maṇḍala of the Kālacakra and revealed the tantras to the assembly of male and female yogins and yoginīs. On other occasions, he appeared as a fully ordained monk to reveal the outer tantras, including most of those of the kriyā and upa classes. When revealing to King Indrabhūti the *Guhyasamāja-tantra*, and to Vajragarbha the *Hevajra-tantra*, he manifested as the principal deities of those maṇḍalas surrounded by the entire assembly of deities. In this way, just as the tantras had previously been fully revealed in the great Akaniṣṭha, they were also introduced in their entirety into many other realms and world systems.

2. After the teachings were compiled, the manner in which they were practiced and upheld:

> ...and compiled by Vajrapāṇi and the retinue of recipients, and elaborated upon by the eight great mahāsiddhas and scholars of India and Tibet.

The manner in which the tantric teachings were compiled and propagated began in the celestial palace of Vajrapāṇi known as Alakāvatī. Vajrapāṇi convened with nine hundred and ninety-six million bodhisattvas to teach all the tantric classes and categories without exception. The disciple Candrabhadra compiled the root *Kālacakra-tantra*, and Vajragarbha compiled the *Diviparīkṣā*, and so forth. Although the retinue of recipients compiled various tantras that appeared to be distinct from their teacher, Vajrapāṇi, from the ultimate point of view they were nondual.

The secret Vajrayāna vehicle was not predicted to enter the world of human beings until a later time. According to prophesy, Vajrayāna entered this world in the following way. In the original translation school of the Nyingma there are two tantric distinctions, those of tantra and accomplishment. The coming of the tantra class was clearly prophesied by Lord Buddha Śākyamuni. Twenty-eight years after he passed into parinirvāṇa, five great sages—Deva Yaśasvī Varapāla of the gods' realm, Nāgarāja Takṣaka the nāga king, Yakṣa Ulkāmukha of the yakṣas, Rakṣa Matyaupāyika of the cannibals, and Vidyādhara Vimalakīrti the Licchavi of the human realm[55]—convened through their clairvoyant powers on the peak of Mount Malaya. In twenty-three verses, they made heartfelt prayers to receive the tantric transmissions. It was then that Vajrapāṇi directly appeared to them and revealed the essence of secret mantra, just as he had revealed it before in Akaniṣṭha, in Tuṣita, and in the thirty-third gods' realm. Rakṣa Matyaupāyika of the cannibals wrote the teachings down on golden parchment with lapis lazuli ink and buried them in the expanse of space.

Then, by the force of these blessings, King Ja of Sahor had seven auspicious dreams, indicating that all the scriptures of the tantric class would descend into this human world; and, in fact, shortly thereafter, all the scriptures of the tantric class of mahāyoga descended upon the roof of his palace. The kriyā class descended in Varanasi, the yogatantra class descended on the peak of Akniparvata Ujjavala mountain, and the anuyoga class descended in Śrī Laṇkā in the Singali forest.

These teachings then progressively spread into the countries of India, Nepal, and Druṣa.[56]

Later, Nubchen Sangye Yeshe accomplished these tantras under the guidance of the great paṇḍitas of these various countries and brought them into Tibet, where they were propagated. The atiyogatantra class was received in the country of Oḍḍiyāna by Garab Dorje through his direct visions of Vajrasattva. Compiling the teachings into volumes of scriptures, he then passed the lineage on to his disciple Mañjuśrīmitra. Mañjuśrīmitra passed it to Śrī Siṃha, and Śrī Siṃha passed it to the second Buddha, Padmasambhava. Padmasambhava passed the teachings to Vimalamitra, who then passed them to the translator Vairocana. Thus, the atiyogatantra was extensively propagated through this line of great realized beings.

The second category of the Vajrayāna vehicle, the accomplishment class, came into the human world in a manner similar to the way in which it was originally revealed in the Akaniṣṭha pure realm. Through the wrathful manifestation of divine presence and with the speech of the natural sound of the nature of truth, Vajra Dharma, a manifestation of Vajrapāṇi, revealed his own self-nature as nine maṇḍalas. The teachings were revealed and the scriptures were compiled. Five commentaries were then written by Vajra Dharma: *Thukje Jang Thakne Kyi Lung* (*Thugs-rJe dPyangs Thag-gNas Kyi Lung*), *Dzepa Chötrul Hlayi Lung* (*mDzad-Pa Chos 'Phrul Lha-Yi Lung*), *Trinley Tharchin Drubpai Lung* (*Phrin-Las mThar-Phyin sGrub-Pa'i Lung*), *Sang-Ngak Ngepa Döngyi Lung* (*gSang-sNags Nges-Pa Don-Gyi Lung*), and *Sangwa Goje Drönmai Lung* (*gSang-Ba sGo-'Byed sDron-Ma'i Lung*).

As it was not yet time to bring these teachings into the human world, they were given over to their caretaker, Ḍākiṇī Lekyi Wangmo (*las kyi dbangmo*; *Mahākarmendrāṇī*). The *ḍākiṇī* then placed the five general tantras of the eight herukas as one maṇḍala in a small case made of eight precious metals and jewels. She placed the ten individual tantras in ten separate little caskets, sealed them, and hid them in the stūpa called Ukhakara Ityasyastūpa in the charnel ground known as Śmaśāna Śītavana (Cool Forest). Then, at the appropriate time, through their clairvoyant powers of awareness, the eight great mahāsiddha paṇḍitas gathered together at this stūpa. By the force of their strong invocation in meditative absorption, Ḍākiṇī Lekyi Wangmo appeared directly before them. She then brought out the individually sealed cases and distributed them in the following way: The golden case containing the cycle for the accomplishment of Mahā Uttama Heruka was given to Vimalamitra; Hūṃkara received the silver case of Samyak Heruka; Mañjuśrīmitra received the iron case of Yamāntaka; Nāgārjuna received the copper case of Hayagrīva; Padmasambhava received the turquoise case of Vajrakīla; Dhana Saṃskṛta received the golden case of Saṃskṛta Preṣaka; Rambuguhya received the multicolored gem case of Lokapūja Stotra; and Śāntigarbha received the stone case of Vajra Mantrabhīru. This distribution was according to prophecy, and each went off to practice and fully realize their individual accomplishments. The small case made of eight precious jewels and metals containing the *Sugatasaṃnipāta* (*Gathering of all the Sugatas*), the combined maṇḍala of the eight herukas, along with the secret essential instructions, was not revealed but was instead resealed and prophesied to be discovered and revealed at a later date.

Later, the great vidyādhara Padmasambhava, according to his own prophetic indication, came to the land of Tibet, where he bestowed all the empowerments and essential instructions upon his own nine heart-sons and the twenty-five disciples. They in turn were prophesied to reincarnate over the centuries to reveal the empowerments and instructions to the karmic aspirants of future times. Moreover, the tantric teachings were extensively propagated throughout India and Tibet through the kindness of many realized mahāsiddhas and scholars.

3. Establishing the main subject, in two divisions:

a. Briefly revealed:

> Although the original translation tradition is known for the lineages of kama and terma, and though the latter tradition has boundless systems, a general explanation of the samaya of the tantric classes will be explained here.

The earlier translation school is well known for its two traditions of kama and terma. The kama is the "distant" tradition, whereas the terma is "near." Both originate through the three extraordinary lineages of mind-to-mind transmission, symbolic indication transmission, and oral transmission. The terma tradition also has three additional lineages: prophetic indication, empowerment through aspiration, and the lineage sealed and entrusted to the ḍākiṇīs.

The later translation school teachings were placed into scriptures by the king of Oḍḍiyāna, Indrabhūti. By introducing these teachings to his kingdom, it came to pass that every living being within Oḍḍiyāna without exception achieved spiritual attainment and vanished in the rainbow body. Later, the country became a great lake filled with serpent beings. Vajrapāṇi traveled there, taught the doctrine, and gradually ripened the minds of the serpents. Eventually they took rebirth as human beings living around the banks of the lake and, through their efforts in practice, later achieved realization. All of them becoming *ḍākas* and ḍākiṇīs, they flew here and there throughout space so that the place became known as Oḍḍiyāna Khandro Ling, the land of space travelers. Later, when the lake evaporated, a self-originating palace of Heruka arose that was filled with the original treasury of scriptures. Later still, each of the great mahāsiddhas, such as King Bipukawa, Nāgārjuna, Ḍombī Heruka, Kukkuripā, Lalita Vajra, the mahāsiddha Tilopa, and others propagated the teachings. Other great realized beings propagated the teachings in other pure realms, such as Śambhala. In short, the eight great and eighty minor mahāsiddhas and countless other scholarakra

s and realized beings composed commentaries and extensively propagated the doctrine. The boundless descriptions of their enlightened deeds will not be presented in detail here. However, readers may refer to the many translations of their inspiring lives and the accounts of their liberation. In this commentary, a general description of the morality practiced by the outer tantric traditions will be given, along with a detailed explanation of the inner practice of morality.

b. Extensively explained, in seven subdivisions:
   1. The essential nature of the mantra words of honor
   2. The distinctions
   3. Obtaining the unobtained
   4. Guarding the obtained from deterioration
   5. The support for generation
   6. The methods of restoration
   7. The benefits of guarding the words of honor

1. The essential nature of the mantra words of honor:

> The essential nature is to maintain awareness of method and wisdom with the three doors and the morality of the vows according to the individual traditions.

The objective of the words of honor is to guard the mind from discursive grasping at the concept of inherent existence, including all subtle habitual propensities arising through the three doors. The way of enacting the words of honor is to maintain the skillful application of the method of great bliss and the wisdom of emptiness. The words of honor are dependent upon receiving empowerment, at which time the initial discipline of the practice is received. Maintenance of primordial wisdom awareness during the blissful experiences of gazing, smiling, joining hands, and union is taught according to each of the four individual tantric distinctions.[57]

2. The distinctions, in two divisions:

2.a The general distinctions of the four tantric classes:

> The distinctions are four: kriyā, upa, yoga, and anuttara. Each has individual enumerations of the fourteen root downfalls. These are explained in the *Kālacakra-tantra* and elsewhere.

The divisions of kriyā, upa, yoga, and anuttara yoga each have their individual enumerations of the fourteen root downfalls, which are elaborated extensively in the *Śrī Kālacakra-tantra.* Briefly, the fourteen root words of honor of the kriyātantra are the following: faith in the Three Jewels, faith in mantra, regard for the Mahāyāna, respect for the lama and vajra family, never despising another worldly or wisdom deity, making offerings to one's own deity at the appropriate times, not offering to other traditions, making offerings to uninvited guests, never forsaking love, making effort to accomplish the purpose of others, perseverance in mantra recitation, maintaining all words of honor according to one's own capacity, not giving secret mantra teachings to immature recipients, and guarding one's own words of honor and realizing their meaning. If one opposes these fourteen, they become root downfalls.

In upa tantra the fourteen root words of honor are to abandon the ten non-virtues and the four roots. The four roots are the rejection of Dharma, the rejection of bodhicitta, a lack of generosity due to avarice, and harm to other sentient beings. In yogatantra the words of honor correspond to the five buddha families. The buddha family words of honor are the three vows of refuge. Those of the vajra family are to maintain a vajra, bell, *mudrā*, and the vajra master. Those of the ratna family are to never forsake the four generosities: the giving of love, material aid, protection from fear, and Dharma. Those of the padma family are to maintain the Dharma in its entirety. Those of the karma family are to maintain all vows and words of honor received and to persevere in making offerings. To persevere in the training and maintenance of these fourteen is to uphold samaya, the words of honor. To oppose any of them is to commit a root downfall.

2.b The specific distinction of the anuttara tradition:

> The anuttara tradition adheres to the twenty-five uncontrived activities, the vows of the five families, the fourteen root downfalls, the major transgressions, and the tradition of the Great Perfection.

The principal subject and explanation given here are for the words of honor of the anuttara yoga tradition. They are distinguished as the common twenty-five uncontrived activities, the specific words of honor of the five buddha families, the fourteen general root words of honor, the eight auxiliary major transgressions, and the root and branch words of honor of the atiyoga Great Perfection tradition.

3. Obtaining the unobtained mantra words of honor, in two divisions:

3.a Briefly revealed:

> First, to explain the manner for receiving the unobtained:

When empowerment is received for the first time, it is characterized as the "causal" initiation. Afterwards, when one receives empowerment from a lama, or if self-initiation occurs, it is the "path" initiation. By purifying the subtle habitual propensities so that the teacher and assembly are realized to be nondual, the "resultant" empowerment occurs. Here, an explanation of the causal and path empowerments will be discussed.

In order to receive empowerment, one must meet with a spiritual master who has the necessary qualifications. Mainly, the teacher must have great respect for his or her teacher and no deterioration of samaya. The teacher must have unfailing love and compassion for all parent sentient beings, as well as the potential and strength to unfailingly uphold the Buddha's doctrine. In addition, the disciple must have faith, diligence, wisdom, generosity, meditation experience, pure samaya, a joyful attitude toward practice and meditation, constant faith in the lama, the ability to make offerings to the lama during the three times, and noble, excellent qualities. In order to bestow empowerment upon such a suitable disciple, the teacher must be skilled in the knowledge of how to unmistakenly arrange and bestow empowerment.

3.b The extensive explanation, in five subdivisions:

3.b.1 A description of maṇḍalas:

> The four types of maṇḍalas are those of colored sand, the *bhaga*, relative bodhicitta, and absolute bodhicitta.

In order to reveal the outer maṇḍala of characteristics to beginning disciples, an external maṇḍala is created. For those of superior scope, the maṇḍala is made of mounds; for those of middling scope, it is drawn on cloth; and for those of inferior scope, it is made out of colored sand. All these are in accordance with the instructions given for the particular deities to which they correspond. The inner empowerments and maṇḍalas are revealed without elaborations. The second empowerment corresponding to the essential nature of mantra is bestowed by drawing the bhaga syllable to indicate the secret center of the consort. (The ultimate bhaga is the sphere of truth.) The third empowerment is the essential nature of the deity as relative bodhicitta, the essence of the male deity. The fourth empowerment is the essential primordial wisdom as ultimate bodhicitta, the essence of which is the maṇḍala of primordial wisdom vital air. Empowerment is bestowed in dependence upon these four maṇḍalas.

3.b.2 A description of the four empowerments:

> The vase, secret, wisdom, and fourth empowerments are progressively bestowed upon qualified disciples.

The vase empowerment is preceded by the ritual for preparing the place, the vase, the deities, and, finally, the disciples. In order to prepare the disciples so that they are suitable vessels to receive the empowerment, they are initially allowed to enter and then must promise to keep all commitments and words of honor. As the actual empowerment begins, the initiating master is recognized to be indivisible with the meditation deity and maṇḍala. After the master invokes the primordial wisdom maṇḍala, the primordial wisdom deities dissolve into the disciples and the empowerment substances, consecrating them with blessings. Then the empowerments for each of the five buddha families are bestowed. These are the water, diadem, vajra, bell, and name empowerments. The sixth empowerment is the vajra method, and the seventh is the source of the method, the vajrācārya empowerment. The vase empowerment includes these seven parts (with auxiliary concluding sections), through which the nondual primordial wisdom of appearance and emptiness is experienced.

The second, secret empowerment is bestowed by the vajra master in his sambhogakāya presence in union with the wisdom consort. All the buddhas and bodhisattvas are invoked to dissolve into their union, from which the red and white bodhicitta nectars are received and experienced by the disciples. Otherwise, the nectar may be taken from the face of a small mirror and placed upon the tongue of the disciples so that it dissolves down into their hearts. From this, they experience the inexpressible primordial wisdom of clarity and emptiness.

The third, primordial wisdom empowerment is bestowed by the vajra master who resides in the vajra nature of the dharmakāya mind. With the support of the disciples in union with consort, the four joys are realized through the descent and ascent of the wisdom nectar as it moves through the networks of wisdom channels. Here, the nondual primordial wisdom of bliss and emptiness is experienced.

The fourth empowerment of the precious ultimate word is bestowed as the vajra master remains in the actual nature of vajra-like primordial wisdom and, through the use of the method, perfects all sixteen joys in order to realize spontaneously arising primordial wisdom.

Introduction to empowerment through rhetoric is the introduction to primordial wisdom through words, whereas the ultimate empowerment is the development of the supreme meditative absorption of the primordial wisdom of great bliss. The experience derived through dependence on the mudrā of union is the support-based empowerment. Meditating upon this is the path, and perfection is the result.

Whoever bestows these four empowerments must have the personal power of these accomplishments so that others are inspired with faith, as well as the power to accomplish the purpose of others with great diligence. In addition, the vajra master must have the power to use, without accepting or rejecting, the specific samaya substances such as the five meats and the five nectars. Finally, the four empowerments may be bestowed individually if necessary. For example, only the outer vase empowerment may be given at one time.

3.b.3 A description of separating and obtaining:

> During the four periods of wakefulness, dreaming, deep sleep, and meditative absorption, subtle stains arising in the three doors are cleared. During generation stage and *tummo* (*gtummo*; *caṇḍālī*) [mystic heat] practice, the potency to meditate on both illustrative and definitive primordial wisdom and to realize the four kāyas occurs.

The bestowal of the four empowerments also corresponds to four periods of time. The first is wakefulness, when appearances are coarse or rough. The second is the dream state, when appearances are subtle due to the distribution of the essential fluid by the vital air. The third is the state of deep sleep, devoid of thoughts, which is the sole experience of the nonconceptual essence of the mind. The fourth is the state of meditative absorption, when all discursive thoughts are arrested within bliss. These four periods correspond first to the body when appearances are rough, second to the speech, third to the mind, and fourth to the extremely subtle, all-pervasive foundation. Otherwise, the four empowerments correspond to the four māras and their elimination. The māra-demon of the aggregates corresponds to the coarse (body), the demon of delusion corresponds to the subtle (speech), the demon of death corresponds to the very subtle (mind), and the demon of grasping at objects corresponds to the extremely subtle (all-pervasive foundation). In addition, obscurations categorized as karmic, deluded, subtle, and extremely subtle habitual propensities are cleansed, and the potential to fully purify them is awakened.

When the vase empowerment is received, this authorizes the initiate to practice the generation stage. The secret empowerment corresponds to the completion stage, tummo, and so forth. The wisdom empowerment introduces illustrative primordial wisdom, whereas the word empowerment introduces ultimate primordial wisdom. The result of all four empowerments is as follows: The vase empowerment ripens as the nirmāṇakāya, the embodiment of manifestation; the secret empowerment ripens as the sambhogakāya, the embodiment of complete enjoyment; the wisdom empowerment ripens as the dharmakāya, the embodiment of ultimate truth; and the word empowerment ripens as the svābhāvikakāya, the embodiment of the essential nature. The potential to realize these four kāyas is ultimately actualized.

3.b.4 A description of how the words of honor are received:

> First, give rise to the three places as the three vajras. Later, at the time when the four empowerments are fully complete, the words of honor of a vidyādhara are received.

The very moment that the mantra words of honor are obtained occurs when the disciple visualizes the three doors marked by the three vajra syllables. The three vajra syllables are a white OM (ཨོཾ) in the crown, a red AH (ཨཱཿ) in the throat, and a blue HUM (ཧཱུྃ) in the heart. This blesses and transforms the ordinary three doors into the three vajra states. As the empowerment begins, the vase and other empowerments are progressively bestowed. At the conclusion of all four empowerments, the vidyādhara words of honor are obtained in their entirety. From that point on, one should recognize that all the words of honor are received and that they must therefore be guarded and maintained.

3.b.5 A description of the margin of receiving:

> Thereafter, persevere in the training of commitments and words of honor.

After obtaining the words of honor of a secret mantra vidyādhara, the disciple must clearly discern what to accept and what to reject.

4. Guarding the obtained from deterioration, in three subdivisions:
   - 4.a Briefly revealed
   - 4.b Extensively explained
   - 4.c Summing up

4.a Briefly revealed:

> In the interim, an explanation of the methods through which to guard the vows from deterioration is as follows:

Just receiving mantra words of honor is not sufficient. Thereafter, one must guard the mind from any deteriorations. All Vajrayāna training is dependent upon the purity of the words of honor. If they are allowed to deteriorate, all further training becomes meaningless. As an analogy, if one's life force is lost, all other sense organs become dysfunctional. Because the methods through which to guard the words of honor are crucial to one's success and development on the mantra path, this is the principal subject of this chapter.

4.b Extensively explained, in five subdivisions:
- 4.b.1 The twenty-five uncommon activities
- 4.b.2 The vows of the five buddha families
- 4.b.3 The fourteen root downfalls
- 4.b.4 The major branch downfalls
- 4.b.5 A specific explanation of the words of honor taken according to the Nyingma tradition of the Great Perfection

4.b.1 The twenty-five uncommon activities, explained in two further subdivisions:

4.b.1(a) Briefly revealed:

> First, according to the *Kālacakra*, the uncommon activity is as follows:

According to the *Śrī Kālacakra-tantra*, the basis for all mantra training is the practice of the twenty-five uncommon words of honor of Vajrasattva.

4.b.1(b) The twenty-five are explained in groups of five each:

4.b.1(b.1) The five to abandon:

> Killing, lying, stealing, adultery, and drinking liquor are the five basic actions to avoid and abandon.

Within the context of mantra, killing means to take the life of even the smallest insect and includes harboring, even for one instant, any harmful intent toward another living being. Lying means to deceive someone else because of one's own desire or needs. Stealing means to take the wealth or possessions of another, even if it belongs to animals. Adultery means to take the wife or husband of another for oneself. Finally, drinking liquor is seen as the basis for the development of all faults. Any activity or thought that even comes close to these five must be abandoned. Guarding oneself with the vajra lasso of awareness so as not to become ensnared in the trap of saṃsāra, one should recognize that broken words of honor naturally destroy all virtue.

4.b.1(b.2) The five to avoid:

> Gambling, eating unwholesome food, engaging in negative speech, and training in the spiritual traditions of elementals[58] and titans are the five activities to avoid.

Gambling means to spend one's time using dice, cards, or other methods to squander money and time in the pursuit of meaningless pleasure. Eating unwholesome food refers specifically to any food that is acquired through nonvirtuous means: for example, food that has been stolen or animal meat that has been butchered for one's own consumption. Engaging in negative speech means to unnecessarily discuss subjects that have to do with war, killing, harming others, and so forth. Following the rituals of spiritual traditions that make sacrificial offerings and training in the philosophies of titans or barbaric spiritual traditions comprise the fourth and fifth activities to avoid. Any of these five activities causes one to be diverted from the path of virtue and thus produces harmful, negative karma.

4.b.1(b.3) The five killings:

> The killing of cows, children, men, and women and the destruction of stūpas are known as the five killings.

These five killings are meant to be abandoned, as specific words of honor, because of the beliefs employed by non-Buddhist schools of thought. In certain non-Buddhist Hindu traditions it is believed that, in order to be reborn in heaven, these killings are performed as offerings that please the gods and thereby cause one's wishes to be fulfilled. They are the following: the sacrificial killing of cows in order to obtain higher rebirth, the killing of children in order to offer their blood to the deity Kālī, the killing of men in order to be reborn as a man, and the killing of women in order to be reborn as a woman. The fifth "killing" is to destroy, desecrate, or otherwise put an end to the supports or images of enlightened body, speech, and mind such as stūpas, temples, statues, and so forth due to holding a barbaric view. These five killings must be completely rejected.

4.b.1(b.4) The five not to have aggression toward:

> The five to avoid feeling aggression toward are virtuous friends, elders, the buddhas, the saṅgha, and one's spiritual mentor.

This category involves any expression of anger or aggression directed toward five specific objects: a virtuous friend with whom either a worldly or spiritual relationship has been established, someone who has greater qualities than oneself and is therefore worthy of veneration, enlightened beings, fully ordained monks, and one's own teacher or khenpo. Feeling anger toward any of these five must be abandoned.

4.b.1(b.5) The five nonattachments:

> The five nonattachments are to have no attachment with the five organs (eyes, ears, nose, tongue, and body) toward form, sound, smell, taste, and touch. These are the twenty-five uncommon activities.

These remaining five correspond to form, sound, smell, taste, and touch, the five objects of the five sense fields or consciousnesses, which, when experienced with attachment, are the condition through which the five mental afflictions arise. If one allows attachment and compulsory attraction to occur, the experience of cyclic existence is intensified. It is an objective of generation stage practice to transform objective appearances into awareness of the primordial wisdom deity. At the completion stage, all objective appearances dissolve into oneself and are no longer pursued externally. One must persevere in the antidote of mindfulness and mental alertness so as to prevent the deterioration of any of these twenty-five words of honor that correspond to the Buddha Vajrasattva.

4.b.2 The words of honor of the five families, in two divisions:
4.b.2(a) The common words of honor
4.b.2(b) The specific words of honor

4.b.2(a) The common words of honor, in two subdivisions:

4.b.2(a.1) Briefly revealed:

> According to the common explanation, there are five words of honor for the five families.

The relative explanation of these words of honor is common, whereas the specific, definitive understanding is extraordinary. Here there is a strong foundational emphasis on the training in aspirational and practical bodhicitta, as well as on the three moralities that are general Mahāyāna practices, thus qualifying them as common. Although all upholders of the Vajrayāna must maintain all words of honor of the five buddha families, it is particularly important to take special care in maintaining the words of honor of the family of one's own tutelary deity.

4.b.2(a.2) Extensively explained:

> The practice of the buddha family is to train in aspirational and practical bodhicitta and the three moralities. The practice of the vajra family is the vajra, bell, mudrā, and reliance upon the lama. The practice of the *ratna* family is the giving of wealth, Dharma, fearlessness, and love. The practice of the *padma* family is to maintain the outer, inner, and secret vehicles. The practice of the karma family is to maintain offerings, torma (*gtorma*; *bali*), and the stages of action.

Each of the five buddha family words of honor will be explained in progressive order. The words of honor of the buddha yoga or central buddha family include the development of aspirational and practical bodhicitta, the three moralities, and training in the practice of refuge. According to the hidden meaning, the Three Jewels are recognized as the originally pure nature of the awakened mind of the indivisibility of emptiness, bliss, and the nature of the mind. Since the lord of the buddha family is Buddha Vairocana, this family corresponds principally to the body. It is upon this body that all realization depends. It is the support, as well, for the noble qualities that arise from pure morality. Thus, refuge is taken in this physical support.

The words of honor of the vajra family are to keep in one's possession the samaya objects of vajra and bell and to maintain awareness of one's nature as the deity with the great mudrā. According to the hidden meaning, the vajra is the nature of the method, the wish-fulfilling jewel of the male. The nature of wisdom is the lotus of the female, symbolized by the bell. The mudrā is the joining of these two into union. When the secret elements of the white and red bodhicitta mix together through the heat and melting, the unchanging nature of great bliss, indivisible with the nature of emptiness, is meditated upon. This experience of nondual primordial wisdom is the great mudrā. One must maintain tremendous respect for the lama who reveals this nature as it is. The vajra family of Buddha Akṣobhya corresponds primarily to the mind, whose nature is illustrated by bringing together the outer objects of vajra and bell, as well as by the secret union of method and wisdom, which introduces the nature of mind.

The words of honor of the ratna family are the four expressions of generosity: the giving of material wealth, spiritual teaching and assistance, protection from fear, and the root perfection of generosity, the giving of great love. These four must be practiced six times during the day and night. According to the hidden meaning, during union practice, when the mystic heat ignites to melt the white bodhicitta which then descends and ascends through the major networks of channels, the experience of the four joys is the generosity of primordial wisdom. Buddha Ratnasambhava is the source of all noble qualities, so this is known as the ratna or jewel family. The nature of generosity is that it is the source of both material enjoyments and endowments.

The words of honor of the padma family include all words of honor of the three outer vehicles of characteristics and the three inner tantric vehicles. According to the hidden meaning, by maintaining the vital air in the central channel, perpetual, unobstructed enlightened speech is accomplished. Buddha Amitābha represents speech as the essence of the lotus family. In addition, Dharma itself is of the nature of speech.

The words of honor of the karma family include maintaining all words of honor previously mentioned, as well as regular outer, inner, and secret offerings, torma and fire offerings, and the activation of the four concerned activities. According to the hidden meaning, all vows are sealed in the nondual union, and through the bliss of the descent of the bodhicitta, all the deities residing in one's aggregates, elements, and organs are satisfied through this offering. Buddha Amoghasiddhi is the essence of all concerned activity, and action is thus the essence of the samaya of this buddha family.

4.b.2(b) The specific words of honor of the five buddha families:

> The specific words of honor of the vajra family are the taking of life with the ten prerequisites, authorization, and realization established. Taking what is not given belongs to the ratna family. It is taught that with the pure intent to accomplish the purpose of oneself and others, one may steal wealth, another's wife, or the profound Dharma of the Mahāyāna. For the padma family it is taught to rely upon a female for action, Dharma, samaya, and mudrā. For the karma family it is taught to speak what is untrue, indicating the nonconceptual lack of true existence of self and sentient beings. The *cakra* (buddha) family must rely upon liquor, the five meats, and all objects. Upholding pure conduct of the outer, inner, and secret stages of the vehicles is the tradition of the unsurpassed (anuttara).

According to the uncommon, extraordinary words of honor of the five buddha families, first, in terms of the generation stage commitment that corresponds to relative truth, killing is required of those who possess the specific power acquired through the depth of meditative realization, or who have received permission from the deity or the lama, and who have the certain motivation of compassion. With these prerequisites, it is the samaya of the generation stage to then perform the activity of killing and liberating the consciousness of an entity who is seriously obstructing the propagation of the Dharma. If a practitioner does not have these prerequisites, the way of understanding this samaya changes. This is why this category of samaya is termed "specific." Otherwise, without the full potency to actually maintain the specific samaya, the practitioner must bring the understanding of each of the five words of honor onto the level of the three inner empowerments and the completion stage level of practice. For example, literally and from the relative point of view, the first vow of killing corresponds to the purified nature of hatred as the samaya of the vajra family, the Buddha Akṣobhya. With the complete ten prerequisites, wrathful concerned activity is activated in order to liberate the consciousness of an obstructor who is unable to be benefitted or tamed through peaceful means. Not only is there no fault, the purpose is a profound expression and actualization of immeasurable mercy. From the ultimate point of view, life is understood as the vital air that moves through the two principal side channels. The method to cut off or obstruct this flow so that it will enter into the central channel and ascend to the crown cakra is the meaning of "to kill." Otherwise, the mind is the very life essence of discursive thoughts. By cutting off or "killing" the mind, the unborn nature of mind is actualized in the sphere of truth.

The second word of honor is the purified nature of pride as the samaya of the ratna family. This word of honor requires one to steal and is understood according to both relative and ultimate truth. Relatively speaking, so that others may accumulate merit and with the objective of alleviating the suffering of poverty, one may take the wealth of another, either physically or through the power of mantra. Such an expression of generosity brings no harm because of its greater purpose.

From the ultimate point of view, in order to realize primordial wisdom through mantra practice, one steals the female of another through the method of summoning and receives the bodhicitta through the strength of one's vital air. Otherwise, according to ultimate truth, the meaning of "consort" is the ultimate meaning of the greater spiritual pursuit, the nature of emptiness. Stealing the essence refers to realizing the nondual primordial wisdom nature through the strength of one's meditation. This gives one the power to accomplish the two purposes, those of self and others.

The purified nature of desire is the essence of the samaya of the lotus family. An individual who has accomplished the depth of meditative realization and who maintains the view of recognizing nonduality must maintain the "three recognitions" during the practice of union. Both male and female are recognized as wisdom deities, the two secret places are recognized as the vajra and lotus, and great bliss and wisdom are recognized as the Dharma. By meditating with the three recognitions, the methods of the three modes of conduct are employed. These three are the ability to cause the essential fluid to descend, ascend, and be evenly redistributed through the networks of channels throughout the body. The action mudrā is a physical consort, while the Dharma mudrā is a visualized consort. The samaya of practicing tummo is the samaya mudrā, through which the bodhicitta melts to realize illustrative as well as primordial wisdom. Ultimately, the term "to rely upon a consort" means to realize the union of unchanging great bliss and the nature of emptiness as the great mudrā.

The fully purified nature of jealousy is the nature of the samaya of the karma family. According to relative truth, a lie may be spoken in order to bring benefit to another. From the ultimate point of view, the liberator and the object to liberate, the sentient being, are both realized to be nonconceptual. Within that nonconceptual nature all sentient beings are understood to have no true inherent existence. With that understanding, one aspires to liberate them from cyclic existence. As it states in the *Guhyagarbha*, "All dharmas are like an illusion. Names, words, and mental labels are false. To make use of that which is a lie is itself a label, and not really true."

According to ultimate truth, when the vital air dissolves into the heart cakra and the unceasing perpetual nature of sound arises, this is the sound of the ultimate nature. Otherwise this is perceived from the point of view of relative truth as the simultaneous revelation of the various Dharma entryways through which all sentient beings are brought to the path.

The fully purified nature of delusion is the samaya of Buddha Vairocana, the cakra family. According to relative truth, this means to drink liquor without the fault of intoxication and, in order to eradicate caste or class arrogance, to partake of the five types of flesh from animals that are usually not killed for consumption. If these five types of animals die a natural death, their flesh becomes a suitable samaya substance. The five are human flesh, elephant flesh, ox flesh, dog flesh, and horse flesh. Similarly, the five nectars are to be partaken of as samaya substances without repulsion or attraction. The five nectars are feces, urine, menstrual blood, marrow, and semen.

From the ultimate point of view, to partake of the five meats is to maintain the pure essence of the five organs. Drinking liquor refers to the descent of the fluid and the experience of coemergent bliss without emission. Partaking of the five nectars refers to maintaining the pure essence of the five elements and to melting the essential fluid to fully purify even the subtlest molecules. The pure essence of the essential fluid must be maintained and brought up to the navel center.

By maintaining these practices as a support, all discursive proliferations are experienced as the one taste of the sphere of equality.

In short, all of these words of honor are to be engaged in the order they are given. Initially, one must maintain and depend upon the twenty-five words of honor corresponding to uncommon activity. The first five words of honor correspond to the abandonment of harming others. The final five correspond to not becoming attached to the objects of one's sense fields by knowing the cause for the development of delusion. These are the outer characteristics that are practiced in the three outer tantric schools of kriyā, upa, and yogatantra. Then, in dependence upon these common words of honor, the specific words of honor of the anuttarayoga are embraced. Here, one begins the practice of maintaining the specific extraordinary samaya of the five families. Understanding the two distinctions of relative and absolute is specific to the tradition of the unsurpassed secret vehicles.

In order that all beings with karmic affinities may engage on these stages of practice without suffering from damaged samaya, they are led upon the path according to the level they can maintain.

4.b.3 The explanation of the root downfalls, in two divisions:

4.b.3(a) Briefly revealed:

The fourteen root downfalls are explained as follows:

The fourteen root downfalls are likened to the trunk of a fruit-bearing tree. In dependence upon the trunk, all the branches and leaves develop. If the trunk deteriorates, the entire tree will tumble down. Likewise, the root vows are like the trunk, and if they are guarded it is through them that all the noble qualities of the path develop. Otherwise, if the trunk is damaged, this becomes the root cause for falling to the lowest hell realm, where there is no chance for liberation and where unbearable suffering is endured. To avoid this, it is necessary to carefully guard against these fourteen.

4.b.3(b) An extensive explanation of the fourteen:

4.b.3(b.1) Disrespecting the vajra master:

> The first concerns heartfelt disrespect for the vajra master who has been kind in the three ways. To belittle him or disturb his mind is the first downfall because of its weight.

The vajra master is one who has bestowed empowerment, transmission, and pointing-out instructions. These are the three expressions of kindness because they make transmission complete according to inner tantric practice. In addition, the vajra master is one who has given a direct introduction to the nature of the mind. Being disrespectful to such a master, either directly through body and speech or indirectly through one's mind, or opposing the advice given by him or harming or disturbing those who are in the lama's immediate retinue, qualifies as the first and heaviest downfall. This is the first of the fourteen root downfalls because of the strength of the weight of negative karma it carries.

The vajra master should be cherished as the essential nature of all buddhas and should, therefore, be the principal object of one's devotion, admiration, and respect. Moreover, in dependence upon one's relationship with the vajra master, all noble qualities of the path, as well as the resultant qualities, are developed. If one allows the precious relationship between oneself, as the disciple, and the irreplaceable vajra master to deteriorate in the ways mentioned above, then whatever meditation one aspires to accomplish will only be the cause for rebirth as a *rudra*.[59] One must therefore be extremely careful.

4.b.3(b.2) Contradicting the Buddha's words:

> The second concerns the utterance of the sugatas, who reveal what to accept and what to reject. This includes the lama's speech. To knowingly contradict it by engaging in unwholesome conduct is the second downfall.

The words of the sugatas clearly reveal the path of what to accept and what to reject in accordance with the advice given by one's lama. The Tripiṭika and the four tantras all qualify as the sugatas' utterance. Ignoring these teachings, acting in opposition to the three trainings (prātimokṣa, bodhisattva, and Vajrayāna), and displaying such conduct in front of others trangresses the Buddha's speech. This downfall is second in weight to directly disrespecting the vajra master.

4.b.3(b.3) Expressing contempt toward the vajra family:

> The third is becoming angry toward general, distant, close, and immediate relatives; holding a grudge; and showing jealousy, disrespect, and so forth.

In general, all sentient beings are considered to be our relatives. Even closer are those who have entered the path of Dharma. Closer still are those who have entered the Vajrayāna, since those who have the same lama are considered to be children of the same father. Those who have received empowerment together at the same time are children of the same parents. Those who received empowerment first are the elders, and those who have received it at the same time are likened to twins born into the maṇḍala simultaneously. To express or to hold anger in one's mind toward any of these near or distant vajra relatives, or out of jealousy to harm them with body and speech, to speak harshly to them, or to argue with them and express their faults, constitutes the third root downfall. It is especially important to be careful toward the innermost vajra family, because to fight with or abuse them in any way accrues extremely negative karma that is very difficult to remove.

4.b.3(b.4) Abandoning love:

> The fourth is wishing that any sentient being should be separated from happiness and losing heartfelt love for them.

To wish that any sentient being should be separated from happiness and to stop feeling heartfelt love for them is the fourth root downfall. The object can be one sentient being or many. To wish for them to be separated from happiness and to meet with suffering or misfortune, thus forsaking them and giving up any love for them at all, constitutes the fourth downfall.

4.b.3(b.5) Abandoning bodhicitta:

> The fifth is, with a desirous mind and at an inappropriate time, intentionally emitting semen, thus forsaking the bodhicitta generated for sentient beings.

The appropriate times to allow seminal fluid to leave the body are during the secret empowerment as an offering to the deities, when increasing the family line of ancestral heritage, and when making special pills or other medicines.

Otherwise, and especially out of desire, to ignore the words of honor and training and emit semen for one's own personal satisfaction outside the context of higher anuyoga practice constitutes the downfall. This also includes the abandonment of bodhicitta for any sentient being, because bodhicitta and the essential fluid are seen as one on the level of generation stage practice (of inner tantra). If aspirational bodhicitta is abandoned, practical bodhicitta is automatically forsaken.

4.b.3(b.6) Disrespecting other religious philosophies and doctrines:

> The sixth is criticizing the philosophical doctrines of heretics searching for a path, śrāvakas and pratyekas on the path, and the great path of Mahāyāna.

The first aspect of this downfall is to disrespect any Buddhist or non-Buddhist, especially if they are searching for a spiritual path and are practicing methods through which they can achieve spiritual understanding or freedom and if one has no intention of guiding them to a higher pursuit. The second is to disrespect those who have entered upon the path that renounces cyclic existence, such as the śrāvakas and pratyekas. In addition, this sixth root downfall concerns those who are on the great path of Mahāyāna, which eliminates the two extremes. To claim that the philosophies of these spiritual pursuits are untrue and pointless, and to then show blatant disrespect toward their practices, constitutes the root downfall.

4.b.3(b.7) Revealing secrets:

> The seventh is openly revealing secret teachings to unsuitable vessels, to those with incomplete and unperfected ritual, or to those with deterioration or who fear the profound.

Teaching certain aspects of secret mantra to spiritually immature individuals is a root downfall. Spiritually immature individuals are those who have not completed prerequisite training; who have not been empowered; who have incomplete practice; who have not received the three higher initiations; who, although having received empowerment, have allowed the words of honor to deteriorate; who are afraid of the profound path; and who, like the śrāvakas and pratyekas, are not mature enough to receive the secret teachings. To intentionally expose such individuals to the uncommon substances and materials of secret mantra and their secret meaning so that they lose faith constitutes the seventh downfall.

4.b.3(b.8) Disrespecting the aggregates:

> The eighth is physically abusing oneself out of disrespect for the five aggregates, which are in actuality the five buddhas.

In inner Vajrayāna practice, the five aggregates are viewed as the five buddhas. At the time of empowerment, the body itself becomes a support for the offering of all desirable objects and the increase of bliss. In dependence upon the body, primordial wisdom is actualized. Not knowing this and so maintaining the view that the body is a source of suffering, and further belittling the body verbally or physically—such as by actually severing one's own limbs and so forth—constitutes the eighth downfall.

4.b.3(b.9) Doubting the Dharma:

> The ninth is explained as doubting the innate purity and liberating nature of the foundation, path, and result.

The foundation, path, result, and all meanings are explained as the natural, perfectly pure nondual clear light bodhicitta, which is the originally pure fundamental essence of the sugatas. To believe that this path of Dharma is merely meant to lead one to a happier state but does not have the ultimate potential to bring about full awareness of one's buddha nature, and to then doubt it so that faith and confidence are lost, constitutes the ninth root downfall.

4.b.3(b.10) Failing to liberate if the ten prerequisites are met:

> The tenth is failing to liberate or express love when there is potential and when the ten prerequisites are complete.

This word of honor concerns that which brings harm to the doctrine, namely the physical enemies of the Three Jewels and more specifically the physical enemies of one's own lama, those who have failed to restore deteriorated words of honor, those who have embraced the view and conduct of mantra and who have then developed incorrect view or have rejected the view and conduct, those who have hatred or anger toward the lama or the vajra family, those who have entered the secret teachings without authorization, those who have brought harm to sentient beings or who are harming pure upholders of samaya, and those who continue to accumulate extremely negative karma. Such individuals qualify as objects of liberation through profound compassion. Any one of these nine causes for suffering must be present, along with the fact that these individuals will surely fall to the three lower realms and experience unendurable suffering as a result of their conduct. Including the point that the results of their negative karma will surely be fatal constitutes the ten prerequisites. If any of these ten are complete, and especially if the potential to liberate exists, failure to accomplish this constitutes the tenth downfall.

4.b.3(b.11) Measuring the Dharma through logic:

> The eleventh is intellectualizing the understanding of substantiality, lack of substantiality, and mental labels as the truth.

This downfall occurs if one attempts to measure or realize the uncontrived, fundamental nature of emptiness, with or without substance, only through the conceptualizing intellect. Believing intellectual understanding to be absolute understanding, when it is only the measure of one's own conceptualizations and mental limitations, constitutes the eleventh downfall.

4.b.3(b.12) Causing someone to lose faith:

> The twelfth is failing to accomplish the needs of any sentient being who possesses the three levels of faith, failing to guard one's own mind, and being deceitful.

The three levels of faith are these: inspired faith, which arises upon recalling the noble qualities of the lama and the Three Jewels; emulating faith, which is the wish to achieve those same qualities; and convinced faith, which is single-pointed devotion. If someone who possesses these three levels of faith needs or asks for spiritual assistance, to then ignore them when one has the potential to help them constitutes the twelfth downfall. In addition, failing to guard one's mind and acting immorally, speaking unkindly, or deceiving someone so as to impair, damage, or reverse their faith also constitutes the twelfth downfall.

4.b.3(b.13) Failing to rely upon the appropriate samaya substances:

> The thirteenth is failing to rely upon necessary word of honor substances at the required time.

During Vajrayāna ceremonies, such as at the *gaṇacakra* feast and on other specific occasions, the gathered disciples are seen as ḍākas and ḍākiṇīs. Those ḍākas and ḍākiṇīs possess mantra materials such as the vajra and bell, partake of the five meats and five nectars, sing special songs of invocation, and dance according to the samaya requirements. Holding the view of the śrāvakas or pratyekas during these times, and thus failing to partake or participate because of that view, constitutes the downfall.

4.b.3(b.14) Disrespecting a wisdom female:

> The fourteenth is both generally and specifically disrespecting a wisdom female, directly or indirectly, in such a way that the female comes to know about it.

This downfall occurs if one tries to trick or blatantly disrespects any female or disrespects one's own wisdom consort. To do this directly or indirectly, to feel satisfaction about it, and for it to then be heard by the woman concerned constitutes the fourteenth downfall.

These fourteen root downfalls are delineated according to gravity. The first carries the heaviest karmic weight, with each decreasing in weight thereafter. However, since they are all root downfalls, the consequence of a break or deterioration is considered to be a failure of mantra morality. The way that these precepts relate to the four levels of mantra empowerment is as follows: the thirteenth relates to each of the four empowerments and the substances that one promises to utilize during each empowerment respectively; the fifth corresponds to the secret empowerment; the fourteenth corresponds to the wisdom empowerment; the ninth and eleventh correspond to the fourth empowerment; and the remaining nine correspond to the vase empowerment. After one receives the vase empowerment, these nine root precepts must be guarded, or they constitute root downfalls. However, if only the vase empowerment has been received, the remaining five, if allowed to deteriorate, do not constitute downfalls. After the remaining three secret empowerments are received, all fourteen root precepts must be guarded.

4.b.4 An explanation of the major branch downfalls, in three divisions:
- 4.b.4(a) Briefly revealed
- 4.b.4(b) Extensively explained
- 4.b.4(c) Summing up

4.b.4(a) Briefly revealed:

> Now the major auxiliary transgressions are explained:

Although similar to the root downfalls in weight, these transgressions do not qualify as causes for the loss of the words of honor. They do, however, create obstructions to the swift accomplishment of spiritual attainments. It is for this reason that they are called major transgressions. For example, if the main branches of a fruit-bearing tree fall, this affects the ability of the tree to bear fruit and may in fact be fatal to the tree.

4.b.4(b) Extensively explained, in two subdivisions:

4.b.4(b.1) The eight major transgressions:

> Relying upon a consort who has not matured through empowerment and samaya; physically or verbally fighting during the gaṇacakra; receiving the nectar of an unauthorized consort; failing to reveal the secret mantra to a qualified recipient; teaching something other than what has been requested by a faithful aspirant; staying seven complete

> days together with a śrāvaka; proclaiming oneself to be a tantric adept when the yoga of primordial wisdom has not been realized; and teaching unsuitable recipients. These are the eight auxiliary transgressions.

The first transgression is relying upon an unqualified consort. An unqualified consort refers to one who has not received the necessary empowerments, who does not purely uphold the words of honor, or whose mind stream is not properly matured. The second transgression occurs if during the gaṇacakra feast or other special Vajrayāna ceremonies one argues with or physically abuses any members of one's vajra family. This transgression occurs even if one does not feel strong aggression or hatred toward them. Displaying any animosity, even in jest, constitutes the transgression. The third transgression refers to reliance upon a consort who does not possess the necessary qualifications, as stated in the scriptures, and who is therefore only an ordinary male or female. Relying upon such a consort without the specific purpose of making relics or realizing the nature of bliss according to *sādhana* practice, but merely using the power of one's vital air to receive the nectar for making pills and so forth, constitutes the downfall. The fourth transgression occurs if, due to avarice, one fails to reveal the secret mantra teachings to a disciple who is a suitable vessel and who has a strong interest to learn. The fifth transgression occurs if a faithful and sincerely interested disciple asks a question about the Dharma, and one not only fails to answer but gives an unrelated or incorrect answer. The sixth transgression occurs if one stays as long as seven days together with someone who blatantly disrespects and disregards Vajrayāna view and conduct, whether this is a śrāvaka or merely one who is a logician.

The seventh transgression occurs if one claims to be a tantric adept when in fact one's self nature has not been actualized as innate primordial wisdom. The eighth and final transgression occurs in the circumstance of a teaching given either to a public gathering or privately to a few disciples. In either case, the transgression occurs if there are students present who are not suitable vessels to receive secret explanations and yet, as the teacher, one openly reveals these explanations regardless of who is present to receive them.

4.b.4(b.2) An explanation of the other enumerations:

> Bestowing empowerment without performing the root recitation; consecrating and engaging in action; showing the body mudrā to someone interested in the outer Dharma; and unnecessarily transgressing the two words of honor based on rules.

There are other faults that qualify as major transgressions. The first is giving empowerments to disciples before one has performed and accomplished both the root and accomplishment mantra recitations of the deity. The second is consecrating supports of the Buddha's body, speech, and mind (such as statues, prayer wheels, stūpas, and so forth) before one has fully accomplished the mantra of the deity and then engaging in spiritual activities such as fire-offering ceremonies and other rituals when one's personal qualifications and requirements are not complete. Moreover, it is a fault to openly reveal secret physical mudrās, postures, and exercises to others who, though unafraid of the profundity of mantra, have a stronger aspiration toward the outer causal vehicle of characteristics, the Sūtrayāna. If one has received prātimokṣa precepts, bodhisattva vows, and Vajrayāna words of honor, it is a major transgression to ignore the first two vow categories such as those prohibiting drinking liquor and eating meals after midday. (The exception to this is a specific Vajrayāna occasion, such as the gaṇacakra feast.)

4.b.4(c) Summing up:

> Although there are many enumerations of major transgressions, the *Kālacakra* explains them as minor faults.

According to this system, there are many other enumerations of the major transgressions. Except for the eight specifically mentioned, the rest are all considered to be less weighty and equal to the degree of harm caused through the deterioration of words of honor. The reasons for this are explained in detail in the great *Kālacakra* commentary. This completes the explanation of the common words of honor of the Nyingma and Sarma traditions.

4.b.5 A specific explanation of the words of honor according to the Nyingma tradition of the Great Perfection, in two divisions:

4.b.5(a) Briefly revealed:

> Specifically in the earlier translation tradition of the Great Perfection,...

"Specifically" refers to the Great Perfection tradition, which is virtually unknown in the tantric systems of the later translation schools. Thus, this explanation of words of honor belongs exclusively to the early translation lineage of the Great Perfection. Generally, "words of honor" means that one is literally bound by the honor of verbal commitment. A word of honor is also described as that which brings ultimate benefit through honorable maintenance and which brings ultimate destruction through deterioration. As is stated in the *Heruka Saṃcayatantra*, "If upheld, it is a cause of the greatest honor; if allowed to deteriorate, it is a cause for one to burn in hell." The uncommon divisions of the Nyingma tantric system are presented according to the tantra class, the transmission class, and the essential oral instruction class. Words of honor, samaya, are further defined in terms of being general, specific, and extraordinary.

First, the general samaya is to guard and maintain all the words of honor that correspond to the prātimokṣa and bodhisattva paths and to the three outer tantras of kriyā, upa, and yoga.

The second, specific samayas are the five root and ten auxiliary words of honor, explained according to the root tantra *Māyājāla* (*The Net of Illusions*). The five root vows have already been included in the explanation of the fourteen root downfalls. The ten auxiliary vows are explained within the context of the twenty-five words of honor. Specifically, these are the five that are not to be abandoned and the five that are to be practiced.

According to the root text of the transmission class *Saṃdhisaṃnipāta*, there are three root and twenty-five auxiliary words of honor. This enumeration has already been incorporated into this (Ngari Panchen's) system. The principal focus of this commentary is to reveal the third, uncommon division, the essential oral instruction class of the atiyoga words of honor. This is the third category of extraordinary samaya, which will be the principal subject of the following explanations.

4.b.5(b) Extensively explained in two divisions:

4.b.5(b.1) The root words of honor:

> ...concerning the root lama's body, speech, and mind, each of these three has nine categories, totalling twenty-seven.

The samaya of the Great Perfection includes two divisions: the simultaneously arising samaya of "nothing to guard" and the progressive stages of samaya maintenance. The first, the simultaneously arising samaya, refers to the primordial nature of all dharmas having transcended the need to accept or reject, an object to protect from, the activity of protecting (vows), and a protector. In the expanse of great bliss where saṃsāra and nirvāṇa are the very nature of equality, this profound awareness of the all-pervasive equality is actualized, and all appearances are nothing more than the play of the great primordial wisdom. Accordingly, there is nothing to guard, since all words of honor are simultaneously perfected.

The second division concerns the progressive stages of samaya maintenance, which are necessary because, although one may have received the profound pointing-out instructions, in order to fully realize the depth of the view and meditation, a faithful, diligent, and wise aspirant must enter the common door of knowing how to guard body, speech, and mind through the stages of progressive development on the path. In this way, the words of honor correspond exactly to the levels of progression as taught in the tantras.

The root words of honor correspond to the root lama's body, speech, and mind. For body, speech, and mind there are outer, inner, and secret words of honor respectively, bringing the total to twenty-seven.

In actuality, the essence of these root words of honor is to realize the indivisibility of one's three doors with the condensed essence of all the buddhas. This is likened to realizing the root lama's body, speech, and mind to be nondual as the three vajras. The very word "guru" implies weight, which can be interpreted here as the weight of the words of honor corresponding to the guru and how, if they are allowed to deteriorate, they will be difficult to restore. The Tibetan equivalent of the word "guru" is "lama," which means "unsurpassed."

Of the nine words of honor that correspond to the body, the first three are outer: to abandon stealing, sexual intercourse, and killing. The three inner words of honor are to abandon abusing one's vajra family, as explained earlier, including one's own body; abusing the Dharma and other individuals and striking one's own body; and forcing oneself to undergo unnecessary hardship, such as extreme ascetic discipline. The three secret words of honor are to abandon striking, or even attempting to strike, the body of a vajra relative (this includes verbal abuse or criticism of ornaments or adornments they may be wearing); making sexual advances toward the lama's consort; and walking on or over the lama's shadow or acting unconscientiously with body and speech in the presence of the lama.

The nine words of honor that correspond to speech begin with the three outer: to abandon speaking falsehoods, slander, and harsh words. The three inner words of honor are to abandon verbally disrespecting a Dharma teacher, anyone who contemplates the meaning, and anyone who meditates upon the fundamental nature. The three secret words of honor are to abandon disrespecting the speech of the vajra family, speaking negative words about the conduct of the lama, and disregarding any of the lama's teachings or advice as well as the words of those in his immediate entourage.

There are nine words of honor that correspond to the mind. The three outer are to abandon craving, ill will, and incorrect view. The three inner are to abandon any unconscientious and incorrect activity, to abandon incorrect meditation practice (practice distorted by dullness, agitation, mental wandering, and other obscurations), and to abandon the incorrect views of eternalism, nihilism, and grasping at the view. In addition, the secret words of honor include the abandonment of failing to maintain awareness of the view, meditation, and conduct throughout the three times of the day and night, as well as of not recalling one's own meditation deity and maintaining deity awareness, not practicing guru yoga, and not striving to develop loving-kindness toward the consort and vajra family.

These are the twenty-seven root words of honor corresponding to body, speech, and mind on the outer, inner, and secret levels.

4.b.5(b.2) The auxiliary words of honor are explained, in two subdivisions:

4.b.5(b.2.1) Briefly revealed:

The twenty-five auxiliary words of honor are the following:

The auxiliary words of honor are methods through which the root words of honor are guarded and maintained on the path. This is why they are auxiliary or branch supports. They are divided into five groups of five vows each, totalling twenty-five.

4.b.5(b.2.2) Extensively explained, in five divisions:

(1) The five actions to practice:

> liberating, union, stealing, speaking untrue words, and idle speech are the five actions to practice.

Concerning each of these five actions to practice, one must be unbound by any personal attachment or grasping. If one has realized the depth of the view arising from meditation, these actions will be performed solely to accomplish the purpose of others. Directly revealed, these five actions called liberating, union, stealing, and speaking untrue words are all performed to bring the minds of those who are extremely unruly and wild to the true spiritual path so as to restore awareness of their inherent buddha nature. This is also the outer meaning of utilizing idle speech. The hidden meaning is that the erratic flow of subtle air is set free as it is sent into the central channel. The desirous conduct of union ignites the heat and melts the essential fluids, which then descend through the major networks of channels to bestow the accomplishment of unchanging great bliss and emptiness. Stealing means to take the nectar from the consort. Speaking untrue words means to give explanations according to relative truth in order to avoid the extreme of nihilism. Idle speech means to speak openly about inexpressible realization.

(2) The five that are not to be rejected:

> Desire-attachment, hatred, delusion, pride, and jealousy are the five not to reject.

Desire, hatred, delusion, pride, and jealousy are well known as the five mental afflictions. Unlike on the path of Hīnayāna, here they are not viewed as threatening, so it is not necessary to reject them. Just as the nature of all dharmas is empty, since an object to reject is unestablished, likewise one need not erect a fence around a mirage of water. As it says in the *Vajra-tantra*, "The nature of all mental afflictions is that they are empty like an illusion. Recognizing the nature of impure awareness is to be liberated. If the method is skillfully maintained, it is not necessary to be bound by the mental afflictions. One can proceed directly on the swift path where rejection itself is unnecessary. If water penetrates inside the ear, adding more water will flush it out."

The primordial nature of the five mental afflictions is in actuality the nature of the five buddhas, expressed as the five primordial wisdoms. There is no need to reject their nature. If sesame oil is needed, one must first acquire sesame seed. Likewise, delusion is the samaya of Buddha Vairocana in that lack of awareness is not to be rejected, just as pure awareness cannot be accomplished, since in the sphere of truth they are both of one taste. Here, the hidden meaning is to understand the pure nature of the five mental afflictions. Similarly, the pure nature of delusion means to realize the nature of equality of all dharmas so that there is no partiality in the view and thus nothing to accept or reject. Desire then means attachment to the pursuit of nonconceptual loving-kindness and compassion. Aggression or hatred means the destruction of incorrect understanding concerning one's own pure primordial wisdom nature. Pride means uncultivated realization of the view of the nature of equality. Jealousy means the truth that dualistic view and conduct cannot be contained in the vortex of total equality. These are the five samayas of nonrejection.

(3) The five to accept:

> Feces, urine, blood, marrow, and semen are the five to accept.

According to direct revelation, if urine, feces, menstrual blood, marrow, and semen are accomplished according to the nature of truth, the essential nature is naturally accomplished, along with the potency of strength and blessings. These five substances also serve as medicines to remove the five illnesses[60] and are the substances through which the mundane and supreme attainments are achieved. Individually, it is understood that feces is Vairocana, urine is Amoghasiddhi, menstrual blood is Amitābha, marrow is Ratnasambhava, and semen is Akṣobhya. The five buddhas are the nature of the five primordial wisdoms, and through these substances the nature is revealed and realized. The hidden meaning is to realize that these five are the pure, inexhaustible, essential nature of the five aggregates, which qualifies them as the five to accept and utilize.

(4) The five objects to recognize:

> The five aggregates, five elements, five objects, five organs, and five colors are the five to be recognized as the deity.

All dharmas primordially exist as the Buddha: the five aggregates are the five male buddhas, the five elements are the five female buddhas, the five objects are the five female bodhisattvas, and the five sense organs and the five corresponding consciousnesses are the five male bodhisattvas. The five colors are the awareness of the five primordial wisdoms. All appearances are the arising of the deity in that all kāyas (pure embodiment) and qualities of primordial wisdom are recognized as the maṇḍala. Recognizing these five objects severs all doubt concerning pure awareness.

(5) The five to accomplish:

> The buddha, vajra, ratna, padma, and karma families are the five to accomplish. At the appropriate time, practice by embracing the enlightened intention.

By ascertaining the certainty of the view of the five objects to recognize, and by combining this realization with meditation, one must experience one's own mind as the nature of the buddha, vajra, ratna, padma and karma families. The direct understanding of these five, as well as their enactment, depends upon whether or not one is a beginner, has some degree of experience, and has realized the depth of the view. This would determine how to proceed, in terms of conduct, if one is in a group of people or in isolation. Otherwise, according to the hidden meaning, one must ascertain the enlightened intention and maintain conduct with skillful awareness.

Additional words of honor correspond to those times when an upholder of general and specific words of honor is proceeding with accomplishment practice or participates in an accomplishment ceremony. There are twenty additional words of honor, explained in indirect analogies, that must be maintained during such times. As it says in the *Mṛtyu-tantra*, "According to the scriptural explanation of the additional words of honor, guard them as extraordinary additions to the samaya!"

"Do not destroy the throne of the king of wild animals" means to never harm the body of the vajra master or disobey his or her words. "Do not pour poison on the rare Zamatok flower" means to not have intercourse with the lama's consort. "Do not cut down a precious new bush" means to not disillusion a faithful new aspirant. "Do not drink boiling lava" means to not use offerings made to the Three Jewels or to scholars and to not drink intoxicating beverages. "Do not expose the pollen heart of a lotus flower" means to not have intercourse with a vajra relative's consort. "Do not pour the essence into a bottomless pot" means to not rely upon a consort with negative characteristics. "Do not rely upon meaningless substances" means to not utilize unqualified and impure substances for practice. "Do not insert a crystal into mud" means to not abuse the noble qualities of the wise. "An impure vessel is not to be considered pure" means to not reveal the secret Dharma to immature recipients. "Do not cut a wish-fulfilling jewel" means to not abandon a qualified consort and suitable qualified disciples. "Do not separate the wings of a *garuḍa*" means to never be separate from the sign of bliss and emptiness (the union of male and female). "Do not strike with a sharp meteorite weapon" means to not fight with one's vajra brothers and sisters, even in jest. "Do not eat the leftovers of wild animals" means to not partake of the leftovers of others. "Do not destroy a great vajra rock" means to not aspire to control the lama's position or seat. "Do not cross the boundary of the corral" means to not enter into the boundaries of another's retreat or leave the boundaries of one's own retreat. "The wind cannot extinguish a butter lamp" means to not allow dullness or agitation to overpower one's meditative absorption.

"Abandon cutting off the flowing river of primordial wisdom" means to not cut off the flow of mantra or sādhana practice by speaking ordinary words. "Do not openly disclose the utterance, indications, and mudrās" means to not transgress the mudrā signs of empowerment or express the indications. "Do not destroy the diamond house" means to not disturb the maṇḍala of a mantra practitioner. "Do not bring the wish-fulfilling crown down to a low place" means to never lose awareness of carrying the vajra master upon the crown of one's head.

The activity of guarding all of these is the maintainance of the additional, extraordinary words of honor.

4.c Summing up:

> Although these and many other descriptions of words of honor have been taught, there is nothing that is not condensed into the root and branch words of honor described herein. In brief, if the three vajras are understood as one's own nature, then all one hundred thousand million classes of mantra samaya are complete.

According to the *Māyājāla,* there are fifteen root and auxiliary words of honor, from which three hundred and sixty are derived. According to the *Ākhyāta-tantra* there are ninety-seven words of honor. In the *Samānya-sūtra* there are four basic words of honor, twenty-eight common words of honor, four additional words of honor, twenty-three of uncontrived conduct, twenty to accomplish, four corresponding to behavior, the abandonment of the five demonic forces, the destruction of the four enemies, and further elaborations of the words of honor that correspond to the view. In addition, each tantra elaborates on individual root and branch words of honor to be guarded.

Further, there are words of honor corresponding to meditative equipoise, behavior, the partaking of food, objects from which never to be separated, and many other countless enumerations. However, concerning all of those root and branch words of honor, there is nothing that has not been condensed into the system of explanations described herein. (The two categories of root and auxiliary refer to that which constitutes the loss or total failure of one's mantra vows and that which causes deteriorations.)

The fourteen root words of honor of the Sarma and Nyingma traditions do not conflict with the specific words of honor of the Nyingma. The fourteen root words of honor are already inherent within the specific root words of honor, so there can be no conflict. The essence is to realize that the innate nature of one's body of channels, winds, essential fluids, and primordial wisdom is originally indivisible as the three vajra states of body, speech, and mind. Self-nature remains as vajra-like primordial wisdom. Recognizing this with wisdom awareness severs all traces of doubt. Here, all of the one hundred thousand million classes of mantra words of honor are spontaneously accomplished, and all faults are purified in the nature-as-it-is.

5. An explanation of the suitable support for the development of the words of honor:

> The support for development includes those who murder a Brahmin daily, those who commit the five heinous nonvirtues, and all others.

Those who qualify as suitable supports for the development of the vidyādhara words of honor are primarily those human beings with all six sense faculties complete. To compare the path of mantra with that of sūtra is like comparing a sharp ax to a dull one. If one wishes to cut down a tree with a dull ax, it will take quite some time to complete the task. On the other hand, if one's ax is very sharp, it is possible to cut the tree down instantly. The sūtra path of characteristics takes many countless lifetimes of merit accumulation before the ultimate result is obtained. On the path of mantra, not only is it unnecessary to first perform the two accumulations of merit, but one can engage in mantra without first specifically engaging in other vehicles. Even those who have killed human beings of high status on a daily basis or who have committed any of the five heinous nonvirtues[61] still qualify as suitable vessels for the development of mantra vows. In particular, through the profound methods found in mantra, individuals with sharp sensibilities, great mental strength, pure fervent regard, and keen aspiration will be able to realize buddhahood in one lifetime.

In addition, those who possess fortunate karmic conditions do not necessarily need the basis or support of a human body. In the tantras it clearly states that *devas* and titans may also qualify as suitable vessels. When the secret mantra was first brought into this world by Vajrapāṇi, who appeared to the five sages convening on the peak of Mount Malaya, four of those sages were nonhuman beings. In the land of Oḍḍiyāna, mantra was broadly propagated to all the nāgas residing there, and even arhats of extraordinary attainment must eventually enter the path of mantra. Therefore, it is taught that all beings with fortunate karmic causes inherently possess the cause for the development of the secret mantra words of honor.

6. If the words of honor deteriorate, the mode of their restoration is explained in two divisions:

6.a Briefly revealed:

> Later, if the words of honor are allowed to deteriorate, the manner of their restoration is taught.

After receiving mantra empowerment, one must persevere in guarding the words of honor from deterioration. If the cause for losing the words of honor results in the deterioration of samaya, the mode of their restoration must be clearly understood.

6.b Extensively explained in two subdivisions:

6.b.1 The methods for restoration

6.b.2 The faults of failing to restore broken words of honor

6.b.1 The methods for restoration are fivefold:

6.b.1(a) An explanation of the antidotes to be applied to the causes that produce downfalls:

> Not knowing what qualifies as a downfall, disrespecting the lama and others, unconscientious behavior, and an abundance of delusion are the four causes of downfalls, as explained by Asaṅga. The antidotes are to train in the words of honor, to develop respect for all, to constantly rely upon mindfulness and awareness, and to diligently train in the antidote for whichever delusion is predominant. In addition to the four actions to abandon, forgetfulness and dullness are included, bringing the total to six causes of deterioration. This is clearly taught in the *Śrī Saṃvara-tantra.*

Although one may have every good intention of maintaining the words of honor, if there is no study or understanding of the limits of what to accept and what to reject in order to avoid a downfall, downfalls will be difficult to avoid. If one has disrespect for the lama and others who hold the words of honor, one's own samaya will have no basis from which to develop. Even if one has respect, if one fails to see one's own faults, one will lack mindfulness and will thereby become careless and conduct oneself unconscientiously. Because of this, deteriorations will occur. Furthermore, although one may be careful, if one allows oneself to be overwhelmed by delusion, deteriorations will again occur. These are explained as the four root causes for deteriorations or downfalls according to the bodhisattva Asaṅga. Therefore, one must know the antidotes to apply to these four causes.

First, if one clearly understands the meaning of the words of honor and thereafter knows what to accept and what to reject, one can train accordingly. By developing joy in the beneficial qualities of both the lama and the disciples, respect for all of them will arise. Like knowing the threat of danger when confronted by enemies, by fearing one's faults and taking control of the mind one must consistently depend upon mindfulness, alertness, and conscientiousness. If one's mind stream becomes deluded in any way at all, immediately recognize this and apply the appropriate remedial force to transform it. Since forgetfulness and mental dullness are both strong causes for the deterioration of samaya, they are included with the four to total six root causes, as taught in the *Śrī Saṃvara-tantra.* The antidotes for the final two are to know and to clearly recall what is permitted and prohibited. One should be able to discern whether words of honor have been transgressed and should have a strong sense of personal shame and concern for how others will react if one allows the words of honor to deteriorate. Furthermore, all of the bodhisattvas of the past, as well as one's root lama, possess extraperceptive powers through which they are able to know what we do and think, so it is very necessary to be careful about faults and to have a sense of shame while in the presence of others, as well as when alone. As it says in the *Saṃvarodaya* (*Source of the Vows*), "If the supreme attainment is truly desired, it will be easy to forsake one's life to achieve it. If the words of honor are pure, the transition of death will be easy as well."

6.b.1(b) The degree of the weight of the downfall:

> A defeat is defined as a combination of object, intention, action, and ultimate deluded motivation; as knowingly contradicting any words of honor; as physically and verbally contradicting the actual practice with clearly recognized behavior and with no remorse; and as exceeding the time for confession. If all these prerequisites are incomplete, it is defined as a "downfall of exceeding the session," which is similar to a remainder. A stage below that is called a major transgression. A fault should be understood to be like a reflection of a downfall.

Here, the difference between a downfall and that which does not qualify as a downfall is explained. A defeat must have four branches to be complete. These four are the object through which the downfall occurs, the intention, the actual activity, and the ultimate fruition of the action, whether this occurs through body, speech, or mind. The three additional prerequisites are to possess a very deluded motivation, such as the certain knowledge that one's physical or verbal action will contradict the words of honor; performance of the action (either physically or verbally) until the nonvirtue is fully established; and clear recognition of the nonvirtue with no regret, thereby allowing the time for confession to pass. If these seven are complete, this constitutes a root defeat, as well as a total loss of samaya. With regard to all root downfalls, if one does not apply antidotes throughout the six times of the day and night, the obstacle of the "duration of the session" will occur. Failing to confess the downfall and allowing the time of the session to pass constitutes a defeat. This means that all antidotes for nonvirtue will have been destroyed or defeated.

A root downfall is defined as the loss of a root word of honor and a confession that is not performed before the session passes by. This is similar to a remainder, according to the prātimokṣa. Next to a defeat, a downfall carries the heaviest accumulation of nonvirtue. The next heaviest karmic negativity is a major transgression. This is defined as a deluded act without all branches complete. All branch failures are similar to downfalls, and all minor faults are similar to the fault category of prātimokṣa. For example, if one expresses anger toward a vajra relative with a truly beneficial intent, this is a mere reflection of a downfall.

6.b.1(c) An explanation of causes that do not constitute a downfall:

> Illness, loss of control, involvement in other activities, an important purpose, firm realization of the unborn nature, an important reason, finding potency, receiving permission, being under command, and avoiding an obstacle: these are all without fault according to the *Garbhālaṅkāra*.

These causes include ill health such that practice cannot be maintained, being overpowered by someone else, becoming involved in an activity that is great and necessary for accomplishing the purpose of others, firm accomplishment of the unborn absolute nature of truth, being led by others to accomplish something extremely meaningful, having accomplished power through meditative realization, having special permission granted by the meditation deity or another extraordinary object such as the root lama, having been given special orders by one's own lama, and avoiding a life-threatening obstacle. According to the *Garbhālaṅkāra*, if what seems to be a downfall occurs, and the cause was any of those mentioned above, this does not even constitute a fault.

6.b.1(d) Exceeding the time allowed for confession:

> Therefore, six times during the day and evening sessions, one must strictly examine the discipline of the words of honor of acceptance and rejection. If one of the six times passes, it is said that the duration of the session has expired. If one day, one month, one year, or two years pass, this is called a contradiction, a deterioration, a transgression, and a tear. However, in all cases, if confession is made from the heart, restoration is possible. The last category is the heaviest. If three years pass, restoration is impossible.

The six times refer to three times during the day and three times during the night. During each of these, one should examine to see whether or not one has contradicted the words of honor concerning what should be accepted and rejected. If any of these six times passes without checking and applying the remedial power if necessary, this qualifies as a transgression of the session. If a downfall occurs and remains unconfessed for one day, this is called a contradiction. If one month passes, this is called a deterioration. If one year passes, this is called a transgression. And if two years pass, this is called a tear. The more time passes, the heavier the negative karma becomes. Still, if any of these are truly confessed from the heart, restoration is possible. However, if three years pass with no confession, restoration is impossible. It is taught that if an individual with broken samaya comes to a teacher after three years and tries to confess the downfall, and if the teacher accepts the confession, both will be reborn in the lowest hell realm to endure endless suffering.

6.b.1(e) The actual restoration has four divisions:

6.b.1(e.1) The restoration method that relies upon the four empowerments:

> If one has received the seven empowerments, each deity's mantra is repeated thirty-six thousand times to purify. If one has received the vase and secret empowerments, if deterioration occurs, first purify through the appropriate method. Afterwards enter the maṇḍala and receive the four empowerments. If one has received the wisdom and word empowerments, if deterioration occurs, except for the generation stage, impeccable morality, the completion stage, and blessing of the mind stream, other methods will not purify.

According to the *Kālacakra-tantra*, for each individual empowerment there are different methods for purifying downfalls, each corresponding to the requirements for that particular empowerment. Within the vase empowerment alone there are seven categories, all of which contain the same antidote to be applied if a downfall occurs. The mantra of each deity in the maṇḍala must be recited thirty-six thousand times. If the words of honor deteriorate after one receives the vase or secret empowerments, then along with the mantra recitations mentioned above one must follow the specific advice for purification given by one's lama. If a deterioration occurs after one receives the fourth empowerment, one must confess the fault and, when a sign of purification is seen,[62] reenter the maṇḍala and again receive the four empowerments from the lama or through self-generation. In particular, if deteriorations of the wisdom and ultimate word empowerments occur, nothing will have the power to effect purification unless one retreats to an isolated place to meditate upon the nondual stages of generation and completion, the untransferable uncommon morality of the completion stage with and without characteristics, and the spontaneous blessing of one's mind. When signs of purification are observed, one should reenter the maṇḍala and once again receive the vows and empowerments. However, while receiving these empowerments and reestablishing the vows, one must not sit together with the senior students or receive offerings from others.

6.b.1(e.2) Restoration based on time:

> If opposition occurs, offer a gaṇacakra. If deterioration occurs, fulfill with possessions. If transgression occurs, offer one's son, spouse, or wealth. If a tear occurs, it is taught that one's life will restore it.

If the fault of a conflict with words of honor occurs, confession should be made while offering the gaṇacakra feast during the gathering of ḍākas and ḍākiṇīs. If the fault of a deterioration occurs, one must offer all of one's possessions to the lama or to the object involved. Confession occurs through this offering. If the fault of a transgression occurs, one's son, spouse, wealth, precious jewels, gold, and so forth should all be offered to the deities of the maṇḍala and to the lama.

If the fault of a tear occurs, then, with no concern at all for one's life, all effort must be directed toward serving the lama and the doctrine. In this way, one's own life becomes an offering—strengthened with intense remorse for one's mistakes—to the lama. This method of restoring the words of honor, which depends upon the degree of one's breakage, is clearly taught in the tantras.

6.b.1(e.3) The method of restoration as taught in the *Garbhālaṅkāra*:

> The restoration ritual found in the *Garbhālaṅkāra* is as follows: confessing before the field of refuge; purifying with mantra, mudrā, and the stages of cleansing, with the burning tummo fire, and with nonconceptual meditation; receiving the four empowerments; confessing to the gathering; speaking to the supports; offering maṇḍalas; constructing stūpas; offering fire and smoke; giving torma and reciting secret mantras; entering into profound meditative concentration; saving lives; reading the Buddha's words; relying upon the lama; practicing self generation; reciting the hundred syllables of the Buddha at auspicious times; reciting the *Triskandhaka*; and meditating on Guru Vajrasattva and the yoga of the subtle essence. All these methods will bring restoration.

According to the *Garbhālaṅkāra*, the mode of restoration is explained according to sādhana practice. After invoking the field of refuge, confession is made in their presence through the application of the four powers. Another method for purifying mantra deteriorations is to use mantra and mudrā. The *Vajra-atta-tantra* says that the six syllables for rebirth in the six classes are cleansed through mantra. Consider that there is a syllable YAṂ (ཡཾ) on the sole of each foot and a RAṂ (རཾ) at the entrance to one's secret place. At one's navel are the six syllables of the six classes, and on a seat in one's heart is PHAṬ (ཕཊ), the essence of body, speech, and mind. From YAṂ, primordial wisdom wind arises, igniting the primordial wisdom fire from the YAṂ in one's navel. This burns the seed syllables and all habitual propensities of the six classes, thus transforming the three doors into enlightened body, speech, and mind. As one recites PHAṬ, they dissolve into the sphere of truth. This is an extremely profound essential instruction.

Another method is to visualize that from the syllable BAṂ (བཾ), the essence of water, the Ḍākiṇī Māmakī arises. With the aspiration that all negativities may be cleansed, one then bathes in the water.

Another method for ordinary individuals on the path to avoid all faults and obscurations is the recitation of the Vajra Vidāraṇī mantra. This is to be recited and accomplished with the vase water, which is then used to cleanse one's body. By giving rise to the appearance of all empowerment deities in the space in front of one and by receiving the five empowerments, the stages of purification occur. Also, one may consider the syllable KHAṂ (ཁཾ) in one's navel, while in the heart one's negativities are visualized as a mass of flesh. By igniting the tummo fire, all negative karma and obscurations are burned. Another method is to meditate upon the wisdom of the three rounds: the nonconceptual awareness of subject, object, and action. By considering one's lama, one may also receive the four empowerments, or during the stages of the gaṇacakra feast one may make offerings and confession to the gathering of ḍākas and ḍākiṇīs. Yet another method is to offer the seven-branch prayer in front of an extraordinary fully consecrated support and to then confess through mantra recitation. This recitation may be performed out of intense sorrow, with a wailing tune. By offering to the maṇḍala one's body, wealth, endowments, and all useful possessions—including the root of all virtue—confession is rendered. Restoration is also possible by building or helping to erect stūpas or clay images of the Buddha and by offering large and abundant peaceful fire-offering ceremonies. One may also offer torma, which is symbolic of offering all of saṃsāra and nirvāṇa to the deities in the maṇḍala.

Other methods include reciting the essence mantra of one's own personal deity; meditating with profound concentration and the application of the meditative absorptions of quiescence and heightened awareness; saving the lives of insects, animals, and fish in springs and ponds; saving bees from honey farms; saving trapped animals; paying hunters not to hunt; assisting people who are ill; protecting others who are under sentence of death; assisting beings who are controlled by weapons; reciting the mantra that is an antidote for negativity and obscurations that is found in the *Mahāmokṣa* (*Sūtra of Great Liberation*); reciting the profound *Vimaladeśanā* (*Tantra of Stainless Confession*); and relying on the lama's presence at the crown of one's head. These are all methods that restore samaya. Still other methods include meditating upon Amoghasiddhi with consort in one's heart, while from the seed syllables in their hearts nectar descends to cleanse all negativity and obscurations; reciting OM AḤ KHAṂ HŪNG and receiving empowerment either from the maṇḍala in front or from oneself; reciting the heart essence mantra of all buddhas or the one-hundred syllable mantra of Vajrasattva at least five thousand times or more; reciting many repetitions of the essence mantra that purifies negative karma during the auspicious lunar days of the eighth and fifteenth; reciting the *Triskandhaka* during the six times of day and night; reciting the one-hundred syllable mantra while visualizing Vajrasattva above the crown of one's head; visualizing self nature as the deity and clearly visualizing the principal channels and cakras in one's body; performing the yoga of igniting heat and bliss by visualizing in the center of the five cakras a tiny hand implement of the corresponding buddha; and performing, with strong awareness, the yogic breathing exercises of the five buddhas. These latter methods are those of the meditation of profound yoga.

6.b.1(e.4) Restoring through the general cleansing of the three yogas:

> As is taught in the *Hasti-upapraveśya-tantra,* the general cleansing yoga of the nest of remorse is the "Stirring the Depths." By confessing in this way, there is nothing that cannot be purified. Practice this accordingly.

According to the tantra called *Hasti-upapraveśya* and the *Vimaladeśanā* contained within it, this is the sole text for practitioners of all three yogas who, having engaged on the path and then allowed their samaya to deteriorate, wish to confess and perfectly restore it. The king of all confessions is *Narakakhadāpravāsaprasphoṭana* (*Stirring the Depths of Vajra Hell*). Here, it is clearly taught that by offering the external gathering of offering substances, the internal gathering of one's own aggregates, and the secret gathering of the awakened mind of bodhicitta on the fifteenth, thirtieth, or eighth day of the lunar month, all deteriorations will be fully purified. If that is not possible, but one still makes prostrations and recalls the deity in order to confess, purification will occur. It is important to persevere in this practice as much as possible.

As is said in this text, "To all the enlightened peaceful and wrathful deities and to their maṇḍalas, I pay homage. I pray that I may cleanse all of my broken commitments without exception. There is no doubt that the five limitless nonvirtues can be cleansed and that even the lower realms can be emptied from their depths and that beings will be led to the well-known pure realm of the enlightened beings of pure awareness. Since Vajrasattva is the essential nature of secret mantra and cleanses all of our karmic obscurations and obscurations caused by broken commitments, in order to empty the realms of cyclic existence, recite the mantra."

Accordingly, if one just hears the names of the deities in this maṇḍala, all deteriorations of one's root and branch words of honor can be repaired. Signs of accomplishing the purification through confession include indications in the dream state; indications from the lama or deity; and dreams of bathing, putting on white clothing, ascending to the peak of a mountain, and the arising of the sun and moon and so forth. Until such signs arise, one should continue to make confession and apply the four remedial powers.

6.b.2 The faults of failing to restore broken words of honor:

> If one fails to make confession in this life, extremely unpleasant consequences will ensue. In the next life, one will be born in the vajra hell of irreversible torment and suffering.

If mantra words of honor are left unconfessed, this becomes a cause for rebirth in what is called "vajra hell." There is no place of greater suffering. As it says in the *Guhyagarbha,* "If the root or branch words of honor deteriorate, the result is that one falls to the lowest realm."

In the *Prakaṭitavicitra-tantra,* it states: "If a root word of honor deteriorates and no effort is made to restore it, one will fall to the vajra hell. If all the suffering of the ordinary hells were to be combined, that suffering would not equal one fraction of one hundred-thousandth of the suffering experienced in vajra hell."

It can thus be understood that even an association with an individual who has accrued this degree of negativity can cause one's own words of honor to deteriorate. Strong adverse effects may occur for those who even come into contact with such an individual. As it says in the *Sarvasamudita,* "Just as spoiled milk will taint all pure milk with which it mingles, a single mantra practitioner who has allowed his words of honor to deteriorate can spoil the words of honor of everyone with whom he comes into contact." Even if one precedes the breaking of samaya by discussing this with others as a means to communicate one's intention, this too must be immediately confessed. As it says in the *Mahānyūha,* "If one harms the lama, his or her retinue, or the vajra brothers and sisters by casually speaking negatively or by just a subtle sign of dissent, even if only in the dream state, this must be confessed and cleared from the mind. Actual and inadvertent neglect of samaya that remains unconfessed will cause one to fall headfirst to the hells."

According to these teachings, it is clear that the loss of any root or branch word of honor is a cause for rebirth in vajra hell. However, there are differences in the degree and duration of suffering experienced, which vary according to the severity of the downfall.

7. The benefits of guarding the words of honor:

> With no deterioration, the maximum will be sixteen consecutive rebirths; the minimum will be in this life, at death, or in the intermediate period. Other benefits include accomplishment of the eight common powers; the eight sovereign qualities; supreme spiritual attainment; and obtainment of the seven features of a divine embrace. For this purpose, spontaneously accomplish the twofold purpose of self and others.

The words of honor are the source of all noble qualities and are the very support for the stability and presence of such qualities. As it says in the *Samānya-sūtra,* "Just as the planting of a seed is dependent upon the earth in order for the result to mature, the life essence of the Dharma remains within the words of honor, which fully mature into the unsurpassed state of awakening as the precious life-essence of virtue."

Temporary benefits include the accomplishment of all that one aspires to obtain; an appearance that is pleasing to all; becoming an object of the veneration of others, including the most powerful worldly gods; and being blessed by the buddhas, bodhisattvas, ḍākas, ḍākiṇīs, and all objects of refuge, who guard one like their own child. Having understood the importance of pure samaya by entering the path of all the buddhas, one will quickly ascend the stages of vidyādharahood to realize enlightenment.

If in one's immediate life one is unable to persevere in the accomplishment of the two stages, yet never allows the words of honor to become defiled, then after taking sixteen successive rebirths enlightenment will be realized. This is the longest possible period of time it will take just through the force and purity of the words of honor alone. After at least seven rebirths, one will meet with the profound path of the two stages and gradually be liberated. The speediest result occurs if one maintains pure words of honor coupled with diligence in the two stages of practice, resulting in the realization of nondual vidyādharahood in that very life. Those of average sensibility will realize the illustrative clear light, which will become the actualization of absolute clear light at the time of their death, and the obtainment of the nondual kāya that arises from training. If the absolute clear light itself is realized, then at death the nondual kāya (arising from no-training) will be obtained. Those of common sensibility, due to their practice, faith in the lama, and strong aspiration for the pure realms, will be liberated in the bardo (*antarābhava*) [intermediate state] by arriving in the natural nirmāṇakāya pure realm.

These are not the only noble qualities that arise from pure samaya. In addition, both extraordinary and mundane spiritual attainments are obtained. The eight mundane spiritual attainments include the power to make an eye medicine, which, when applied, allows one to see without impediment or physical obstruction; speed walking; the sword accomplishment; seeing underground; making power pills; flying in space; disappearing; and extracting the essence. These eight powers are called mundane, or common, because they are still of this world and can also be accomplished by non-Buddhists. They qualify as accomplishments belonging to paths that are both worldly and transcendental. According to Vajrayāna, these qualities are developed during the two yogic stages and are thus termed common because they are not the ultimate result. In addition, the eight sovereign qualities are achieved.[63]

The supreme spiritual attainment is the attainment of self nature as the four kāyas, the five primordial wisdoms, and the nondual kāya that occurs without training. The different aspects of this attainment include the seven features of a divine embrace: the ability to completely utilize all aspects of the Mahāyāna doctrine; the perception of all form and all appearances as pure presence; the experience of unchanging great bliss; seeing that all dharmas are naturally without existence and beyond elaborations, and hence are of the nature of emptiness; the all-pervasive origin of mercy as nonconceptual great compassion; the experience of unchanging loving-kindness and constant engagement in the activation of its nature; and the ability, in accordance with the aspirations of each individual being, to ceaselessly manifest limitless embodiments of pure presence and entryways to the Dharma. The first four of these supreme spiritual attainments accomplish one's own purpose, whereas the latter three are expressions of the fully endowed ability to accomplish the purpose of others.

Summing up the chapter:

> This completes the fourth chapter, the explanation of the different levels of the vidyādhara words of honor of secret mantra.

The description of the vidyādhara words of honor and how to practice the uncommon extraordinary vehicle of secret mantra has now been explained according to the progressive stages of development.

Chapter Five: An Explanation of How to Practice the Three Vows Together without Conflict

III. Chapter Five: A Concise Explanation of the Manner in which an Individual May Practice the Three Vows Together without Conflict, in three divisions:

A. Briefly revealing the main subject
B. A detailed examination and explanation of the six branch categories
C. In conclusion, a brief explanation of how to practice all three vows

A. Briefly revealing the main subject:

> An individual who upholds all three vows must not confuse their distinctions, must fully perfect what to reject and what to accept, and must transform the nature, as the noble qualities increase with the higher vows. The crucial point is never in conflict when what is most important is maintained according to circumstances.

An individual who wishes to uphold and who purely maintains the prātimokṣa, bodhisattva, and secret mantra vows at the same time must know how to practice all three without conflict. The explanation given here is based on the sūtras, tantras, commentaries, and unmistaken teachings of the greatest scholars and realized masters of India and Tibet.

One must take care not to confuse one's understanding of the distinctions of the three vows. In addition, one must be knowledgeable concerning what to avoid and how to practice. One's practice must be fully perfected. One must also understand how it is that the essence of the lower vows transforms into that of the higher vows and the manner in which lower qualities are elevated as the higher vows are obtained. Although there may at times appear to be a conflict, the essential point will never be in doubt if one's practice is pure and complete. At all times and in all situations, one must examine to see whether it is suitable to employ the method of the lower or higher vow.

As it says in Longchenpa's *Samten Ngalso* (*bSam-gTan Ngal-gSo*) [*Relaxing in Concentration*], "The prātimokṣa, bodhisattva, and vidyādhara vows are purely kept without conflict by binding one's own mind, accomplishing the purpose of others to the best of one's ability, and recognizing whatever appears to be the path of pure perception."

Here, what is most important is an awareness of the six points, which will now be explained in detail.

B. A detailed examination and explanation of the six branch categories:

1. The method through which the three vows are understood, without confusing their distinctions:

> Without confusing their distinctions, the vows, the intention, and the rituals are all individually accomplished.

Each category of vows is received according to the intention maintained while receiving them. The rituals through which the vows are received are all different. At the time that one receives a vow, one embraces the nature of that vow. Then, as the next vow is received, the essence of what one already holds transforms into the next, without presenting any conflict. Each vow category will never deteriorate if it is maintained according to its own status. For example, the prātimokṣa precepts are taken for the duration of a lifetime, whereas the bodhisattva and mantra vows are taken until the essence of enlightenment is realized.

2. Perfect awareness of what to abandon and what to practice:

> Delusion is to be abandoned, and one's purpose should be uncontrived so that total perfection of the essence of each individual path prevails. Although there exist the individual paths through which to abandon and transform, all learned ones agree: that which is characterized as delusion must be abandoned.

According to all three vows, the object to abandon is the deluded state of mind from which all unwholesome accumulations arise. Dharma is that which serves the function of eliminating desire and attachment from the mind stream; and if something is introduced that does not eliminate desire, it is not Dharma. That which is understood to be necessary is the disassociation of the mind from deluded mental afflictions. For example, in prātimokṣa, sexual intercourse must be abandoned, whereas the two higher vow categories view sexual intercourse as a method. However, as a method, intercourse must be unstained by desire so that it is performed as a practice. Each vow category is maintained without conflict so that the qualities of each path concerning what to accept and what to reject can be fully perfected. According to the vehicle of the śrāvakas and the prātimokṣa precepts, delusion must be abandoned. The bodhisattvas recognize that delusion has no true inherent existence and thus transform it into the nature of truth, dharmatā. In secret mantra, the primordial wisdom nature of delusion is recognized and is thereby maintained as the path. In this way, while all agree that delusion itself must be abandoned, each individual approach and method is employed. For example, poison can be used in three different ways: it can be rejected, used as a component for making medicine, or blessed by mantra and partaken of. All three methods seek to make the poison harmless.

3. The essence transforms:

> If the prātimokṣa is practiced with the motivation of bodhicitta, this is known as the morality of abstaining from harmful deeds. Upon one's obtaining empowerment, it then becomes the vajra training. Its essence transforms accordingly, as is clearly established in the transmission of the *Pañcaśatasahasra.*

If delusion is left in its place, it will arise to affect the three doors, such that the karma that binds one to cyclic existence continues to accumulate. For this reason, one takes the vow to abstain from harmful conduct, which brings the temporary result of higher rebirth and ultimately leads to liberation. This is the prātimokṣa vow. Then, when one gives rise to the bodhicitta intention and great wisdom and engages in activities that are beneficial to others, this brings the result of the great awakened state. This is the bodhisattva's morality of abstaining from harmful activities, which brings together the essence of both prātimokṣa and bodhisattva practice.

With this practice as the basis, one then receives empowerment and maintains the great combination of method and wisdom to spontaneously accomplish the unsurpassed great awakening, and one's practice is transformed into the training of a vidyādhara. At this time, both prātimokṣa and bodhisattva practices—for one's own purpose with ordinary perception and to benefit others—transform into the nature of the mantra words of honor. This is clearly explained in the transmission known as the *Pañcaśatasahasra.*

Accordingly, once the mantra vows have been received, the two lower trainings are brought into the awareness of extraordinary wisdom and method. Ordinary perception is no longer present, and the essence of the vows becomes the general words of honor of Buddha Vairocana, which include the vows of all five buddha families.

4. The higher possess noble qualities:

> Due to the different intellectual capacities of the worldly, the practiced, and the fully practiced, the higher are capable of what is below. They possess noble qualities that suppress through splendor all that is below.

Just as there are differences between ordinary worldly people, practitioners with some experience, and advanced practitioners in the three trainings, those who have developed extraordinary abilities to skillfully employ the great method and wisdom give rise to the noble qualities they inherently possess. The display of this advanced level of skillful means is an expression of the development of qualities that are primordially perfected.

As it says in the *Guhyagarbha,* "In the supreme words of honor of the unsurpassed, the morality of the prātimokṣa and bodhisattvas is completely perfected without exception."

5. The essential point is not in conflict:

> If a yogin performs intercourse with the three recognitions, then the object, intent, action, and result are incomplete like a dream. It is impossible for this to oppose the essential point.

Here again, we must consider how the two lower vow categories are absorbed into the higher. According to prātimokṣa, the four defeats must be abandoned; bodhi-sattvas, while abandoning harming others, aspire only to bring them benefit. Although externally it may seem that the five words of honor to accomplish according to mantra are in conflict with this, in actuality they are not.

For example, one of the four root downfalls is sexual intercourse. If, according to the mantra words of honor, one engages in the practice of the three recognitions, although externally the activity appears to be intercourse it does not qualify as such. A qualified mantra practitioner has transformed both object and subject into the recognition of male and female wisdom deities, so that the first of the four prerequisites is incomplete. If any of the four prerequisites is incomplete, the act does not constitute a defeat. If ordinary desire is transformed into the recognition of great bliss, the intention is incomplete. The activity of union is incomplete because one is maintaining the words of honor concerning method and wisdom. Ultimately, the loss of seminal fluid and the experience and attachment that arise from sexual satisfaction are transformed into the experience of primordial wisdom awareness, within which the essential fluid is maintained as the ultimate result. The prerequisite of the result is thereby incomplete as well.

When one recognizes that all dharmas arise from the nature of the mind, like the experience of a dream, it will be impossible to contradict the essential point of mantra practice. As it says in the *Guhyagarbha,* "Unattached attachment, the nature of which is unattached, is the supreme king of all desire, the experience of great bliss."

6. That which is most important is maintained according to circumstances:

> When one is in a gathering or public circumstance, the lower vows have precedence concerning any negative action or nonvirtue. When

> free from desire, at the appropriate time and in isolation, practice secret mantra. If there is no internal conflict, perfectly guard them all. The wise teach that if there is a conflict, weigh what is necessary with what to abandon. Concerning beginners, the advanced, the accomplished, and even the all-knowing, their activities must be carried out with appropriate timing. This is explained in the *Kālacakra.*

As an upholder of all three vows, whenever one is in a gathering of others who are beginners on the path, one should refrain from activity that may appear to be negative. At such times, the code of prātimokṣa morality and behavior should be applied. Otherwise, if one is in isolation, and solely for the benefit of others, a bodhisattva is permitted to commit the seven nonvirtues of body and speech. The secret mantra practitioner is permitted to engage in secret practices which, although they externally appear as one thing, are only the reflection of a downfall and consequently bear no fault at all. In fact, these modes of conduct are necessary as methods on the path. As Guru Rinpoche said, "To internally maintain the conduct of the common tradition of secret mantra, it is necessary to connect with the absolute meaning of the generation and completion stages. Secretly, in order to be liberated in the body of light in one lifetime, it is necessary to maintain the tradition of the great secret atiyoga."

It is always taught to be extremely careful concerning one's conduct in the presence of others. Any conduct that would cause others to lose faith must be abandoned, and all conduct that is suitable to accept and incorporate must be perfected without conflict or confusion. If, in one's own mind, a conflict does arise concerning what is to be rejected and what is to be accepted, one must apply the antidote to remove delusion from one's mind stream. In such cases, it is important to consider the most appropriate action to take, depending upon the weight of the action and its result. For example, if one decides to abandon a certain response, this decision should be made by considering the potency of the effect. That response with the most potent result should be employed. If, by rejecting nonvirtue and harm, virtue and other qualities arise, it is then absolutely necessary to abandon the negativity. Understanding the general approach and the flexibility of exceptions is extremely important.

A vajra holder of the three vows does not behave thoughtlessly or casually. All actions are intentionally performed according to the appropriateness of the circumstance. A beginning vajra holder of the three vows is one who is still unable to transform the potency of alcohol through mantra or meditative absorption and who has not developed the power to transform poison. Even an advanced practitioner must approach the words of honor according to his or her level of development. If one has firm realization arising from the accomplishment of the two stages, one is then permitted to engage in conduct without acceptance or rejection.

One who has achieved these results has the temporary accomplishment of conduct free from the need to accept and reject, whereas one who has actualized the ultimate result of the primordial awareness of full awakening experiences every action as the natural expression of bringing boundless benefit to others. All of these individuals on their various levels—beginner, experienced, accomplished, or fully awakened—must still engage in conduct with appropriate and conducive timing and care. This is clearly explained in the *Kālacakra-tantra*, which states, "Beginners should not perform the conduct of yogins. Yogins should not perform the conduct of mahāsiddhas. Mahāsiddhas should not perform the conduct of the fully awakened."

C. In conclusion, a brief explanation of how to practice all three vows:

> The foundational support of all noble qualities is the prātimokṣa; according to potential, the awakened mind is generated upon that. These are branches of mantra practice. After receiving the ripening empowerment, the three vows must be guarded like one's eyes. With the generation stage of the recognition of the three seats as the deity, meditate upon the completion stage with characteristics and without. By uniting the stages of the conduct of close causes, in this life, at death, and in the bardo, perfect enlightenment will occur in the natural manifestation realm.

By clearly recognizing the faults of cyclic existence, the śrāvakas and adherents of the common path will develop renunciation as the basis for the seven categories of the prātimokṣa training. At least one of these vow categories must be taken as the basis for all further Buddhist training. Upon that ground, by recognizing the suffering of all sentient beings and wishing to accomplish the ultimate purpose by establishing them all in full awakening, the bodhisattva vows are received. Both of these categories are branches of the secret mantra words of honor. Although the nature of all sentient beings is originally pure, by failing to recognize their own nature they are caught in the snare of the suffering of negative causes and results. Recognizing this, and through the strength and depth of mercy and compassion for all sentient beings and in dependence upon the ripening empowerment, the words of honor of a vidyādhara are taken. Thereafter, one must understand the essential points of what to accept and what to reject as an upholder of all three vow categories, and must guard this training like one's own eyes. With awareness of the actions to guard against and the basis of the purification and the purification itself, and without separating from the view of the awareness of the three seats of the deity, one then meditates on the profound generation stage. Following that, one meditates upon the channels, winds, and essential fluids, which is the path of the method, the completion stage with characteristics.

After accomplishing each of these stages, one then meditates on the completion stage without characteristics. When the inexhaustible result is swiftly achieved through meditation, this is called the practice, or conduct, of close causes. In the case of one with superior sensibilities, the nondual kāya will be realized in this very life. The average practitioner will give rise to the nondual kāya at the moment of death. The common practitioner will be blessed by the truth of the dharmatā in the intermediate period between lives and will take rebirth in the natural pure realms of the nirmāṇakāya buddhas. One will then meet directly with Vajrasattva and the five buddhas and so forth, receive empowerment and prophecies concerning one's own time of enlightenment, and from there swiftly achieve the state of perfected buddhahood.

This completes the fifth chapter, a general examination of the progressive stages of the three vows.

Third: The Concluding Virtue

Having completed this explanation of the three vows, there are five remaining activities that will bring this text to perfect completion.

I. The cause for composition—great loving-kindness and compassion, how it was born in the mind stream:

> These days, without training, there is much talk about great accomplishments. This is a time when, without realizing even an atom's worth of their own primordial wisdom nature, deluded ones are satisfied with their own fabricated rituals. Thinking of the true source of refuge, tears arise from my heart.

These days, it is a common practice for those with great delusion to claim to be scholars and to boast of their abilities without first training well in hearing and contemplating the meaning of the scriptures and commentaries. In these times, many who have absolutely no realization of their own fundamental primordial wisdom nature, which arises only through practice, take great joy in practicing fabricated sādhanas they have created for themselves. To even think of these victims of these degenerate times, who have lost sight of the true and only refuge of themselves and others, causes unbearable pity and compassion to arise in the hearts of those with great realization. For the author, Ngari Panchen, uncontrollable tears well up from the depths of his heart.

II. The necessity of this composition:

> Although the paths of sūtra and tantra are seemingly without end, the Buddha taught them all as unmistaken paths to enlightenment. In this Land of Snow, this is unanimously agreed upon. However, the three vows still remain as mere names.

The limitless paths of sūtra and tantra relate to sentient beings' various receptivities and capabilities so that they may be led on the path to perfect liberation. Although this is the teaching of Lord Buddha, here in Tibet there are many with empty heads who say that sūtra and tantra contradict one another, like putting fire and water together, and who assert that one cannot maintain both without conflict. Even though the learned, who have investigated, unanimously agree that the three vows can be practiced by one individual, the ability to actually train in all three without conflict is still so rare that it remains a mere name. It is for this reason that these comprehensive explanations have been compiled.

III. The manner in which it was composed:

> Here, drawing from the many excellent explanations given by scholars and accomplished ones, I have arranged this with an attentive single-pointed mind. It is for this reason that I can boast that not even the scent of a fault is present here!

This composition was prepared by fully ascertaining the meaning of the sūtras and tantras according to the excellent explanations given by great scholars and mahāsiddhas and was done without any personal fabrication or bias. Therefore, I am certain that this text does not conflict with anything found in the sūtras, tantras, or essential instructions. Furthermore, I can claim that nothing explained here is misunderstood or mistakenly stated. Because of this, I do not possess even the slightest trace of the stain of remorse. All fortunate followers of this, the supreme path, can have total, heartfelt confidence in this text as an excellent treasure of unrivaled wealth.

IV. Dedication of the virtue obtained:

> By this virtue, may the status of the primordial buddha be swiftly obtained!

May the space-like mass of merit and virtue arising from the composition of this marvelous *Ascertaining the Three Vows* bring about the swift obtainment of the self-originating original state of the primordial buddha, indivisible as the five states of pure presence and the five primordial wisdoms, for the purpose of all sentient beings as limitless as space.

V. Finally, revealing how and where this commentary was composed:

> This explanation of the stages of *Ascertaining the Three Vows* was composed by the renunciate Ngari Panchen Pema Wangyal, born in the southern part of the snow-capped mountain range land of Tibet. At all times and in all directions, may there be the potency to engage in the activity of spreading the doctrine of the natural Great Perfection!

This commentary in five chapters is short and concise as a treasure of knowledge, transmission, and essential instruction. At the time that this text was perfectly completed without obstacles, all deities throughout space acknowledged their joy by sending a rain of flowers that fell from all directions. The place of composition was the cool land of snow mountain ranges. Within this land of Tibet, in the south in a place called Ngari Lowotang, a learned scholar of unequalled wisdom and compassion was born with the purest motivation of establishing all beings in the unsurpassed state of awakening. He was versed in all methods that accomplish the purpose of others and was fully accomplished in the five major and minor sciences. He became well known as Ngari Paṇḍita, Pema Wangyi Gyalpo, Dorje Drakpa Gyaltsen Palzangpo.

All individuals who wish to be liberated should immediately take up and wholeheartedly practice this expertly composed commentary, which is based entirely on the supreme speech of the Buddha himself.

May whatever virtue has been gained by this work contribute to the propagation of the doctrine of the Buddha throughout all realms in this world and throughout the three times and the ten directions. In particular, may the activities of the pinnacle of all paths, the natural Great Perfection atiyoga, be like powerful great waves of benefit, bringing ultimate bliss to all who come in contact with it.

Commentator's Note

The following prayer is made by the author of this commentary, Jigdral Yeshe Dorje, His Holiness Dudjom Rinpoche.

By distinguishing the initial, intermediate, and final virtues of the path,
like an all-pervasive wish-fulfilling treasure,
this is the supreme tradition of the fourth Buddha to come.
If not for you, King Trisong Detsen, who would have upheld it?

The initial virtue is to abstain from causing harm through the three doors.
The intermediate virtue is the primary accomplishment of the purpose of others.
The final virtue is the spontaneous accomplishment of the two purposes,
the great breath of the stage of unfailing invincibility.

Although still dwelling in delusion myself,
I have unerringly understood the meaning of this text.
Accordingly, I am able to make some small contribution of clarity
to this, your superior path.
By this, may the continuity of this unmistaken supreme path
perfectly remain until the fifth incarnation, Maitreya, appears.
By accomplishing this profound tradition of teaching, hearing, and meditation,
although the time of the five dregs has arrived,
this Dharma, never declining, will again illuminate this world with clarity
to bring the great fortune of benefit and happiness.
May there be the glorious auspiciousness of this doctrine
prevailing throughout all realms of existence!

At the age of twelve, I received an in-depth teaching on the root text *Ascertaining the Three Vows* from my lama of unequaled kindness, Orgyan Chöjor Gyatso, one of the principal lineage holders of *dzogchen,* Paltrul Jigme Chökyi Wangpo (Dza Paltrul Rinpoche). At the time of receiving these teachings, I made notes in the manner of a word-for-word commentary, and although my understanding of the meaning was unerring, some sections were somewhat obscured and repetitive. Because of this, when I reread the notes, their meaning was unclear and incomplete. Generally, due to my young age, the strength of my training and wisdom qualities were still underdeveloped. Then, as I was overcome by other circumstances and commitments, the writing of this commentary was postponed indefinitely.

Much later, due to the persistent requests of several lamas and tulkus who are disciples of mine, I decided while I was engaged in the revision of the Nyingma Kama to write this commentary as an addition to the Nyingma Kama with the hope that it would be of some benefit, although I myself have no such capabilities. In my eighty-first year, the Year of the Wood Rat, during the tenth month, I, Jigdral Yeshe Dorje, lay yogin of the Śākya family of the Devas, completed this in a Western country at Gawa Kyilwai Jang (the Center of Joy). My attendant Losal Sönam Norbu initially wrote it down, and the final copy was later completed by my disciple Ngaktsun Kunzang Wangdu, who possesses the fortunate karmic ripening of past virtuous habits.

> May the supreme secret tradition of Padmasambhava never deteriorate, and by continually increasing and expanding, may it arise to spontaneously and permanently prevail everywhere!

Sarva Maṅgalam

TRANSLATION OF THE ROOT TEXT

Ascertaining the Three Vows

A Branch on the Path of the Natural Great Perfection Called Ascertaining the Three Vows

Namo Guruve!

Homage to the Guru-Lama!

By churning the treasure ocean of the glorious two accumulations, the white light of knowledge and loving-kindness brings forth the all-pervasive rain of the definitive secret vehicle. To the supreme crown jewel of all scholars and accomplished masters of Tibet's Land of Snow, to the guide of all sentient beings, the Lake-born Vajra (Guru Padmasambhava), I pay homage!

This sage, skilled in knowing how to cleanse the mental stains of beings and upholding the lapis lazuli vase of supreme intelligence, bestows the ambrosia-like explanations of the three vows. May all those with sincere interest gather here to partake of this!

The general expression of primordial wisdom is the Great Perfection atiyoga. The perfectly pure embodiment, kāya, of the great Vajradhara is ultimate fruition, the oneness of buddha.

Although the ways of entry into the profound and extensive Dharma are beyond number, without relying upon the great secret path of maturation and liberation (Vajrayāna), there is no attainment, the perfected Buddha said.

Just as mental engagements are unceasing, one cannot possibly engage in all the inconceivable numbers of vehicles. As places to rest leading to the only true path, each one possesses its own corresponding pinnacle and result. Although these are obtainable as the individual renunciations of each vehicle, what result will be obtained without entering the one path of all vehicles?

Here, according to the tradition of the Great Perfection, the śrāvakabuddhayāna, pratyekabuddhayāna, and bodhisattvayāna are the three causal vehicles of characteristics; kriyātantra, ubhayatantra, and yogatantra are the three outer tantras; and the unsurpassed father tantra of mahāyoga, that known as the mother tantra (anuyoga), and the nondual tantric class of atiyoga are the three inner tantras (completing the nine vehicles).

It is taught that the individual upholders of the śrāvakabuddhayāna, pratyeka-buddhayāna, and bodhisattvayāna can enter the path of the vajra-holders. This is clearly documented in the *Tantra of Five Hundred Thousand Verses* (*Pañcaśatasahasra*). Since the mode of entering mantra depends on distinctions of sensibility, there exist many entranceways. However, this is not the principal subject of discussion.

Here, those of superior, average, and common sensibility, those fortunate ones of superior intelligence who have previously perfected all training, by receiving empowerment, instantaneously develop all three vows. As was the case with Indrabhūti, realization and liberation are simultaneous.

The average rely upon the individual ritual for each of the three vows, obtaining them progressively like Nāgārjuna.

The less fortunate common aspirants, whose minds are more difficult to tame, must gradually familiarize themselves with the purification training of the ten precepts, the four philosophical doctrines, kriyātantra, ubhayatantra, and yogatantra, after which they engage in the unsurpassed. This is taught in the *Tantra of the Two Investigations* (*brTag-pa gNyis-pa*).

Now, the specific method for the average will be discussed. Upholders of full, novice, and lay ordination qualify as superior, average, and common vajra-holders respectively. This is taught in the *Vajrakīlaya* and *Kālacakra-tantras.* However, those who possess primordial wisdom are held as foremost.

According to the root text of the earlier translation tantric class, the *Sarvasamudita-sūtra*: "One's own purpose, the purpose of others, and great benefit" are explained as the nature of prātimokṣa, bodhicitta, and abhiṣeka respectively. The individual upholders are well known among the learned as śrāvakas, bodhisattvas, and vidyādharas.

Therefore, the two lower, common vows are understood here to be branches of the unsurpassed anuttara empowerment. This is taught according to the ocean-like explanations of the tantric classes.

Penetrating the inner meaning and source of each of the three vows; initially, the way to receive vows that have not been previously obtained; afterwards, how to protect them from deterioration; and finally, if they become impaired, the way to restore them: These are the four steps that apply to each vow.

This general explanation of the stages of the main teaching completes the recapitulation of the first chapter.

In Varanasi, the Buddha primarily taught the Four Noble Truths and the practice of higher morality to the Five Excellent Ones. The teachings were compiled by Kāśyapa and others. The arhats composed the *Treasury of Particular Explanations* and other texts, which were propagated by Yönten Öd (*Guṇaprabha*) and Shakya Öd (*Śākyaprabha*). The precept lineage of the earlier translations was propagated by Śāntarakṣita and later by Śākya Śrī.

The nature is to take up the thought of renunciation; the foundation is to abstain from harming others. If born from the body and speech, it is objective by belief. In addition, it is believed to be the seed of the continuum of the "abandoning mind." In our school, this is according to individual views of higher and lower traditions.

The twenty-four-hour and lay ordination for male and female are the categories for laymen. Novice (male and female), female novice in training, and full ordination (male and female) are the five categories for the completely renounced. These are the eight divisions of prātimokṣa. According to the *Abhidharmakośa* tradition, if condensed according to type, there are four categories.

First, the manner for receiving vows not previously obtained is explained according to two traditions.

In the ritual of the past, through self-origination, primordial wisdom realization, a message, promising the Buddha, coming forward, the four requests, in response to the questions, taking the promise of the heavy dharmas, and so forth, the aspirants had pure minds and the preceptor was an arhat.

In the present-day ritual one must be free from the five certain circumstances (as well as from the obstacle of birth, such as birth as a neuter and so forth), and of circumstances such as not receiving permission from the ruler and so forth; in particular, not having the potential to drive away a crow; and the obstacle of appearance, such as having blond hair and so forth. Those with excellent karma have developed renunciation.

The abbots and others must possess knowledge of the excellently spoken vast and perfectly complete vinaya and be well versed in all of the one hundred and twenty-one disciplines.

Full ordination is received in progressive stages. However, permission is granted in the sūtras to "receive without doing the former." At the conclusion of three repetitions, the vows are obtained.

In the interim, the obtained must be guarded from deterioration.

The three uncommon refuge precepts are to not search for refuge elsewhere, to abandon harming sentient beings, and to not accompany a heretic. Respect must be generated for each.

To never forsake the Three Jewels, even for one's life or rewards; to not search elsewhere, regardless of how pressing the need may be; to not fail to make offerings at the correct time; to actively establish oneself and others in refuge; and, before traveling, to bow to the buddha of that direction: These are the five common precepts as taught by Lord Atīśa.

The abandonment of the four roots establishes morality. The abandonment of liquor establishes conscientiousness. To establish uncontrived conduct is to abandon three things: expensive and high beds, dancing and ornamentation, and eating after noon. These are the twenty-four-hour precepts. Because these eight branches do not remain permanently, they do not qualify as a prātimokṣa support for noble qualities. Only the seven precept categories qualify. Although guarding these eight branches for the duration of one's life is gomi lay ordination, according to the explanations of Vasubandhu in the *gomi Sthavira* (*gNe-brTen sDe-pai*) tradition, this does not exist in the Sarvāstivāda tradition.

The precepts of lay ordination are to abandon killing, stealing, lying, adultery, and all intoxicants.

To wish and promise according to enumeration is to maintain one vow, several vows, almost all, and complete training. This means the abandonment of either one, two, three, or five.

In addition, to abandon sexual intercourse is to hold "lay ordination of pure conduct." Scholars assert that both this and gomi lay ordination qualify as neither lay nor full ordination.

The six remaining nonvirtues and similar activity must be abandoned.

An upholder of lay ordination who is also a pure-awareness holder must, except for the signs and rituals of complete ordination, practice all that remains. This is explained in the *Subāhuparipṛcchā-sūtra* .

The abandonment of killing, stealing, lying, sexual intercourse, drinking alcohol, dancing, wearing ornaments and so forth, sleeping on expensive or high beds, eating after noon, and possessing gold and silver are the ten basic precepts (condensed as such to avoid discouragement).

Separating from the saffron robe and begging bowl, digging the earth, touching jewels and touching fire, eating after stopping, climbing trees, cutting trees, taking offerings, urinating or defecating upon grass, eating stored food, and destroying seeds are the thirteen exceptions permitted without fault. Otherwise, the practice of acceptance and abandonment is identical to that of the fully ordained.

Similar to "owning," possessing unstitched fabric for thirty days; similar to "separating," separating in the monastery; similar to "harboring," harboring is permitted.

Failing to reject the sign of a layman, failing to maintain the sign of a renunciate, and disrespecting the abbot are the three downfalls. Renunciation is to train in the precepts of a novice.

In addition to novice ordination, to refrain from traveling alone, swimming, touching a man, staying together, arranging a marriage, and concealing faults are the six root precepts.

To abandon possessing gold, shaving pubic hair, digging in the earth, eating unoffered or harbored food, and cutting grass are the six corresponding precepts.

The bhikṣu precepts total two hundred and fifty-three. The four root downfalls are known as the basis for all precepts. The basis is the body. All parts capable, in the birth canal, with a capable male organ, with an attached mind devoid of shame and fear, and engaging in the activity with the ultimate obtainment of satisfaction are the factors that comprise the total loss of pure conduct.

The basis of stealing is the wealth of another human being. The thought is to benefit oneself through the intention to steal. The object is one of value in its country of origin; and the activity is stealing with the ultimate thought to steal or to receive the object, even if another is engaged to obtain it.

The basis of killing is an unmistaken awareness of the object as another human being. The intention is to kill, with recognition of the object, and the activity is killing without hesitation or reversal, ultimately bringing about the cessation of life. This includes the condition of engaging another to kill, or expressing delight.

The basis for a lie is a human being with the ability to comprehend the meaning of words. The intention is to say something that will affect and change their understanding. The subject is one's own clairvoyance or noble qualities, which, although nonexistent, are promoted as an "unsurpassed" lie. Ultimately, if the object hears the lie, the vow is lost. Since any of these four root downfalls will defeat a bhikṣu, they are known as the four root downfalls or defeats, as taught by the All-Knowing One.

The thirteen remainders of the saṅgha are the following: emitting seminal fluid apart from the previously mentioned orifices; holding any part of a woman's body with attachment; due to attachment to a female, openly discussing sex; encouraging a female to engage in sexual contact with oneself as a form of offering; encouraging sex in order to arrange a marriage between a male and a female; for personal welfare, constructing a dwelling place larger than the permitted size; building a large house; uttering baseless or factual slander about a bhikṣu; dividing the saṅgha; supporting a schism and opposing one's precepts; causing laymen to lose faith; ignoring expulsion; and disregarding advice given to restore downfalls.

The thirty abandoning downfalls are explained as: keeping extra cloth for personal use for longer than ten days; separating from the saffron robe for the duration of one night; keeping unstitched robe fabric for longer than one month; allowing a bhikṣuṇī to wash the robes; receiving fabric from a bhikṣuṇī; asking for and receiving fabric from an unrelated lay householder; if offered, accepting more than one upper or lower garment; with the hope of receiving a saffron robe, enquiring as to measurements and value; begging for cloth by indirectly reminding others to offer; and receiving valuable jewels for the purchase of robes. Making a cushion with expensive silk; making a cushion solely composed of rare black wool; making over half of a cushion out of rare black wool; before six years of use, making a new seat cover; although owning a suitable cover, making a new one; accepting black wool and carrying it beyond three miles; allowing a fully ordained female to spin and wash wool; accepting gold or silver; receiving interest payments or profit; intentionally engaging in business.

Keeping an unblessed begging bowl for longer than ten days; keeping a pair of begging bowls; asking others to weave cloth without payment or gift; extending the size of the loom; taking back cloth given to a bhikṣu; receiving cloth before the given time; remaining for more than seven days in a secluded, frightful place without the three robes; keeping the rainguard more than one month after gagyei (*dgag dbye*; *pravāraṇā*) [the ceremony that concludes the traditional rainy season retreat]; personally receiving and keeping offerings dedicated to the saṅgha; harboring medicine for longer than seven days.

The ninety solitary downfalls are: knowingly lying; expressing the faults of a bhikṣu; slandering a bhikṣu in order to create a schism (although an intermediary has established harmony); reviving a quarrel; teaching Dharma to a laywoman; practicing Dharma with the unordained; verbalizing another bhikṣu's downfall (that leads to lower realms); truthfully expressing unsurpassed spiritual development; making accusations, ignoring the foundational training.

Destroying viable seeds; blaming to avoid personal abuse; not listening to instructions and responding incorrectly when one's downfalls are told; failing to put away the seats; leaving the cover spread out; expelling a bhikṣu; overpowering to harm; puncturing with the bed stand; tossing water and grass that contain living beings; knowingly constructing a temple with two layers of bricks.

What follows pertains to relationships with fully ordained females. Teaching Dharma without authorization; although authorized, teaching after sunset; teaching Dharma for food; having cloth sewn; giving away the saffron robe; traveling together for the same purpose; traveling here and there, together, in a boat; sitting together in solitude; standing together in solitude; and eating food requested to be made. These are the actions to abandon.

Eating repeatedly; staying and eating with a heretic for longer than one day; eating the contents of two full begging bowls; eating after completing a meal; intentionally lying concerning a downfall about rejected food; without permission, gathering and eating at the incorrect time; untimely eating in the afternoon; eating harbored food; swallowing any of the four medicines of unoffered food; and begging to receive delicacies.

Utilizing water containing living beings; sleeping close to cohabitation; standing in isolation; naked dwellers; watching the military; staying more than two days in a military camp; making arrangements for the military; beating a bhikṣu; attempting to strike another; concealing downfalls leading to lower rebirth.

Obstructing a bhikṣu from receiving food; causing to touch fire; speaking incorrectly about affiliation with the saṅgha's activities; sleeping more than the duration of two nights with the unordained; failing to reject the views of negative traditions; making friendly conversation; sleeping near a novice who has failed to reject negative views; wearing cloth of an unsuitable color; touching jewels, weapons, and musical instruments; unnecessarily bathing.

Taking the life of animals; causing a bhikṣu to develop regret toward ordination; tickling; playing with water; sleeping in the same area as a woman; frightening a bhikṣu; hiding a bhikṣu's possessions; with uncertainty, again using previously given objects; baseless abuse; traveling with a female who is unaccompanied by her spouse.

Similarly, accompanying a thief; bestowing full ordination before age twenty; digging the earth; although invited, staying and eating more than four months; claiming not to know; listening to discord; leaving without saying one has committed no harm; disrespectfully contradicting; drinking liquor; and, during the incorrect time of afternoon, going to town.

Accepting food in the afternoon from more than three families; sleeping in the palace of the king and queen; during sūtra recitation, claiming to understand; making an expensive needle-sheath; making a seat higher than the required measurement; with a harmful intent, spreading cotton on a cushion; making a seat cover, undergarment, rainguard, or saffron robe larger than the required measurement.

In the category of individual confession, there are four: in town, receiving and eating food received from a bhikṣuṇī in a household; eating without reversing a bhikṣuṇī's order; receiving and partaking of unfit food (according to the precept training); receiving and eating food in the monastery, rather than guarding the forest. These are the four.

The one hundred and twelve faults are known as: wearing the lower garment unevenly, too high, too low, like an elephant's trunk, with uneven folding, with bulging, and unnecessarily protruding. These are the seven corresponding to the lower garment. Uneven, too long, and too short are the three corresponding to the upper garment. These total ten.

Undisciplined, improperly dressed, chattering, gazing distractedly, gazing at a distance, covering the head, hiking up the garments, hanging over shoulders, clasping hands behind one's head, clasping hands at the nape of the neck, jumping, striding, walking on the balls of the feet, walking on the heels, embracing the hips, twisting the body, tossing the arms, twisting the head, embracing the shoulders, and holding hands. These comprise the twenty behaviors to avoid when going to a layman's home.

Sitting without permission; sitting without checking; dropping forcefully; stretching with legs crossed; crossing legs at the thighs; placing one ankle upon the other; hanging legs below the seat; sitting with legs spread; exposing the genitals. These are the nine to abandon while sitting.

Receiving improperly; receiving to the brim; receiving together; not receiving in order; glancing sideways at the begging bowl; opening the bowl too early; hiding the received and reopening; opening over another's bowl. These are the eight to abandon when receiving food.

Eating inappropriately, too much, too little, improperly, with an open mouth, or while talking; swishing; snapping; sucking; blowing; licking; eating individual grains; complaining about the food; shifting a mouthful around; smacking the lips; regurgitating; licking the hand; licking; shaking the hand; swirling; shaping the food like stūpas. These are the twenty-one to abandon while eating.

Looking at a begging bowl so as to poke fun; touching a water vessel with food stuck to the hand; sprinkling water; throwing dirty water without permission; keeping leftover food; placing the bowl on the bare earth, an edge, a steep hill, or steps; washing the bowl at an edge, a precipice, a steep hill, while standing, or in a strong current. These are the fourteen to abandon.

Teaching Dharma while standing or (while listeners are) lying down; while sitting too low; while following behind others; at the path's edge; with a listener's head covered or with clothing hiked up; with cloth hanging; with hands crossed at the neck or behind the head; with hair tied up; while wearing a hat, a diadem, or a mālā on the head; on an elephant; while riding a horse or in a palanquin or carriage; while wearing shoes; while carrying a staff, umbrella, weapon, sword, fighting materials, or arrows; or while wearing armor. These are the twenty-six to abandon while teaching.

The three manners to accomplish are to avoid the emission of feces and urine while standing; to avoid the emission of feces, urine, or mucus in water; and to avoid emission on grass.

To avoid climbing a tree higher than a human is the single vow pertaining to movement.

A fully ordained female has eight root downfalls, twenty additional remainders, thirty-three rejected downfalls, one hundred and eighty downfalls, eleven individual confessions, and one hundred and twelve faults. The total, therefore, is three hundred and sixty-four.

The manner through which to purify all lapses in discipline is sojong (*so sbyong*; *uposatha*) [confessional ceremony], yarney (*g. yar gnas*; *vārṣika*) [rainy season retreat], and gagyei (*dgag dbye*; *pravāraṇā*) [the ceremony that concludes the rainy season retreat].

The foundations of cloth, dwelling places, medicine, and so forth are taught elsewhere.

In brief, originally there were no sanctions or prohibitions. If something is suitable, it is permitted. If it is unsuitable, it is prohibited. If it corresponds to the unsuitable and contradicts what is right, it is taught to completely reject it.

With the exception of heretics, committers of heinous crimes, human inhabitants of the northern continent, nymphs, hermaphrodites, the five classes of neuters, those who change sex three times, and manifestations, the desirable supports for the vows to take birth include all male and female human inhabitants of the three continents.

Afterwards, in case of damage, the explanation of precept restoration follows: For the precepts to be lost, they are offered back, death occurs, two sex organs simultaneously develop, or sex change occurs three times. The weightiest cause of all, severing the vows from their root, is to hold the view that there is no cause and result.

Receiving ordination before age twenty and learning of it later terminates the vows of full ordination. A female novice in training who transgresses her promise in order to serve (beyond one night) loses her precepts. Each of these is uncommon.

If a root downfall occurs or the Dharma vanishes, the precepts are lost. According to the Vaibhāṣika of Kaśmīr, a vow-holder who commits a root downfall "possesses two," like having both wealth and debts. Some say that all vows deteriorate if one root downfall is committed.

Beginners, mental instability, intense illness, and inability to accomplish are without fault. Concealment is defined as not expressing a secret. It is not possible to make good a concealed root downfall in this life.

If there is no concealment and the act is openly revealed through confession to the saṅgha, recognition of the fault, and a vow not to repeat it, the fault is purified and the vow is retaken.

The vows pertaining to the thirteen remainders and others are gradually restored through confession according to their weight.

In brief, without bringing together the four powers there can be no confession. The power of remorse consists of a remorseful confession of previous deeds: a regret from one's heart, as though one had taken poison. The power of the antidote, like a medicine for poison, consists of an intensive activation of virtue in order to purify the fault. The power of restoration consists of the strength of the conviction never to repeat the fault, like never drinking poison again. Like reliance on a doctor, taking refuge and making confession (and so forth) with intense faith comprise the power of the support. These are the four to apply.

However, if even one powerful negative downfall occurs, the obtainment of a bhūmi is indefinitely postponed. The precepts must be guarded like one's eyes!

Receiving precepts in order to cure an illness or escape punishment, although clearing these conditions, is the morality of protection from fear. Receiving precepts for the sake of future lifetimes is the morality of excellent aspiration. Although the result—the bliss of gods and humans—is obtained, liberation is not.

If the vows are held with the morality of full renunciation, arhatship is obtained, as in the life story of Nanda.

The noble qualities of refuge in the Three Jewels and others are supreme in the latter (precepts). Since the initial precepts are the foundation for the later ones, the aspirants of bodhicitta and mantra must follow them accordingly. Thus, they are the basis for all noble qualities.

This explanation of the stages of the prātimokṣa-vinaya completes the second chapter.

Mahā Muni, the guide of sentient beings in this fortunate eon, at Vulture's Peak and elsewhere boundlessly taught the extremely extensive piṭaka to those of the Mahāyāna class. The *Gambhīradarśanaparamparā* (*Tradition of the Profound View*) was compiled by Mañjuśrī, elaborated upon by Nāgārjuna and others, and propagated by Śāntideva. The *Udāracaryāparamparā* (*Tradition of Extremely Vast Conduct*) was compiled by Maitreya, elaborated upon by Asaṅga and his brother, and propagated by Atīśa. Our tradition of Padmasambhava follows that of Nāgārjuna.

The nature is a mind moist with love and compassion that wishes to obtain full awakening for the sake of others, together with the intention to abandon all faults of the three doors.

The distinctions are well known as the two traditions of Nāgārjuna and Asaṅga. Each has from one to six, with two each.

First, compassion as the essence of emptiness; second, training in the two accumulations of merit, relative and absolute; third, the three trainings of morality, meditative equipoise, and wisdom, the motivation engaged in the aspiration of accumulation and preparation; and fourth, the seven impure stages with residual purity, full maturation of the three pure stages, and great loving-kindness as the complete abandonment of obscurations, the awakened mind of the state of buddha. These constitute four. The fifth is the five paths, and the sixth is the six transcendent virtues.

Earth, gold, the moon, fire, and so forth are the twenty-two examples of the levels of accomplishment within the ten bhūmis. All are condensed into the two categories of aspirational and practical awakened mind, within which the wish and action are complete, like wishing to go and actually embarking.

Initially, the manner in which to receive unobtained vows is from a virtuous, vow-upholding spiritual mentor, a disciple who is a suitable vessel for the Mahāyāna, inspired by faith. After the seven-branch offering, both aspirational and practical awakened mind are simultaneously received. Then, the meditation upon joy for oneself and others follows, in the tradition of Nāgārjuna.

Asaṅga's tradition is explained in this way: Although it is not necessary to have prātimokṣa ordination in order to receive the vow of the aspirational awakened mind, in order to fully receive all the vows, one of the seven categories of prātimokṣa must be received first. By enquiring about obstacles, promising to train, and so forth, aspirational and practical awakened mind are received through their individual rituals.

Both traditions agree that it is appropriate to use the conquerors as a support.

The vows are received at the conclusion of the third repetition.

The development of ultimate awakened mind through ritual occurs in the tradition of secret mantra. If explained according to sūtra, it is the nature of the promise that develops through the force of meditation.

After receiving the vows, the methods for guarding them from deterioration are the three moralities of the bodhisattvas: namely, refraining from harm, amassing virtue, and fulfilling the purpose of sentient beings.

To embezzle the property of the Three Jewels, to abandon the Dharma, to punish or expel a moral or immoral bhikṣu, to commit a heinous nonvirtue, and to hold incorrect views are the five pertaining to rulers.

The destruction of a dwelling, village, city, metropolis, or nation are the five that pertain to administrators.

Prematurely talking about emptiness to the untrained, thus causing them to take interest in the śrāvaka path; turning from full awakening in order to develop the Hīnayāna motivation; abandoning the prātimokṣa in order to train in Mahāyāna; as a śrāvaka, failing to reverse attachment and so forth and reversing, yet bringing no results; overpowered by jealousy, praising oneself and disparaging others; promoting oneself for the sake of gain and respect; instigating the punishment of a bhikṣu; taking the possessions of a renunciate and giving them to someone merely reciting prayers, thus causing someone to give up śamatha practice. These are the eight root downfalls that relate to common people.

Although the vows are specifically categorized, they pertain to everyone. They are mentioned as eighteen and classified as fourteen.

To forsake the aspirational and practical mind constitutes a root downfall.

The eighty auxiliary faults and others are minor in comparison and are not explained here. Refer to the *Śikṣāsamuccaya* (*Compendium of Precepts*).

Aspirational training according to the tradition of Asaṅga is to never mentally forsake any sentient being, to recall the benefits of the awakened mind, to accumulate merit and persevere in purifying the mind, and to aspire to correctly accept and reject the eight white and black dharmas.

To deceive an object of veneration, to develop unnecessary regret, to abuse the exalted, and to behave with an ulterior motive toward sentient beings are the four black dharmas to abandon. The opposite are the four white dharmas to fully accept.

Out of attachment to personal gain and respect, to praise oneself and belittle others; out of avarice, to not give ordinary material wealth and Dharma; out of anger, to harm others and fail to reverse the harm; and to teach impurely, fabricating the Dharma. These are the four root downfalls of practical training.

The forty-six minor auxiliary faults are explained elsewhere.

The amassing of virtue is the training in the six transcendent virtues. In order to alleviate poverty, give wealth, Dharma, and protection from fear. With a renounced mind, train in the three moralities. Patience is the endurance of anger, suffering, and the profound. Bring together the ceaseless effort that is armor-like, that amasses virtue, and that benefits others. Practice meditative concentration that is both worldly and transcendental. Maintain the profound wisdom of hearing, contemplation, and meditation. The morality of accomplishing the purpose of sentient beings is the practice of the four means of gathering. Initially, through generosity, the objects to tame are brought together. Then, through pleasing speech, their attentiveness is captured. They are then led through the nine vehicles, and their purpose is fulfilled. In order to guide them, one's own discipline is upheld. Train in all that is wholesome. Completely abandon all that is contrary. Continually rely upon mindfulness, alertness, and conscientiousness in the four activities of moving about, remaining still, eating, and sleeping. Purify all conduct in accordance with the sūtras, and pray to accomplish all that is conducive.

According to the sovereign of supreme knowledge, Longchenpa (*Klong chenpa*), the vows for aspirational awakened mind are the meditation of the four immeasurables, and the vows for the practical awakened mind are the practice of the six transcendent virtues. In brief, it is taught that these are condensed into the eight white and black dharmas.

Here, practicing all activities that bring benefit and bliss and rejecting all that is nonbeneficial and harmful is the essence of the training of both traditions that disregards nothing.

The support for development includes gods, nāgas, spirits, and others. Nāgārjuna taught that development occurs even in great sinners. Asaṅga taught that the prātimokṣa is a necessary support. In general, it is taught in the *Ratnolkānāmadhāraṇī* that, with faith in the Buddha and the Dharma and belief in the resultant unsurpassed awakening as well as the ocean-like pure conduct of the bodhisattvas, the awakened mind will be born.

If the vows deteriorate after they are received, this will explain how to restore them: Whoever fails to examine what is correct or incorrect, whether to do something or not, or whether to be indifferent contradicts what is correct and commits a downfall. In order to accomplish a greater purpose, the lesser may be forsaken. This is a reflection.

If there is no potential, there are no downfalls. To apply effort when there is no potential is also a reflection.

If they benefit others, the seven nonvirtues of body and speech are permitted because the purpose is virtue. If vows are allowed to deteriorate beyond a session, make prayers to Ākāśagarbha in the predawn. Confess all downfalls that occur in dreams. To purify remainders, recite the *Triskandhakanāmamahāyāna-sūtra* three times in the day and in the night. This is the tradition of Nāgārjuna.

The causes for losing aspirational awakened mind are the four black dharmas and the heartfelt abandonment of any sentient being. With unceasing shameless conduct and joy regarding the deed, to think that it is positive is a great delusion that destroys the vow. This is known as a defeat. It is not so if small or medium.

If a defeat occurs, the vow must be received again. State and confess the fault in front of three if medium, one if small. If there is no suitable person, confess with the mind. This is the incomparable tradition of *Udāracaryāparamparā* (*Extremely Vast Conduct*).

If the awakened mind is maintained accordingly, even while sleeping and during unconscientious behavior, the strength of merit unceasingly arises.

One becomes a bodhisattva, and in three, seven, or thirty-three countless eons, enlightenment is obtained.

This completes the third chapter, the explanation of the bodhisattva's training in the awakened mind.

The sovereign teacher, the vajra-holder Samantabhadra, taught the ocean-like classes of tantra in the great Akaniṣṭha. Later, at Dhānyakaṭaka and elsewhere, the teachings were once again revealed and compiled by Vajrapāṇi and the retinue of recipients, and elaborated upon by the eight great mahāsiddhas and scholars of India and Tibet.

Although the original translation tradition is known for the lineages of kama and terma, and though the latter tradition has boundless systems, a general explanation of the samaya of the tantric classes will be explained here.

The essential nature is to maintain awareness of method and wisdom with the three doors and the morality of the vows according to the individual traditions.

The distinctions are four: kriyā, upa, yoga, and anuttara. Each has individual enumerations of the fourteen root downfalls. These are explained in the *Kālacakra-tantra* and elsewhere.

The anuttara tradition adheres to the twenty-five uncontrived activities, the vows of the five families, the fourteen root downfalls, the major transgressions, and the tradition of the Great Perfection.

First, to explain the manner for receiving the unobtained:

The four types of maṇḍalas are those of colored sand, the bhaga, relative bodhicitta, and absolute bodhicitta. The vase, secret, wisdom, and fourth empowerments are progressively bestowed upon qualified disciples.

During the four periods of wakefulness, dreaming, deep sleep, and meditative absorption, subtle stains arising in the three doors are cleared. During generation stage and *tummo* (*gtummo*; *caṇḍālī*) [mystic heat] practice, the potency to meditate on both illustrative and definitive primordial wisdom and to realize the four kāyas occurs.

First, give rise to the three places as the three vajras. Later, at the time when the four empowerments are fully complete, the words of honor of a vidyādhara are received.

Thereafter, persevere in the training of commitments and words of honor.

In the interim, an explanation of the methods through which to guard the vows from deterioration is as follows:

First, according to the *Kālacakra*, the uncommon activity is as follows: Killing, lying, stealing, adultery, and drinking liquor are the five basic actions to avoid and abandon.

Gambling, eating unwholesome food, engaging in negative speech, and training in the spiritual traditions of elementals and titans are the five activities to avoid.

The killing of cows, children, men, and women and the destruction of stūpas are known as the five killings.

The five to avoid feeling aggression toward are virtuous friends, elders, the buddhas, the saṅgha, and one's spiritual mentor.

The five nonattachments are to have no attachment with the five organs (eyes, ears, nose, tongue, and body) toward form, sound, smell, taste, and touch. These are the twenty-five uncommon activities.

According to the common explanation, there are five words of honor for the five families.

The practice of the buddha family is to train in aspirational and practical bodhicitta and the three moralities. The practice of the vajra family is the vajra, bell, mudrā, and reliance upon the lama. The practice of the ratna family is to give wealth, Dharma, fearlessness, and love. The practice of the padma family is to maintain the outer, inner, and secret vehicles. The practice of the karma family is to maintain offerings, torma (*gtorma*; *bali*), and the stages of action.

The specific words of honor of the vajra family are the taking of life with the ten prerequisites, authorization, and realization established. Taking what is not given belongs to the ratna family. It is taught that with the pure intent to accomplish the purpose of oneself and others, one may steal wealth, another's wife, or the profound Dharma of the Mahāyāna. For the padma family it is taught to rely upon a female for action, Dharma, samaya, and mudrā. For the karma family it is taught to speak what is untrue, indicating the nonconceptual lack of true existence of self and sentient beings. The cakra (buddha) family must rely upon liquor, the five meats, and all objects. Upholding pure conduct of the outer, inner, and secret stages of the vehicles is the tradition of the unsurpassed (anuttara).

The fourteen root downfalls are explained as follows:

The first concerns heartfelt disrespect for the vajra master who has been kind in the three ways. To belittle him or disturb his mind is the first downfall because of its weight. The second concerns the utterance of the sugatas, who reveal what to accept and what to reject. This includes the lama's speech. To knowingly contradict it by engaging in unwholesome conduct is the second downfall. The third is becoming angry toward general, distant, close, and immediate relatives; holding a grudge; and showing jealousy, disrespect, and so forth. The fourth is wishing that any sentient being should be separated from happiness and losing heartfelt love for them. The fifth is, with a desirous mind and at an inappropriate time, intentionally emitting semen, thus forsaking the bodhicitta generated for sentient beings. The sixth is criticizing the philosophical doctrines of heretics searching for a path, śrāvakas and pratyekas on the path, and the great path of Mahāyāna. The seventh is openly revealing secret teachings to unsuitable vessels, to those with incomplete and unperfected ritual, or to those with deterioration or who fear the profound. The eighth is physically abusing oneself out of disrespect for the five aggregates, which are in actuality the five buddhas. The ninth is explained as doubting the innate purity and liberating nature of the foundation, path, and result. The tenth is failing to liberate or express love when there is potential and when the ten prerequisites are complete. The eleventh is intellectualizing the understanding of substantiality, lack of substantiality, and mental labels as the truth. The twelfth is failing to accomplish the needs of any sentient being who possesses the three levels of faith, failing to guard one's own mind, and being deceitful. The thirteenth is failing to rely upon necessary word of honor substances at the required time. The fourteenth is both generally and specifically disrespecting a wisdom female, directly or indirectly, in such a way that the female comes to know about it.

Now the major auxiliary transgressions are explained:

Relying upon a consort who has not matured through empowerment and samaya; physically or verbally fighting during the gaṇacakra; receiving the nectar of an unauthorized consort; failing to reveal the secret mantra to a qualified recipient; teaching something other than what has been requested by a faithful aspirant; staying seven complete days together with a śrāvaka; proclaiming oneself to be a tantric adept when the yoga of primordial wisdom has not been realized; and teaching unsuitable recipients. These are the eight auxiliary transgressions.

Bestowing empowerment without performing the root recitation; consecrating and engaging in action; showing the body mudrā to someone interested in the outer Dharma; and unnecessarily transgressing the two words of honor based on rules.

Although there are many enumerations of major transgressions, the *Kālacakra* explains them as minor faults.

Specifically in the earlier translation tradition of the Great Perfection, concerning the root lama's body, speech, and mind, each of these three has nine categories, totalling twenty-seven.

The twenty-five auxiliary words of honor are the following: liberating, union, stealing, speaking untrue words, and idle speech are the five actions to practice. Desire-attachment, hatred, delusion, pride, and jealousy are the five to not reject. Feces, urine, blood, marrow, and semen are the five to accept. The five aggregates, five elements, five objects, five organs, and five colors are the five to be recognized as the deity. The buddha, vajra, ratna, padma, and karma families are the five to accomplish. At the appropriate time, practice by embracing the enlightened intention.

Although these and many other descriptions of words of honor have been taught, there is nothing that is not condensed into the root and branch words of honor described herein. In brief, if the three vajras are understood as one's own nature, then all one hundred thousand million classes of mantra samaya are complete.

The support for development includes those who murder a Brahmin daily, those who commit the five heinous nonvirtues, and all others.

Later, if the words of honor are allowed to deteriorate, the manner of their restoration is taught.

Not knowing what qualifies as a downfall, disrespecting the lama and others, unconscientious behavior, and an abundance of delusion are the four causes of downfalls, as explained by Asaṅga. The antidotes are to train in the words of honor, to develop respect for all, to constantly rely upon mindfulness and awareness, and to diligently train in the antidote of whichever delusion is predominant. In addition to the four actions to abandon, forgetfulness and dullness are included, bringing the total to six causes of deterioration. This is clearly taught in the *Śrī Saṃvara-Tantra.*

A defeat is defined as a combination of object, intention, action, and ultimate deluded motivation; as knowingly contradicting any words of honor; as physically and verbally contradicting the actual practice with clearly recognized behavior and with no remorse; and as exceeding the time for confession. If all these prerequisites are incomplete, it is defined as a "downfall of exceeding the session," which is similar to a remainder. A stage below that is called a major transgression. A fault should be understood to be like a reflection of a downfall.

Illness, loss of control, involvement in other activities, an important purpose, firm realization of the unborn nature, an important reason, finding potency, receiving permission, being under command, and avoiding an obstacle: these are all without fault according to the *Garbhālaṅkāra.*

Therefore, six times during the day and evening sessions, one must strictly examine the discipline of the words of honor of acceptance and rejection. If one of the six times passes, it is said that the duration of the session has expired. If one day, one month, one year, or two years pass, this is called a contradiction, a deterioration, a transgression, and a tear. However, in all cases, if confession is made from the heart, restoration is possible. The last category is the heaviest. If three years pass, restoration is impossible.

If one has received the seven empowerments, each deity's mantra is repeated thirty-six thousand times to purify. If one has received the vase and secret empowerments, if deterioration occurs, first purify through the appropriate method. Afterwards enter the maṇḍala and receive the four empowerments. If one has received the wisdom and word empowerments, if deterioration occurs, except for the generation stage, impeccable morality, the completion stage, and blessing of the mind stream, other methods will not purify.

If opposition occurs, offer a gaṇacakra. If deterioration occurs, fulfill with possessions. If transgression occurs, offer one's son, spouse, or wealth. If a tear occurs, it is taught that one's life will restore it.

The restoration ritual found in the *Garbhālaṅkāra* is as follows: confessing before the field of refuge; purifying with mantra, mudrā, and the stages of cleansing, with the burning tummo fire, and with nonconceptual meditation; receiving the four empowerments; confessing to the gathering; speaking to the supports; offering maṇḍalas; constructing stūpas; offering fire and smoke; giving torma and reciting secret mantras; entering into profound meditative concentration; saving lives; reading the Buddha's words; relying upon the lama; practicing self generation; reciting the hundred syllables of the Buddha at auspicious times; reciting the *Triskandhaka*; and meditating on Guru Vajrasattva and the yoga of the subtle essence. All these methods will bring restoration.

As is taught in the *Hasti-upapraveśya-tantra*, the general cleansing yoga of the nest of remorse is the "Stirring the Depths." By confessing in this way, there is nothing that cannot be purified. Practice this accordingly.

If one fails to make confession in this life, extremely unpleasant consequences will ensue. In the next life, one will be born in the vajra hell of irreversible torment and suffering.

With no deterioration, the maximum will be sixteen consecutive rebirths; the minimum will be in this life, at death, or in the intermediate period. Other benefits include accomplishment of the eight common powers; the eight sovereign qualities; supreme spiritual attainment; and obtainment of the seven features of a divine embrace. For this purpose, spontaneously accomplish the twofold purpose of self and others.

This completes the fourth chapter, the explanation of the different levels of the vidyādhara words of honor of secret mantra.

An individual who upholds all three vows must not confuse their distinctions, must fully perfect what to reject and what to accept, and must transform the nature, as the noble qualities increase with the higher vows. The crucial point is never in conflict when what is most important is maintained according to circumstances. Without confusing their distinctions, the vows, the intention, and the rituals are all individually accomplished. Delusion is to be abandoned, and one's purpose should be uncontrived so that total perfection of the essence of each individual path prevails. Although there exist the individual paths through which to abandon and transform, all learned ones agree: that which is characterized as delusion must be abandoned.

If the prātimokṣa is practiced with the motivation of bodhicitta, this is known as the morality of abstaining from harmful deeds. Upon obtaining empowerment, it then becomes the vajra training. Its essence transforms accordingly, as is clearly established in the transmission of the *Pañcaśatasahasra*.

Due to the different intellectual capacities of the worldly, the practiced, and the fully practiced, the higher are capable of what is below. They possess noble qualities that suppress through splendor all that is below.

If a yogin performs intercourse with the three recognitions, then the object, intent, action, and result are incomplete like a dream. It is impossible for this to oppose the essential point.

When one is in a gathering or public circumstance, the lower vows have precedence concerning any negative action or nonvirtue. When free from desire, at the appropriate time and in isolation, practice secret mantra. If there is no internal conflict, perfectly guard them all. The wise teach that if there is a conflict, weigh what is necessary with what to abandon. Concerning beginners, the advanced, the accomplished, and even the all-knowing, their activities must be carried out with appropriate timing. This is explained in the *Kālacakra*.

The foundational support of all noble qualities is the prātimokṣa; according to potential, the awakened mind is generated upon that. These are branches of mantra practice. After receiving the ripening empowerment, the three vows must be guarded like one's eyes. With the generation stage of the recognition of the three seats as the deity, meditate upon the completion stage with characteristics and without. By uniting the stages of the conduct of close causes, in this life, at death, and in the bardo (*antarābhava*)[intermediate state], perfect enlightenment will occur in the natural manifestation realm.

This completes the fifth chapter, a general examination of the progressive stages of the three vows.

These days, without training, there is much talk about great accomplishments. This is a time when, without realizing even an atom's worth of their own primordial wisdom nature, deluded ones are satisfied with their own fabricated rituals. Thinking of the true source of refuge, tears arise from my heart.

Although the paths of sūtra and tantra are seemingly without end, the Buddha taught them all as unmistaken paths to enlightenment. In this Land of Snow, this is unanimously agreed upon. However, the three vows still remain as mere names.

Here, drawing from the many excellent explanations given by scholars and accomplished ones, I have arranged this with an attentive single-pointed mind. It is for this reason that I can boast that not even the scent of a fault is present here!

By this virtue, may the status of the primordial buddha be swiftly obtained!

This explanation of the stages of *Ascertaining the Three Vows* was composed by the renunciate Ngari Panchen Pema Wangyal, born in the southern part of the snow-capped mountain range land of Tibet. At all times and in all directions, may there be the potency to engage in the activity of spreading the doctrine of the natural Great Perfection!

OUTLINE OF THE COMMENTARY

Outline of the Commentary

This outline is divided into three major sections:

The Initial Virtue
The Intermediate Virtue
The Concluding Virtue

Within these three distinctions of virtue there are five chapters that comprise the commentary:

Chapter One:	A Brief Explanation of the Stages of the Main Teaching
Chapter Two:	An Explanation of the Prātimokṣa-Vinaya
Chapter Three:	The Bodhisattva Vows
Chapter Four:	Secret Mantra
Chapter Five:	A Concise Explanation of the Manner in which an Individual May Practice the Three Vows Together without Conflict

First: The Initial Virtue

I. The title of the text
II. Homage
A. General homage to the supremely kind guru
B. Specific homage to the great master, Padmasambhava
III. The commitment to compose

Second: The Intermediate Virtue

The actual text is divided into three sections:

I. A brief explanation of the stages of the main teaching
II. An extensive explanation of the nature and training of each of the three vows
III. A concise explanation of the manner in which an individual practices the three vows together without conflict

I. Chapter One: A Brief Explanation of the Stages of the Main Teaching, in three subdivisions:
A. Recognizing the basis for purification and the ultimate result
B. A general explanation of the different aspects of the path to accomplish

C. A specific explanation of how the average receive vows

A. Recognizing the basis for purification and the ultimate result
B. A general explanation of the different aspects of the path to accomplish, in three subdivisions:
1. A brief revelation of the one and only path
2. A specific explanation of how vehicle distinctions are merely steps on the path, in two subdivisions:
a. An explanation of the general characteristics of the foundational vehicles
b. A specific explanation of how all paths leading to liberation are included in the nine vehicles
3. Revealing the manner in which the prātimokṣa and bodhisattva categories are branch precepts of mantra vows, in three subdivisions:
a. Showing how upholders of each of the three categories qualify to enter the path of mantra
b. Although the path of mantra has many entranceways, this is not the present subject of discussion
c. Recognizing and establishing the purpose of this subject, in two subdivisions:
    1. A general explanation of the manner in which the superior, average, and common receive the vows
    2. A specific explanation of how the average aspirants receive the vows

    1. A general explanation of the manner in which the superior, average, and common receive the vows, in two subdivisions:
      1.a Briefly revealed
      1.b An extensive explanation in three parts:
      1.b.1 The manner in which the superior receive all three vows simultaneously
      1.b.2 The manner in which the average receive the three vows individually
      1.b.3 The manner in which the common aspirants are led to gradually engage in the three vows

C. A specific explanation of how the average receive vows, in five divisions:
1. An explanation of the higher and lower supports as well as the exception
2. Revealing the individual philosophies of each of the three vows
3. The manner in which the lower two are branches of the higher
4. In order to easily understand each of the three vow categories, the following three chapters set forth each vow as follows
5. A recapitulation of the first chapter

II. An extensive explanation of the nature and training of each of the three vows in three divisions, which comprise the second, third, and fourth chapters

A. Chapter Two: Prātimokṣa

B. Chapter Three: Bodhisattva
C. Chapter Four : Secret Mantra

A. Chapter Two: An Explanation of the Prātimokṣa-vinaya, in three subdivisions:
1. The manner in which Lord Buddha taught the precious doctrine of the vinaya
2. After the teachings were compiled, the way in which the teachings and accomplishments were upheld
3. The main topic of discussion, in two subdivisions:
a. A general explanation of the nature and distinctions of vows
b. A specific explanation of the format for the vow-receiving ritual

a. A general explanation in two additional subdivisions:
   1. The nature of the vows
   2. The distinctions of the vows
b. The specific explanation of the format for the vow-receiving ritual in five additional subdivisions:
   1. The manner in which to receive vows previously unobtained
   2. The methods that guard the vows from deterioration
   3. The physical support necessary to receive the vows
   4. The methods for restoring damaged vows
   5. The benefits of guarding the vows

   1. The manner in which to receive vows previously unobtained, in two subdivisions:
      1.a Briefly revealed
      1.b An extensive explanation, in two subdivisions:
      1.b.1 The ritual of the past
      1.b.2 The present-day ritual

      1.b.1 The ritual of the past
      1.b.2 The present-day ritual, in three divisions:
         1.b.2(a) The qualifications of the individual practitioner
         1.b.2(b) The qualifications of the preceptors, abbots, and others
         1.b.2(c) The manner of accomplishment

   2. The methods that guard the vows from deterioration, in two subdivisions:
      2.a Briefly revealed
      2.b An extensive explanation, in two subdivisions:
      2.b.1 An extensive explanation of the actual training in what to reject and accept
      2.b.2 Briefly revealing what is thereafter considered acceptable

      2.b.1 An extensive explanation of the actual training in what to reject and accept, in two subdivisions:

2.b.1(a) Training for lay householders
2.b.1(b) Training for the fully renounced
2.b.2 Briefly revealing what is thereafter considered acceptable

2.b.1(a) The first, training for lay householders, in three categories:
2.b.1(a.1) The refuge vows
2.b.1(a.2) The twenty-four-hour vows
2.b.1(a.3) The lay householder vows

2.b.1(a.1) The refuge vows are twofold:
2.b.1(a.1.1) The uncommon training for each of the Three Jewels of Refuge
2.b.1(a.1.2) The common training for each of the Three Jewels of Refuge

2.b.1(a.2) The twenty-four-hour vows, in two subdivisions:
2.b.1(a.2.1) An actual explanation of these vows, based on restriction of time
2.b.1(a.2.2) If taken as permanent vows, the manner in which they become known as gomi lay ordination

2.b.1(a.3) The lay householder precepts, in three subdivisions:
2.b.1(a.3.1) Recognizing the five abandonments of lay ordination
2.b.1(a.3.2) An explanation of the divisions of lay ordination based on enumeration in two divisions:
(1) The tradition of the Vaibhāṣika
(2) The tradition of the Sautrāntika
2.b.1(a.3.3) The corresponding training, in two subdivisions:
(1) The actual corresponding training
(2) Instructions concerning the training a tantric lay householder must follow

2.b.1(b) Training for the fully renounced, in three divisions:
2.b.1(b.1) An explanation of novice precepts for male and female
2.b.1(b.2) An explanation of the precepts for the female novice in training
2.b.1(b.3) An explanation of full ordination precepts for male and female

2.b.1(b.1) The novice precepts, in three subdivisions:
2.b.1(b.1.1) The actual precepts of the novice
2.b.1(b.1.2) Corresponding practice to avoid deteriorations
2.b.1(b.1.3) Corresponding precepts received at the time of preparatory ordination

2.b.1(b.1.1) The actual precepts of the novice, in two subdivisions:
(1) The four root precepts

(2) The six branch precepts
2.b.1(b.1.2) Corresponding practice to avoid deteriorations
2.b.1(b.1.3) Corresponding precepts received at the time of preparatory ordination

2.b.1(b.2) The explanation of the precepts for the female novice in training in two divisions:
2.b.1(b.2.1) Briefly revealed
2.b.1(b.2.2) Extensively explained, in two subdivisions:
(1) The six root precepts
(2) The six branch precepts

2.b.1(b.3) The explanation of full-ordination precepts for male and female, in two subdivisions:
2.b.1(b.3.1) That which must be rejected
2.b.1(b.3.2) That which must be accomplished

2.b.1(b.3.1) That which must be rejected, in two subdivisions:
(1) Briefly revealed
(2) Extensively explained in six categories:
(2.a) The category of root downfalls
(2.b) The category of remainders
(2.c) The category of rejected downfalls
(2.d) The category of solitary downfalls
(2.e) The category of individual confession
(2.f) The category of faults

(2.a) The category of root downfalls has three divisions:
(2.a.1) Revealing the basis in brief
(2.a.2) An extensive explanation of the basis
(2.a.3) Summing up

(2.a.1) Revealing the basis in brief
(2.a.2) An extensive explanation of the four root defeats:
(a) The root downfall of sexual intercourse
(b) The root downfall of stealing
(c) The root downfall of killing
(d) The root downfall of an "unsurpassed" lie
(2.a.3) Summing up

(2.b) The category of remainders, in two divisions:
(2.b.1) Briefly revealed
(2.b.2) Extensively explained
(2.c) The category of rejected downfalls, in two divisions

(2.c.1) Briefly revealing the enumerations
(2.c.2) An extensive explanation of the divisions has three categories:
(a) The category concerning clothing
(b) The category concerning cushions and seats
(c) The category concerning the begging bowl and so forth

(2.d) The category of solitary downfalls, in two divisions:
(2.d.1) Briefly revealed
(2.d.2) Extensively explained
(a) The category of intentional action
(b) The category of seeds and so forth
(c) The category of unauthorization and so forth
(d) The category of repetitive behavior and so forth
(e) The category corresponding to water and so forth
(f) The category corresponding to dwelling places and so forth
(g) The category corresponding to intention and so forth
(h) The category corresponding to visitors, thieves, and so forth
(i) The category of teaching Dharma and so forth

(2.e) The category of individual confession, in two divisions:
(2.e.1) Briefly revealed
(2.e.2) Extensively explained

(2.f) The category of faults has two divisions:
(2.f.1) Briefly revealed
(2.f.2) Extensively revealed:
(a) The one hundred and twelve faults are divided into nine categories. The first category concerns the wearing of clothing.
(b) The category concerning conduct while traveling
(c) The category concerning sitting on cushions or seats
(d) The category concerning receiving food
(e) The category concerning partaking of food
(f) The category concerning begging bowls
(g) The category concerning teaching the Dharma
(h) The category concerning etiquette to establish
(i) The single precept concerning movement

2.b.1(b.3) An explanation of full ordination precepts for male and female
2.b.1(b.3.1) The explanation of what a fully ordained female must train to abandon
2.b.1(b.3.2) The corresponding training to accomplish is in three divisions:
(1) The three foundations for all training
(2) The five foundational conditions for staying comfortable
(3) A concise, indirect revelation of what is permitted and conducive

3. An explanation of the physical support necessary for the vows to take birth

4. An explanation of the restoration of vows in the case of deterioration, in two divisions:
   4.a Briefly revealed
   4.b Extensively explained:
   4.b.1 The causes for losing precepts
   4.b.2 The actual restoration

4.b.1 The causes for losing precepts, in two subdivisions:
   4.b.1(a) The common causes
   4.b.1(b) The uncommon causes, in three categories:
   4.b.1(b.1) Specific individual causes for the loss of the precepts
   4.b.1(b.2) The specific differences of opinion concerning the loss of precepts
   4.b.1(b.3) An explanation of the causes that disqualify the development of a precept in order to discern whether or not this qualifies as a root defeat

4.b.2 The actual restoration, in three subdivisions:
   4.b.2(a) An explanation of the restoration divisions
   4.b.2(b) Revealing the manner in which all methods of purification are condensed into the four powers
   4.b.2(c) Instructions on how to carefully guard the precepts by recognition of faults

4.b.2(a) An explanation of the restoration divisions, in two subdivisions:
4.b.2(a.1) Recognizing the fault of concealment
4.b.2(a.2) An explanation of the actual distinctions, in two subdivisions:
4.b.2(a.2.1) Restoration of vows pertaining to root downfalls
4.b.2(a.2.2) Restoration of vows pertaining to remainders and so forth

4.b.2(a.2.1) Restoration of vows pertaining to root downfalls, in two subdivisions:
   (1) A concealed root downfall cannot be made good
   (2) If not concealed, it can be made good
4.b.2(a.2.2) Restoration of the vows pertaining to the thirteen remainders

4.b.2(b) Restoration through the application of the four powers
4.b.2(c) Instructions on how to guard the precepts through recognition of faults

5. The benefits of guarding the precepts have three divisions:
   5.a The benefits of morality alone

5.b The benefits of the prātimokṣa precepts
5.c The benefit of how the precepts are the basis for all noble qualities

B. Chapter Three: The Bodhisattva Vows, in three divisions:
1. The manner in which the Buddha taught the Pāramitā Piṭaka
2. After it was compiled, the manner in which it was taught and practiced
3. The principal subject, in two subdivisions:
a. A general explanation of the nature and distinctions of the vows to be received
b. A specific explanation of how to receive the vows

a. A general explanation of the nature and distinctions of the vows to be received, in two further subdivisions:
 1. The nature of the vows
 2. The distinctions of the vows, in three subdivisions:
  2.a Briefly revealed
  2.b Extensively explained
  2.c Summing up

  2.a Briefly revealed
  2.b The extensive explanation, in two subdivisions:
  2.b.1 The divisions ranging from one to six
  2.b.2 The analogies that exemplify the stages of awakened mind
  2.c Summing up

b. A specific explanation of how to receive the vows, in five subdivisions:
 1. How to receive unobtained vows
 2. Guarding obtained vows from deterioration
 3. The physical support for the generation of the vows
 4. If they deteriorate, the method of restoration
 5. The benefits of guarding the vows

 1. How to receive unobtained vows is taught in two subdivisions:
  1.a An explanation of the ritual for developing relative awakened mind
  1.b An explanation of how it is not necessary to perform a ritual to develop ultimate awakened mind

  1.a An explanation of the ritual for developing relative awakened mind, in two further subdivisions:
  1.a.1 Briefly revealed
  1.a.2 Extensively explained
   1.a.2(a) The manner in which to receive the vows is explained according to the two traditions:
   1.a.2(a.1) The tradition of Nāgārjuna
   1.a.2(a.2) The tradition of Asaṅga

1.a.2(a.1) The tradition of Nāgārjuna, in two subdivisions:
1.a.2(a.1.1) The type of individual qualified to receive the vows
1.a.2(a.1.2) The vow-receiving ritual

1.a.2(a.2) The tradition of Asaṅga, in two subdivisions:
1.a.2(a.2.1) An explanation of the type of individual who qualifies to receive the vows
1.a.2(a.2.2) The vow-receiving ritual

1.a.2(b) The explanation of receiving vows from a support (as an exception)
1.a.2(c) Recognizing the margin that indicates that the vows have been received
1.b An explanation of how it is not necessary to perform a ritual to develop absolute awakened mind

2. Guarding the obtained vows from deterioration, in three subdivisions:
2.a Briefly revealed
2.b Extensively explained
2.c Summing up

2.a Briefly revealed
2.b Extensively explained as the three divisions of morality:
2.b.1 The morality of refraining from harm
2.b.2 The morality of amassing virtue
2.b.3 The morality of accomplishing the purpose of others

2.b.1 An explanation of the morality of refraining from harm is given first and is explained according to the two traditions of Nāgārjuna and Asaṅga:
2.b.1(a) Nāgārjuna's tradition, in two subdivisions:
2.b.1(a.1) An explanation of the root downfalls
2.b.1(a.2) The auxiliary faults are explained elsewhere

2.b.1(a.1) An explanation of the root downfalls, in three further subdivisions:
2.b.1(a.1.1) An explanation of the actual root downfalls
2.b.1(a.1.2) A concise categorization of the supports for the vows and of their downfalls
2.b.1(a.1.3) Revealing how the abandonment of common aspirational and practical awakened mind qualifies as a root downfall

2.b.1(a.1.1) There are three divisions of actual root downfalls:
(1) The first division, the five that are closely related to rulers
(2) The second division, the five that are closely related to administrators
(3) The third division, the eight that closely relate to ordinary people
2.b.1(a.1.2) A concise categorization of the supports for the vows and of

their downfalls

2.b.1(a.1.3) Revealing how the abandonment of common aspirational and practical awakened mind constitutes a root downfall

2.b.1(a.2) The auxiliary faults are explained elsewhere

2.b.1(b) The tradition of Asaṅga is explained in two subdivisions:
2.b.1(b.1) Training in aspirational awakened mind
2.b.1(b.2) Training in practical awakened mind

2.b.1(b.1) Aspirational training is explained in two further subdivisions:
2.b.1(b.1.1) A general explanation
2.b.1(b.1.2) A specific explanation of the eight white and black dharmas

2.b.1(b.2) The training in practical awakened mind, in two subdivisions:
2.b.1(b.2.1) An explanation of the root downfalls
2.b.1(b.2.2) The auxiliary faults are mentioned elsewhere

2.b.2 An explanation of the morality of amassing virtue, in two subdivisions:
2.b.2(a) Briefly revealed
2.b.2(b) Extensively explained, in six subdivisions:
2.b.2(b.1) The transcendent virtue of generosity (*dāna-pāramitā*)
2.b.2(b.2) The transcendent virtue of morality (*śīla-pāramitā*)
2.b.2(b.3) The transcendent virtue of patience (*kṣānti-pāramitā*)
2.b.2(b.4) The transcendent virtue of ceaseless effort (*vīrya-pāramitā*)
2.b.2(b.5) The transcendent virtue of concentration (*dhyāna-pāramitā*)
2.b.2(b.6) The transcendent virtue of wisdom (*prajñā-pāramitā*)

2.b.3 The morality of accomplishing the purpose of sentient beings, in two subdivisions:
2.b.3(a) The actual practice
2.b.3(b) An explanation of the vows that correspond to the three moralities

2.b.3(a) The actual practice, in two further subdivisions:
2.b.3(a.1) Briefly revealed
2.b.3(a.2) Extensively explained
2.b.3(b) An explanation of the vows relating to all three moralities

2.c Summing up, in two divisions:
2.c.1 Repeating what other scholars assert
2.c.2 Establishing our own assertion
3. The suitable support for the development of the vows

4. If the vows deteriorate, the manner in which to restore them, in two subdivisions:

4.a Briefly revealed
4.b Extensively explained in three subdivisions:
4.b.1 The description of a downfall is given by revealing the "four dogmas."
4.b.2 Revealing how the seven nonvirtues of body and speech are permitted if they accomplish the purpose of others
4.b.3 The general way to restore damaged vows, in two divisions:
4.b.3(a) The tradition of Nāgārjuna
4.b.3(b) The tradition of Asaṅga, in two divisions:
4.b.3(b.1) Recognizing what constitutes the loss of a vow
4.b.3(b.2) Restoration of a downfall

5. The benefits of guarding the bodhisattva vows, in three divisions:
5.a The benefit of the development of unceasing merit
5.b The benefit of the transformation of name and purpose
5.c The benefit of attaining the unsurpassed status of awakening

C. Chapter Four: Secret Mantra, an explanation of the third root, the vajra vehicle of secret mantra, the training of all the vidyādharas, and the progressive stages of the samaya words of honor. The vajra vehicle is taught in three divisions:
1. An explanation of how the doctrine of the vajra vehicle originated
2. After the teachings were compiled, the manner in which they were practiced and upheld
3. Establishing the main subject, in two divisions:
a. Briefly revealed
b. Extensively explained, in seven subdivisions:
1. The essential nature of the mantra words of honor
2. The distinctions
3. Obtaining the unobtained
4. Guarding the obtained from deterioration
5. The support for generation
6. The methods of restoration
7. The benefits of guarding the words of honor

1. The essential nature of the mantra words of honor
2. The distinctions, in two divisions:
2.a The general distinctions of the four tantric classes
2.b The specific distinction of the anuttara tradition
3. Obtaining the unobtained mantra words of honor, in two divisions:
3.a Briefly revealed
3.b The extensive explanation, in five subdivisions:
3.b.1 A description of maṇḍalas
3.b.2 A description of the four empowerments
3.b.3 A description of separating and obtaining
3.b.4 A description of how the words of honor are received

3.b.5 A description of the margin of receiving

4. Guarding the obtained from deterioration, in three subdivisions:
   - 4.a Briefly revealed
   - 4.b Extensively explained
   - 4.c Summing up

4.a Briefly revealed

4.b Extensively explained, in five subdivisions:

4.b.1 The twenty-five uncommon activities

4.b.2 The vows of the five buddha families

4.b.3 The fourteen root downfalls

4.b.4 The major branch downfalls

4.b.5 A specific explanation of the words of honor taken according to the Nyingma tradition of the Great Perfection

4.b.1 The twenty-five uncommon activities, explained in two further subdivisions:
   - 4.b.1(a) Briefly revealed
   - 4.b.1(b) The twenty-five are explained in groups of five each:
   - 4.b.1(b.1) The five to abandon
   - 4.b.1(b.2) The five to avoid
   - 4.b.1(b.3) The five killings
   - 4.b.1(b.4) The five not to have aggression toward
   - 4.b.1(b.5) The five nonattachments

4.b.2 The words of honor of the five families, in two divisions:
   - 4.b.2(a) The common words of honor, in two subdivisions:
   - 4.b.2(a.1) Briefly revealed
   - 4.b.2(a.2) Extensively explained:
   - 4.b.2(b) The specific words of honor of the five buddha families

4.b.3 The explanation of the fourteen root downfalls, in two divisions:
   - 4.b.3(a) Briefly revealed
   - 4.b.3(b) An extensive explanation of the fourteen:
   - 4.b.3(b.1) Disrespecting the vajra master
   - 4.b.3(b.2) Contradicting the Buddha's words
   - 4.b.3(b.3) Expressing contempt toward the vajra family
   - 4.b.3(b.4) Abandoning love
   - 4.b.3(b.5) Abandoning bodhicitta
   - 4.b.3(b.6) Disrespecting other religious philosophies and doctrines
   - 4.b.3(b.7) Revealing secrets
   - 4.b.3(b.8) Disrespecting the aggregates
   - 4.b.3(b.9) Doubting the Dharma
   - 4.b.3(b.10) Failing to liberate if the ten prerequisites are met

4.b.3(b.11) Measuring the Dharma through logic
4.b.3(b.12) Causing someone to lose faith
4.b.3(b.13) Failing to rely upon the appropriate samaya substances
4.b.3(b.14) Disrespecting a wisdom female

4.b.4 An explanation of the major branch downfalls, in three divisions:
4.b.4(a) Briefly revealed
4.b.4(b) Extensively explained
4.b.4(c) Summing up

4.b.4(a) Briefly revealed
4.b.4(b) Extensively explained, in two subdivisions:
4.b.4(b.1) The eight major transgressions
4.b.4(b.2) An explanation of the other enumerations
4.b.4(c) Summing up

4.b.5 A specific explanation of the words of honor according to the Nyingma tradition of the Great Perfection, in two divisions:
4.b.5(a) Briefly revealed
4.b.5(b) Extensively explained in two divisions:
4.b.5(b.1) The root words of honor
4.b.5(b.2) The auxiliary words of honor are explained, in two subdivisions:
4.b.5(b.2.1) Briefly revealed
4.b.5(b.2.2) Extensively explained, in five divisions:
(1) The five actions to practice
(2) The five that are not to be rejected
(3) The five to accept
(4) The five objects to recognize
(5) The five to accomplish

4.c Summing up

5. An explanation of the suitable support for the development of the words of honor

6. If the words of honor deteriorate, the mode of their restoration is explained in two divisions:
6.a Briefly revealed
6.b Extensively explained in two subdivisions:
6.b.1 The methods for restoration
6.b.2 The faults of failing to restore broken words of honor
6.b.1 The methods for restoration are fivefold:
6.b.1(a) An explanation of the antidotes to be applied to the causes that produce downfalls
6.b.1(b) The degree of the weight of the downfall

6.b.1(c) An explanation of causes that do not constitute a downfall
6.b.1(d) Exceeding the time allowed for confession
6.b.1(e) The actual restoration has four divisions:
6.b.1(e.1) The restoration method that relies upon the four empowerments
6.b.1(e.2) Restoration based on time
6.b.1(e.3) The method of restoration as taught in the *Garbhālaṅkāra*
6.b.1(e.4) Restoring through the general cleansing of the three yogas

6.b.2 The faults of failing to restore broken words of honor

7. The benefits of guarding the words of honor

III. Chapter Five: A Concise Explanation of the Manner in which an Individual May Practice the Three Vows Together without Conflict, in three divisions:

A. Briefly revealing the main subject
B. A detailed examination and explanation of the six branch categories:
C. In conclusion, a brief explanation of how to practice all three vows

A. Briefly revealing the main subject
B. A detailed examination and explanation of the six branch categories:
1. The method through which the three vows are understood, without confusing their distinctions
2. Perfect awareness of what to abandon and what to practice
3. The essence transforms
4. The higher possess noble qualities.
5. The essential point is not in conflict.
6. That which is most important is maintained according to circumstances.
C. In conclusion, a brief explanation of how to practice all three vows

THIRD: THE CONCLUDING VIRTUE

Having completed the explanation of the three vows, there are five remaining activities that will bring this text to perfect completion.

I. The cause for composition—great loving-kindness and compassion, how it was born in the mind stream
II. The necessity of this composition
III. The manner in which it was composed
IV. Dedication of the virtue obtained
V. Finally, revealing how and where this commentary was composed

COMMENTATOR'S NOTE

Notes

1. Commentaries of *sDom-gSum rNam-Nges* by Tulku Tsultrim Zangpo, p. 695, and by Dzogchen Khenpo Yönten Gyatso, p. 84a/5–6.

2. See *Sems-Nyid Ngal-gSo* by Longchen Rabjam, p. 33b/5.

3. *Lam-Rim Chen-Mo* by Je Tsongkhapa, p. 518a/5.

4. *Lam-Rim Chen-Mo* by Je Tsongkhapa, pp. 518a/5.

5. *sDom-gSum rNam-Nges* by Panchen Pema Wangyal, p. 2b/2.

6. *bSam-gTan Ngal-gSo* by Longchen Rabjam, p. 4b/2.

7. Autocommentary of *bSam-gTan Ngal-gSo* by Longchen Rabjam, p. 14a/4.

8. Names up to this point are according to the *sDom-rGyun rNam-Thar* by Dharmaśrī, Vol. *ga*, *Lochen Sungbum* (The Collected Works of Lochen Dharma Śrī), and *Chos-'Byung* by Guru Trashi, p. 349/9.

9. *Chos-'Byung* by Guru Trashi, p. 715.

10. *Chos-'Byung* by Shechen Gyaltsab, p. 209b/2.

11. *Chos-'Byung Blo-gSal mGrin-Pa'i mDzes-rGyan* by Kongtrul Yönten Gyatso, p. 5a/5.

12. These names are from the *gSang-Yig* by Zhuchen Tsultrim Rinchen, p. 59b/4, *Deb-Ther sNgon-Po* by Golo Zhönupal, pp. 1-57/17, and *Chos-'Byung* by Pawo Tsuglak Trengwa, p. 505/11.

13. *sDom-gSum Nam-Thar* by Dharmaśrī, p. 29a/2 and *Chos-'Byung Blo-gSal mGrin-Pa'i mDzes-rGyan* by Kongtrul Yönten Gyatso, p. 6a/5.

14. *sDom-gSum rNam-Thar* by Dharmaśrī, p. 29a/2 and Commentary of *sDom-gSum Nam-Nges* by Dzogchen Khenpo Yönten Gyatso, p. 22b/3 and others.

15. Nāgārjuna and Asaṅga received the transmissions from Mañjuśrī and Maitreya

directly and in person, not in human forms but in wisdom bodies.

16. The four baskets are the following: the basket of moral discipline, vinaya; the basket of general discourses, sūtra; the basket of metaphysical instructions, abhidharma; and the basket of secret mantra (combining the essence of the preceding three). The eighty-four thousand categories correspond to these four in the following way: twenty-one thousand are concerned with the elimination of desire, vinaya; twenty-one thousand are concerned with the elimination of hatred, sūtra; and twenty-one thousand are concerned with the elimination of delusion, abhidharma. The remaining twenty-one thousand serve to equally eliminate all three.

17. The five major sciences are the following: the mechanical arts, healing or medicine, language, logic, and spiritual knowledge of the four baskets.

18. The term "vajra" is synonymous with space. There are seven qualities possessed by a vajra that qualify it as being of the nature of emptiness or space. A vajra is invulnerable, indestructible, authentic, incorruptible, stable, unobstructed, and invincible.

19. The five states of pure presence are the following: dharmakāya, the embodiment of ultimate reality; sambhogakāya, the embodiment of rapture; nirmāṇakāya, the embodiment of manifestation; svābhāvikakāya, the embodiment of the absolute nature; and vajrakāya, the embodiment of the unchanging vajra nature. The five primordial wisdoms are the following: ādarśajñāna (*me-long ye-shes*) [mirror-like]; samatājñāna (*mnyam-nyid*) [the nature of equality]; pratyavekṣaṇājñāna (*sor-rtog*) [discriminating awareness]; kṛtyānuṣṭhānajñāna (*bya-grub*) [fully accomplished action]; and dharmadhātujñāna (*chos-dbyings*) [the sphere of truth].

20. The three appearances are the appearance of the white flash of light, the arising of the red flash of light, and the near-attainment of the experience of blackness. These are the three final appearances just prior to the moment of death.

21. The path of seeing is one of five paths that lead to perfect liberation. When aspirants reach the level of spiritual development whereby they are able to see the meaning of absolute truth, they enter the path of seeing. This qualifies as the first level of the achievement of arhatship. Specifically, they realize the identitylessness of "self" according to the wisdom-knowledge that ascertains the nature as it is. However, on this level there is only a partial realization of the wisdom-knowledge that ascertains all knowable things. The principal meditation practice is the seven branches of awakening. These seven are the following: mindfulness, discriminating awareness, diligence, joyful gratitude, physical and mental suppleness, meditative absorption, and equanimity. The abandonment is the level of delusion corresponding to this level of spiritual development. The result is freedom from the five states

of fear and the development of the one hundred and twelve noble qualities. These are elaborated upon in the *Abhisamayālaṅkāra* (*Ornament of Direct Realization*).

22. The Five Excellent Ones are Ājñātakauṇḍinya, Aśvajit, Vāṣpa, Mahānāman, and Bhadrika. These five were the direct recipients of the Buddha's first Dharma discourse at Varanasi, India (present-day Sarnath).

23. Yarney (*g. yar gnas*; *vārṣika*) is explained extensively in the corresponding training section of the fully ordained.

24. According to the *Vinaya-kṣudraka*, the ten basic activities that were not permitted are the following: exclamations of astonishment; rejoicing if a saṅgha member commits a remainder; partaking of a small amount of intoxicating beverage if one is sick; digging in the earth with one's hands only; using salt at an inappropriate time of eating; after completing a meal, walking one kilometer's distance and partaking of food again; taking and eating food with both hands; mixing solid food with liquids and partaking of this at an inappropriate time; making a new cushion without a patch from a cushion that is at least six years old; and begging for gold or silver.

25. Sojong (*so sbyong*; *uposatha*) is explained extensively in the corresponding training section of the fully ordained.

26. The five foundational discrepancies originated with a monk who was actually a demon appearing in monk's robes, and who claimed that to answer others' questions (in other words, to take satisfaction in giving incorrect answers), to have ignorance, to have doubt, to imagine, and to nourish one's concept of a "self" are the five foundations of the Buddha's teaching. Other monks whose minds were influenced by his demonic energy believed in this, and for a time the saṅgha community adhered to these five points.

27. Within the Hīnayāna school are the two vehicles of the śrāvaka and pratyeka. The śrāvaka school includes the four root schools mentioned earlier as well as the eighteen minor schools that arose from the original four. The śrāvaka philosophical doctrine includes the tenets of the Vaibhāṣika and Sautrāntika philosophical systems. The Mahāyāna school includes the causal vehicle of the bodhisattvas, which maintains the tenets of the Cittamātra and Madhyamaka philosophical doctrines.

28. Abhidharma is defined as all aspects of inexhaustible wisdom, including the scriptures on developing the wisdoms of hearing, contemplation, and meditation in order to actualize inexhaustible wisdom. The spoken teachings of the Buddha as well as the commentaries that reveal the training in wisdom all fall under the category of abhidharma.

29. These eight are the following: receiving ordination from a male member of the saṅgha; seeking advice from a fully ordained male every half month; participating in yarney (*g. yar gnaṣ*; *vārsika*) [summer rainy retreat] with fully ordained males; participating in gagyei (*dgag dbye*; *pravāraṇā*) together with fully ordained males; not speaking out when a fully ordained male has impaired his morality; not teasing or ridiculing a fully ordained male; even though a fully ordained male is new, prostrating and showing due respect; confessing before a fully ordained male if any of the eight heavy dharmas have been committed.

30. The three states of nirvāṇa are the nirvāṇa of a śrāvaka, pratyeka, or bodhisattva.

31. "Stealing a valuable article" is basically an undetermined point in terms of what is considered to be of value. Usually this would be determined by the country of residence at the time in question. The value of the object under consideration should be according to the place and time it exists, so that it would be considered valuable enough to be missed if stolen or taken from one's possession.

32. Gagyei (*dgag dbye*; *pravāraṇa*) is one of the three principal ceremonies performed in order to purify the prātimokṣa precepts. (The other two are sojong (uposatha) and yarney (vārṣika)). During the time of yarney the bhikṣus are not allowed to speak of the faults or downfalls of other bhikṣus, to be punished for downfalls, or to distribute the offerings received. In addition, they are not allowed to spend one night outside the confines of the monastery. When all of these rules are lifted at the conclusion of yarney this is called gagyei (to lift the restrictions). There is a special ceremony performed at this time that the entire saṅgha participates in. Gagyei itself has three divisions. The first of these is time-based, the second is uncertain, the third is a gathering of bhikṣus.

33. The term "naked dweller" refers to one of the non-Buddhist philosophical schools known as Jain. The Jain do not think nakedness is shameful. They must go out begging for alms in any and all directions, at which time they do not cover their bodies with any garments.

34. It is said that the Buddha's body was extremely large, some three times larger than an ordinary human being's body of the present day. (An ordinary height would be considered to be roughly five feet five inches.) The length and width of the Buddha's saffron robe was five by three cubits measured according to his own arm's length. Therefore, if an ordinary bhikṣu were to make a robe the same as these measurements it would be fifteen by nine cubits in size. This would be to commit the tenth downfall.

35. Śamatha (quiescence) is the basis for any meditation that employs single-pointed absorption. Śamatha is practiced in order to reverse the mind from pursuing

objective appearances with distraction and to allow the mind to remain upon its object of meditation. The mind that remains single-pointedly absorbed upon its object is called śamatha. Vipaśyanā (heightened awareness) is the ability to perceive the true nature of substances with the eye of penetrative insight.

36. The five paths are the following: the path of accumulation, the path of preparation, the path of seeing, the path of meditation, and the path of no more learning.

37. The thirty-seven limbs of enlightenment include the four close contemplations, the four perfect abandonments, the four miraculous legs of transformation, the five purified mental faculties, the five forces, the seven limbs of enlightenment, and the eight noble paths. The four close contemplations are visualizations employed while meditating on vipaśyanā (heightened awareness). This involves visualizing the body, feeling, mind, and all knowable things. The four perfect abandonments are to purely abandon all nonvirtue that arises in the mind, to prevent any nonvirtue from developing, to develop virtue that is undeveloped, and to increase all virtue that has been developed. The four miraculous legs of transformation are achieved on the first stage of the most advanced level of the path of accumulation. They are the absorption of aspiration, perseverance, thought, and analysis. The five purified mental faculties are faith, virtuous effort, mindfulness, concentration, and wisdom. The five forces are the force of faith, enthusiastic perseverance, mindfulness, concentration, and wisdom. The seven limbs of enlightenment are the practice of nondual concentration and wisdom, which are auxiliaries to enlightenment. They are mindfulness, wisdom, effort, joy, suppleness, concentration, and equanimity. The eight noble paths are perfectly pure view, thought, speech, action, livelihood, effort, mindfulness, and concentration.

38. The fourfold accomplishment of the śrāvakas refers to the level of constantly abiding on the path as an enterer, the level of an enterer who is a once-returner, the level of an enterer as a never-returner, and abiding as a foe-destroyer (arhat).

39. The *Treatise on the Three Aggregates* is a collection of sūtras that deal with the three subjects of homage, confession, and dedication.

40. The five types of hermaphrodites are the following: an individual who possesses neither male nor female genitals; an individual who changes sexual gender every half month (after fifteen days, changing from male to female or from female to male); an individual who at the time of a sexual encounter changes gender spontaneously; a male individual who, overcome by jealousy when seeing a female, experiences a transformation of sexual gender or a female, or who, overcome by jealousy upon viewing a male, experiences a spontaneous sex transformation; and an individual who initially possesses genitals and later loses them.

41. The Nyingma school follows the vinaya tradition of the Sarvāstivāda school of the śrāvakas. Accordingly, the vows are lost according to the common and uncommon causes elaborated upon in the text.

42. Arhatship is defined as the total elimination of the four māras (negative forces), resulting in the achievement of the status of a foe-destroyer, or arhat. A śrāvaka arhat is one who has completely eliminated all gross or coarse deluded obscurations. A pratyeka arhat is one who has actualized a partial realization of the identitylessness of "self" and appearances based on his or her own personal practice without reliance upon a spiritual guide. This is done by investigating the nature of truth based on interdependency. A fully awakened arhat is one who has fully abandoned the two obscurations (gross and subtle) and all habitual propensities that remain. In addition, the two states of omniscient wisdom knowledge are fully developed.

43. Nirvāṇa "without traces" occurs at the very moment that all deluded obscurations are eliminated. Simultaneously, life terminates and the consciousness no longer relies upon the aggregates, thus passing beyond the suffering of cyclic existence.

44. The twelve miraculous deeds of the Buddha are the following: descending from the Tuṣita pure realm, entering the womb of his mother, taking birth, displaying his skill in the worldly arts, enjoying pleasure with the women of the harem, renouncing the world and receiving ordination as a monk, practicing arduous asceticism, meditating under the Bodhi tree, defeating the host of māras (demonic forces), attaining perfect enlightenment, turning the wheel of the doctrine, and finally passing into the state of permanent peace, parinirvāṇa.

45. The six treatises on the Middle Way are the following: *Prajñanāmamūla madhamaka-śāstra* (*The Fundamental Treatise on the Middle Way*), *Ratnāvalī* (*The Precious Garland*), *Yuktiṣaṣṭika* (*The Sixty Verses of Reasoning*), *Śūnyatāsaptati* (*Seventy Verses on Emptiness*), *Vigrahavyāvartanī* (*The Refutation of Wrong Views*), and *Vaidalyasūtra* (*The Thorough Investigation*).

46. These Five Great Commentaries are the following: *Mahāyāna Sūtrālaṃkāra* (*The Ornament of Mahāyāna Discourses*), *Abhisamayālaṃkāra* (*The Ornament of Clear Realization*), *Madhyāntavibhaṅga* (*Clear Distinction Between the Middle Way and Extremes*), *Dharmadharmatāvibhaṅga* (*Clear Distinction Between Phenomena and Reality*), and *Uttaratantra* (*The Sublime Continuum*).

47. The eight *Prakaraṇas* (works of Vasubandhu) are the following: *Mahāyāna Sūtrālaṃkārabhāṣya* (*Explanation of the Ornament of Mahāyāna Discourses*), *Madhyāntavibhaṅgaṭīkā* (*Commentary on the Clear Distinction Between the Middle Way and Extremes*), *Dharmadharmatāvibhaṅgavṛtti* (*Commentary on the Clear

Distinction between Phenomena and Reality), *Triṃśikakārikā* (*The Thirty Verses*), *Viṃśatikakārikā* (*The Twenty Verses*), *Pañcaskandhaprakaraṇa* (*Clear Distinction of the Five Aggregates*), *Vyākhyāyukti* (*Distinctions of Knowledge*), and *Karmasiddhiprakaraṇa* (*Clear Distinction of Accomplishing Action*).

48. The six transcendent virtues are generosity, discipline, patience, enthusiastic perseverance, concentration, and wisdom.

49. The four means of assembling disciples are the following: generosity expressed whenever necessary, pleasant speech, assistance given to others, and consistency between words and deeds.

50. The ten nonvirtues are killing, stealing, adultery, lying, slander, harsh speech, idle speech, craving, ill will, and incorrect view. The eight worldly concerns are concern for gain, loss, pleasure, misery, praise, degradation, fame (reputation), and infamy. The five wrong livelihoods are based on incorrect motivation. They are the use of flattery, hinting, seeking reward for favor, pretentious behavior, and contrived means.

51. A cakravartin ruler is a rebirth that occurs only when the life span of human beings of the four continents is from eighty thousand to countless years. Such a rebirth has the power to overcome, conquer, and rule all inhabitants of the four continents. In ancient times this was considered an example of the most powerful rebirth possible within cyclic existence.

52. On the path of preparation, the four levels that arise are temporary levels of accomplishment. The heat experience refers to the initial sign of the development of the fire of the primordial wisdom on the path of seeing. The peak refers to the level of the development of the root of virtue, which reaches its highest point of expansion at this stage of preparation. Forbearance refers to the state of mind on this level that no longer has any fear or restraint toward the profound meaning of the nature of emptiness. The supramundane refers to the fact that on this level the highest possible accumulation of worldly merit and virtue is accrued. This is the last state of practice that is still mundane.

53. The Akaniṣṭha pure realm is the pure realm of Buddha Samantabhadra appearing in the aspect of the sambhogakāya in order to display the five certainties. The certainty of the place is the Akaniṣṭha pure realm. (This is not the Akaniṣṭha of the seventeen regions of the form realm.)

54. Orgyan refers to Oḍḍiyāna, which literally means the land of "travel by flying." Over time the original sound of Oḍḍiyāna began to be pronounced as Orgyan. This was the kingdom of the well-known ruler of India, King Indrabhūti.

55. The five great sages came from five different realms. The yakṣa realm is within the desire realm, and its inhabitants are a variety of harmful spirit. The rakṣa realm is inhabited by a type of cannibal demon. The nāga realm contains a variety of serpent spirits, regarded as belonging to the animal class and residing in subterranean realms.

56. Druṣa is the name of a region close to present-day Tibet and Turkestan.

57. These four stages correspond to the inner practice of deity generation as practiced according to kriyā, upa, yoga, and anuttara. The kriyā practice corresponds to "gazing," upa to "smiling," yoga to "joining hands," and anuttara to "union." For further information one must receive empowerment, authorization, and oral instructions.

58. The word "elementals" refers to beings who are unable to discern the truth of what should be accepted as the true spiritual path and what should be rejected. Elementals are considered to be a type of negative spirit.

59. The term "rudra" refers to the type of rebirth taken by those who have entered the path of Dharma and accumulated considerable merit and potential and who then break their words of honor with the vajra master by developing wrong view towards the master or by developing an incorrect view of emptiness. In their very next lifetime, such individuals will be reborn in the desire realm as very powerful negative spirits with an uncertain appearance. From the ultimate point of view, the actual stage of "rudra" arises from the intensity of grasping at a "self."

60. The five illnesses are the imbalances that arise from energies, bile, phlegm, all three together, and two together.

61. The five heinous nonvirtues are to kill one's father, mother, or an arhat, to divide the saṅgha by creating a schism, and, with a negative intention, to draw blood from the body of a buddha.

62. A sign of purification may be an actual or dream experience of any of the following: to experience the healing of an illness or disease or to have pus or unclean substances issue from one's body in the form of sores, blisters, or oozing liquid. In the dream state one may dream of such a purging or purification occurring or of white nectar or light entering one's body and removing illness, obscurations, and nonvirtues in the form of black, dark liquid or other substances. Otherwise, one may dream of donning white or new clothing, taking a shower, or cleansing the body in other ways.

63. The eight sovereign qualities are those of body, speech, mind, miracles, free movement, abode, wish-fulfillment, and noble qualities.

Wisdom Publications

Wisdom Publications is a non-profit publisher of books on Buddhism, Tibet, and related East-West themes. We publish our titles with the appreciation of Buddhism as a living philosophy and the special commitment of preserving and transmitting important works from all the major Buddhist traditions.

If you would like more information, a copy of our mail order catalogue, or to be kept informed about our future publications, please write or call us at:

361 Newbury Street
Boston, Massachusetts, 02115
USA
Telephone: (617) 536-3358
Fax: (617) 536-1897

The Wisdom Trust

As a non-profit publisher, Wisdom is dedicated to the publication of fine Dharma books for the benefit of all sentient beings. We depend upon sponsors in order to publish books like the one you are holding in your hand.

If you would like to make a donation to the Wisdom Trust Fund to help us continue our Dharma work, or to receive information about opportunities for planned giving, please write to our Boston office.

Thank you so much.

Wisdom Publications is a non-profit, charitable 501(c)(3) organization and a part of the Foundation for the Preservation of the Mahayana Tradition (FPMT).

Care of Dharma Books

Dharma books contain the teachings of the Buddha; they have the power to protect against lower rebirth and to point the way to liberation. Therefore, they should be treated with respect—kept off the floor and places where people sit or walk—and not stepped over. They should be covered or protected for transporting and kept in a high, clean place separate from more "mundane" materials. Other objects should not be placed on top of Dharma books and materials. Licking the fingers to turn pages is considered bad form (and negative karma). If it is necessary to dispose of Dharma materials, they should be burned rather than thrown in the trash. When burning Dharma, first recite OM, AH, HUNG. Then, visualize the letters of the texts (to be burned) absorbing into the AH, and that absorbing into you. After that, you can burn the texts.

These considerations may be kept in mind for Dharma artwork, as well as the written teachings and artwork of other religions.